The Wizard's Illusion

The Wizard's Illusion

A Conversation from Oz with
Sallie McFague and Others

KATHERINE ABETZ

RESOURCE *Publications* • Eugene, Oregon

THE WIZARD'S ILLUSION
A Conversation from Oz with Sallie McFague and Others

Copyright © 2022 Katherine Abetz. All rights reserved. Except for brief quotations in critical publications or reviews, no part of this book may be reproduced in any manner without prior written permission from the publisher. Write: Permissions, Wipf and Stock Publishers, 199 W. 8th Ave., Suite 3, Eugene, OR 97401.

Resource Publications
An Imprint of Wipf and Stock Publishers
199 W. 8th Ave., Suite 3
Eugene, OR 97401

www.wipfandstock.com

PAPERBACK ISBN: 978-1-6667-3602-1
HARDCOVER ISBN: 978-1-6667-9380-2
EBOOK ISBN: 978-1-6667-9381-9

05/02/22

Scripture quotation is from Revised Standard Version of the Bible, copyright © 1946, 1952, and 1971 National Council of the Churches of Christ in the United States of America. Used by permission. All rights reserved worldwide. https://nrsvbibles.org/index.php/licensing/

Contents

Acknowledgments | vii
Introduction | ix

1. **Two Kinds of Screen** | 1
    The Screen That Hides | 3
    Screen of the Peep-Hole View | 5
    Knocking Over the Screen | 11
    The Wizard's Perspective | 16

2. **"Is" and "Is Not"** | 19
    Oshtrans | 20
    Three Steps to Home | 25
    Losing the "Is" | 28
    Metaphorical Truth | 35

3. **The *Via Negativa*** | 40
    The Wizard's Cinema | 42
    The Frame of Non-Reference | 46
    The Power of Speech | 50
    Mostly Fiction | 54

4. **The *Via Analogia*** | 61
    The Lost Covenant | 63
    The Lost Coin | 68
    The Tower of Babel | 72
    The Yellow Brick Road | 76

5. **"Beam Me Up, Scotty"** | 83
    Identity and Exteriority | 86
    In Search of the Subject | 88
    Nature Which Isn't | 96
    St. Francis and St. Clare | 99

6. **The Other Side of Barth?** | 104
    Philosophers' God | 105
    The Cathedral | 110
    Myth or Minster? | 113
    Master's Metaphor? | 117

7. **Making Sense?** | 123
    Relativism | 126
    Two Stories | 129
    The Possibility of the Incarnation | 135
    The Wizard and Science | 140

8. **"A Reality Comes to Language"** | 147
    Second Naïveté and Nature Writing | 149
    Parable | 155
    Vocational Autobiography | 160
    Myth | 163

9. **Three Kinds of Sacramentalism** | 169
    Dresden China Country | 172
    An Integrated Sensibility? | 178
    Horizontal Sacramentalism | 181
    Coming Alive | 189

10. **Metaphor or Better-For?** | 195
    Why Better? | 198
    Allegory and a Moral Revolution | 205
    A Linguistic Mistake? | 208
    Looking Outwards | 215

Conclusion | 219
Bibliography | 233
Index | 237

Acknowledgments

THERE IS MUCH THAT goes into the compilation of a book of this nature. It is hard to do justice to all the contributions in their various manifestations but I will try.

I acknowledge all conversation partners, in particular my chief sparring partner, Sallie McFague. I acknowledge the breadth of research and the academic history represented. I submit that the conversation needs to continue with rigor.

My thanks are due to those who have walked with me on my journey. I am grateful for all the advice and encouragement by my supervisor, Dr. Charles Sherlock, from the Master of Theology to the doctorate to support of the book proposal. I am grateful for support from my examiner, Professor Benjamin Myers. I am grateful to Dr. Robert Brennan for pioneering this foray in publishing and offering his support for mine. I am grateful for encounters with the University of Divinity, and its various associated colleges, during my postgraduate studies and afterwards. I am grateful for assistance from the Dalton McCaughey Library staff in chasing up obscure points and clemency in seemingly endless book borrowing at a distance. I am grateful to Wipf and Stock for taking on my project and promptly answering my questions. I am grateful to my various support networks. I am grateful to my husband for his patience, backing, technical assistance and academic feedback. I am grateful to God for indispensable guidance.

I acknowledge L. Frank Baum for the incidents in *The Wizard of Oz* which I have borrowed to supply illustrations for my arguments and for the sage comments by the Wizard himself on the inadequacy of his devices. I thank my supervisor, Dr Charles Sherlock for suggesting the sub-title.

Lastly, I am grateful in advance to those who will read this book and continue the conversation.

Introduction

Even with eyes protected by the green spectacles Dorothy and her friends were at first dazzled by the brilliancy of the wonderful City. The streets were lined with beautiful houses all built of green marble and studded everywhere with sparkling emeralds . . . even the sky above the City had a green tint, and the rays of the sun were green.[1]

'But isn't everything here green?' asked Dorothy.
'No more than in any other city,' replied Oz; 'but when you wear green spectacles, why of course everything you see looks green to you.'[2]

THE GREENNESS OF THE City of Oz is an illusion produced by wearing green spectacles. Dorothy and her friends find out that the Wizard of Oz is a "humbug" but the inhabitants of Oz do not. They continue to believe that the Emerald City is really green. This device is pivotal to the plot of the story. The question is: is a similar device pivotal to the way language works? When we say something and in particular when what we say depends on a metaphor, do we rely on an illusion or are we actually claiming to say something about what is out there? Is it or is it not the nature

1. Baum, *The Wizard of Oz*, chapter 11.
2. Baum, *The Wizard of Oz*, chapter 15.

of metaphor to point beyond itself to something else? The question may seem simple but the thinking behind it is not simple.

This book is an appraisal of Sallie McFague's "metaphorical theology." In describing what she means by metaphor, McFague appeals to the green spectacles of the Wizard of Oz.[3] How pivotal then is this illustration to her theory of the *modus operandi* of metaphor? If, in her understanding, metaphor deals in illusion rather than points to a reality what does this say about her theology and her use of language? The question is important because McFague has been influential as a source of theory about theological language, in feminist circles in particular. Language about God often relies on metaphor. It is important to be clear about the function of such language and how reliable it claims to be.

I have said that the thinking behind theory about the operation of metaphor is not simple. Under discussion is the efficacy of a particular use of language, not the efficacy of any particular metaphor. If one describes one woman as a rose and another as a violet by a mossy stone half hidden from the eye, the metaphors may be judged apt or they may not.[4] But judging whether a particular metaphor is appropriate in the case of a particular woman is different from appreciating that metaphor is an effective means of describing something. It would not otherwise be possible to decide that the metaphor of a rose gave a poor idea when applied to a particular woman. It is because metaphor is a powerful linguistic tool that judgment about its success in a particular case is possible. In this context, the appeal to the Wizard's spectacles demonstrates an interesting proposition. In itself it is a powerful metaphor for a particular understanding of how metaphor works. But if the operation of metaphor is understood in this way, this particular metaphor would convey no more about its referent (how metaphor works) than the green spectacles would convey about the City of Oz. To think otherwise would be to fall for the Wizard's illusion.

The plot of *The Wizard of Oz* turns on the unmasking of an illusion. Parallel to this, McFague wishes to unmask the theological metaphor "God the father."[5] In the book, unmasking the Wizard's trick is in the end a simple affair. McFague's journey is a rather more complex matter.

---

3. See McFague, *Metaphorical Theology*, 41.

4. C. S. Lewis draws attention to these metaphors in "The Language of Religion," 168, citing Robert Burns, "A red, red Rose," line 1 and William Wordsworth, "She dwelt among the untrodden ways," line 5.

5. See McFague, *Metaphorical Theology*, 29; cf. 150.

Introduction

She does not unmask a timid and elderly ventriloquist or, if she does, she would not put it in those terms. In fact, the character of the linguistic Wizard bears little relation to that of the Wizard in the book. In entering a discussion about McFague's treatment of metaphor, I disclaim any attempt to enter a discussion of the story. Once borrowed as an illustration, the linguistic Wizard takes on a different role. It is here that my discussion begins.

In terms of my own journey, however, it would be truer to say that this discussion is an unanticipated precursor to my starting-point as I originally conceived it. I began by asking: what does it mean for a woman to be created in God's image? I then realized that one must ask what is meant by being in the image of something or Someone, how the language of analogy functions, in short how metaphor works. If such language reduces to green spectacles it is clear that what is supposedly referred to as "out there" is really in the eye of the beholder. The case is not that woman is made in the image of God but that God is in the image of woman. Some feminists, Rosemary Ruether for example, would assert this kind of framework unashamedly.[6] This then throws theological discussion on its head: "God" becomes a kind of construct in the imagination of those who interest themselves in such things. Further, if what is meant by metaphor is at the back of the upheaval, theology is not the only field at stake.

McFague would agree that the question of how metaphor can be said to operate must be asked in a wide context. This book engages with McFague's series: *Metaphorical Theology*; *Models of God*; *The Body of God*; *Super, Natural Christians*. In these works her theory of metaphor is not confined to theology but also embraces scientific models. She goes so far as to attempt to "make sense" of theology and science in a postmodern world.[7] In support of her thesis she appeals to Paul Ricoeur and C. S. Lewis, writers with an acknowledged cross-disciplinary breadth of purview. I question the legitimacy of the appeal. It would take a bold writer to claim the expertise of a Ricoeur or a Lewis, but since both men also go some way towards trying to make sense in a broad field, it would seem allowable to test McFague's thesis against their observations and this is what this book aims to do.

---

6. See Ruether, "Christian Tradition and Feminist Hermeneutics," 286–87 and 291 n. 42. Ruether describes feminist theology in terms of the method outlined in McFague, *Metaphorical Theology* and *Models of God*.

7. See McFague, *The Body of God*, 150.

To my mind, McFague's concept of metaphor owes most to Colin Turbayne. It is Turbayne who supplies the illustration of the Wizard. McFague's acknowledgement of both Turbayne and the Wizard is admittedly brief. She draws attention to the Wizard in the first book of her series.[8] She does not refer to him directly again. But this does not mean that the Wizard is a minor player since he is the kind of character who operates behind the scenes. I have mentioned that it is necessary to consider approaches to metaphor across a wide field of disciplines. It is also necessary to consider the nature of metaphor against a history of linguistic study. In terms of discussion of language the stage is already set before the Wizard's brief public appearance in McFague's book.

The early half of the twentieth century saw the rise of a surmised dichotomy about the efficacy of language. The distinction was introduced by the positivists for whom cognitive or "literal" language was verifiable and consequently objectively reliable while other kinds of language (including metaphor) were non-verifiable and therefore without external reference, "sensed purely 'within' the subject" to use Ricoeur's phrase.[9] One may recognize the affinity between sensed within the subject and green spectacles. Since this era metaphor has acquired new prominence, its presence in the formation of "literal" language now widely acknowledged. But on what terms? This is where McFague's theory is of key importance. If the Wizard has anything to do with it, any supposed efficacy attached to metaphor is likely to be illusory.

For McFague, the first point about the illusion is that it must be unmasked. Unlike Dorothy and her friends, McFague begins her journey on this assumption. She does not attempt an analysis of the operation of metaphor for its own sake but for the sake of exposing a particular metaphor because she finds the metaphor "God the father" to be unduly influential in the Christian faith. In short she begins with a feminist ethic. Analysis of the operation of metaphor is a means to that end. This is one source of complexity in McFague's project. The second point is something of a non-sequitur. Unmasking metaphor does not merely affect the metaphor "God the father." It affects all metaphors. Nothing daunted, McFague goes on to declare her intention of "remythologizing" the Christian faith. She affirms the importance of metaphor in theology. But here, I believe, metaphor is on a new footing.

---

8. McFague, *Metaphorical Theology*, 41; cf. 150. McFague cites Turbayne, *The Myth of Metaphor*, 24–25.

9. Ricoeur, *The Rule of Metaphor*, 226–27.

Introduction

In this new approach to metaphor, McFague seems both to agree and to disagree with a positivist position. A positivist would treat metaphor with caution on the grounds that it leads in the direction of illusion.[10] While apparently agreeing about the illusory propensity of metaphor, McFague would nonetheless advocate its use. Unlike the positivist approach McFague uses the language of science (and models) in connection with her treatment of metaphor. Thus a positivist might say that if one refers to a woman as a rose one is describing one's feelings and not the woman herself. McFague might say that if one refers to "God the father" one is describing one's hypothesis about God and not the Godhead itself.[11]

Such an emphasis opens the door to what I term the Wizard's illusion. In some ways the effect on language is not new. The process of unmasking linguistic reference predates twentieth century positivism. One must go back to the nineteenth century for the beginnings of demythologizing and linguistic deconstruction. It is probably not possible to understand a writer like Jacques Derrida without taking cognizance of earlier French symbolists, Stéphan Mallarmé and Arthur Rimbaud. What is striking here is not only non-commitment to symbolic reference except within the bounds of language itself but also the strong ethical component. Rimbaud was a visionary poet who looked forward to a new moral outlook for humanity. For Rimbaud as for McFague the subjectivized nature of linguistic reference is no apparent bar to ethical effect.

A discussion of metaphor begins with linguistic and literary theory. Before moving on to the wider implications of McFague's approach to metaphor, it is important to be clear about the standard meaning of terms. It is customary to make a distinction between metaphor and simile. Likewise analogy is often differentiated from metaphor. This book is not the place for this sort of distinction except as it may arise incidentally. In general I don't find fine-spun distinctions along these lines in McFague either. Of these terms "metaphor" is perhaps the most poetic in its use of nuance in words: a familiar word is used to portray something that cannot easily be described directly. If a woman is referred to as a rose, this invokes a certain quality about the woman that is not easy to elicit in any other way.

10. See McFague, *Metaphorical Theology*, 76–77. Cf. Thiselton, *New Horizons in Hermeneutics*, 353: "Ricoeur rejects . . . the positivistic view . . . that metaphor constitutes a generally misleading abuse of language, which encourages illusion."
11. See McFague, *Models of God*, 192 n. 37.

In this connection McFague cites I. A. Richards' distinction between "vehicle" and "tenor."[12] In the case above, the rose is the "vehicle" or means of description. The woman is the "tenor," meaning the referent described. The rose-like quality of the woman sits in between the rose and the woman. What is in between vehicle and tenor is often described as "metaphorical tension." It is clear that the rose and the woman do not share other attributes. Apprehending the metaphor requires sifting out irrelevancies and focusing on the metaphorical interaction. In this regard, McFague quotes Richards' definition of metaphor which, she says, "is a good beginning":

> In the simplest formulation, when we use a metaphor we have two thoughts of different things active together and supported by a single word, or phrase, whose meaning is a resultant of their interaction.[13]

McFague goes on to say: "The most important element in this definition is its insistence on *two active thoughts which remain in permanent tension or interaction with each other.*"[14] But this, I believe, is to bypass what Richards calls the "resultant" of the interaction, that is to say the new meaning generated in the process. Etymologically, "metaphor" comes from the Greek for "with" (*meta*) and "carry" (*phero*). A certain meaning is carried by the vehicle and applied to the tenor. In some sense McFague may seem to incorporate the concepts of "vehicle" and "tenor" in her treatment of metaphor. How she might reconcile this with the Wizard's illusory tactics is explored in chapter 1.

I have said that this book is not the place for fine-spun literary distinctions. Nevertheless the terms "symbol" and "allegory" do have a place in this discussion. "Symbol" has a similar function to "metaphor." The point is raised already in the mention of two French symbolists of the nineteenth century. While a metaphor is primarily to do with words, a symbol is primarily to do with something visible. To use a contemporary example, the golden arches of the "M" are symbolic of McDonald's fast food chain. As with metaphor, the irrelevant aspects of the letter "M" must be bypassed in order to apprehend the particular meaning. The case is altered with the French symbolists because "symbol" is not required to

---

12. McFague, *Metaphorical Theology*, 37–38.

13. McFague, *Metaphorical Theology*, 37. McFague cites Richards, *The Philosophy of Rhetoric*, 93.

14. McFague, *Metaphorical Theology*, 37. McFague's italics.

refer to anything beyond the confines of language. In this way of thinking the golden arches would have an internalized meaning. One may see a similarity between the thinking of the French symbolists and the Wizard's illusion. For this kind of symbolist thinking it would be something of an illusion to assume that the golden arches betokened a fast food outlet.

Despite the term "symbolist" it is clear that the French symbolists do not use symbols in a standard sense. There is another literary term, however, which functions in a somewhat similar way to the internalized meaning of the French symbolists. This is allegory. In terms of linguistic reference, allegory does not point beyond itself to something else. Rather, the concept behind it generates its own picture. The referential tension is between the concept and the imaginary figure which illustrates it. While metaphorical terms may be used in connection with allegory, the vehicle does not in the first instance point to the tenor. Rather, the tenor projects an imaginary vehicle. In *The Pilgrim's Progress*, for instance, the emotion of despair (tenor) is portrayed by the figure of a giant (imaginary vehicle).[15] Allegory is a fictional device but not all fiction is allegory. The example from *The Wizard of Oz* may in fact serve to illustrate the difference. Even in fictional terms the giant has no existence outside the emotion of despair. In fictional terms the City of Oz does have existence outside the green glasses.

One may compare the greenness of Oz with the Giant Despair on the grounds that both are projected from something. The difference is that the greenness is projected onto the City. The Giant Despair is not projected onto anything else. But the process of unmasking is similar in both cases. One can unmask the greenness of the City by demonstrating that it relies on the spectacles. One can unmask the Giant Despair by demonstrating that he relies on the underlying concept. One cannot, however, unmask the metaphor "the woman is a rose" in the same manner even though its aptness in a particular case may be open to dispute. My question is: where does McFague's understanding of the metaphor "God the father" sit with these instances? For Rosemary Ruether, "God" is made in the image of humanity, rather than the other way round. "God" is then a projection from an underlying concept, in literary terminology a kind of allegory. Does "God the father" operate in a similar way for McFague?

---

15. Bunyan, *The Pilgrim's Progress*, 151–57.

Further to a discussion of terms, the word "literal" rates a mention. If the metaphor "the woman is a rose" is taken literally, the vehicle (rose) will be applied to the tenor (the woman) without any sifting out of irrelevancies. This will lead to a false understanding but it is of a different type to the falsity associated with the Wizard's spectacles. In the case of "the woman is a rose" there is a correct way of apprehending the metaphor: one must sift out the irrelevancies. But the Wizard's spectacles are in themselves deceptive. There are no irrelevancies to sift out. In this regard, the use of the term "literal" must be treated with care. As noted, the Wizard's spectacles function in a similar way to a positivist conception of "metaphor." In this way of thinking, "metaphor" belongs to language which is sensed within the subject. Cognitive or "literal" language, on the other hand, can be taken to point reliably to the external world. This distinction has the potential to add something to the notion of "literal" which has nothing to do with a failure to sift out irrelevancies. For a positivist, the metaphor "the woman is a rose" would tend to be a statement of feelings about the woman, not a means of describing the woman. Taking metaphorical language literally could then be equated with the false supposition that such language points reliably to something "out there."

In the metaphor "the woman is a rose" the rose-like quality is attributed to the woman. Once denied as a valid comparison, the alleged rose-like quality of a particular woman would not take on an independent existence. At least this is the case in the standard usage of metaphor. In a positivist tendency, however, one would be mistaken in thinking the metaphor "the woman is a rose" would refer to the woman. Rather, it would express what might be termed "rose feelings" about the woman. While this is not the positivist tendency, it is conceivable that "rose feelings" could then take on a kind of independent existence. As will be seen, the linguistic Wizard would seem to play the part of the positivist in detaching the metaphor from its referent. But he goes further in giving the resultant "picture" a currency of its own. This is what I think McFague means by "remythologizing." Put in terms of green spectacles, the linguistic Wizard continues to bedeck the inhabitants of Oz. But the focus is now on the spectacles, not the City.

Admittedly, focus on the spectacles of the viewer rather than what is "out there" has a long history in Western thinking. C. S. Lewis writes:

> The process whereby man has come to know the universe is from one point of view extremely complicated; from another it is alarmingly simple. We can observe a single one-way

Introduction xvii

progression. At the outset the universe appears packed with will, intelligence, life and positive qualities; every tree is a nymph and every planet a god. Man himself is akin to the gods. The advance of knowledge gradually empties this rich and genial universe: first of its gods, then of its colours, smells, sounds and tastes, finally of solidity itself as solidity was originally imagined. As these items are taken from the world, they are transferred to the subjective side of the account: classified as our sensations, thoughts, images or emotions.[16]

An "eye of the beholder" approach to the universe is not new. What is new is to apply this kind of thinking to the definition of metaphor.

While this book begins with an appraisal of a subjectivist notion of metaphor, the consequent approach to language has far-reaching effects. Chapter 1 looks at the mechanics of metaphor in terms of the proposed illustration of green glasses. Chapters 2 and 3 engage with the effect on ontology. Chapter 4 considers the presence, or absence, of what George Steiner terms cognitive ballast in language: "is there anything *in* what we say?"[17] Chapter 5 assesses McFague's admission that her theological models are mostly fiction alongside the ethical vision which they promote. Chapters 6 and 7 evaluate McFague's theological method in relation to an evolutionary paradigm. In terms of method, McFague appears to owe something to Barth but unlike Barth she states a wish to make sense between theology and evolutionary history. Chapter 8 reconsiders the nature of fiction in terms of metaphorical reference. Chapter 9 compares McFague's and Lewis's notion of "sacramentalism." Chapter 10 suggests that McFague's idea of metaphor more closely equates to what I term an ethical "better-for."

The "rich and genial universe," as described by Lewis above, is a pagan universe. While Lewis conceives the transfer "to the subjective side of the account" as a process of emptying, there is a possibility that such a transfer could take on a new vitality. Erich Neumann sums up such an approach to the "rich and genial universe" as it appears in a Jungian kind of thinking:

The stages of the self-revelation of the Feminine Self, objectivized in the world of archetypes, symbols, images and rites, present us with a world that may be said to be both historical and

---

16. Lewis, "The Empty Universe," 81. (The essay was first published as a Preface to D. E. Harding, *The Hierarchy of Heaven and Earth.*)

17. Steiner, *Real Presences*, 121. Steiner's italics.

> eternal. The ascending realms of symbols in which the Feminine with its elementary and transformative character becomes visible as Great Round, as Lady of the Plants and Animals, and finally as genetrix of the spirit, as nurturing Sophia, correspond to stages in the self-unfolding of the feminine nature . . . . But these manifestations of the Archetypal Feminine in all times and all cultures . . . appear also in the living reality of the modern woman, in her dreams and visions, compulsions and fantasies, projections and relationships, fixations and transformations.[18]

While McFague's "metaphorical theology" begins with Christian theology, her deconstruction of the metaphor "God the father" opens the door to gods in a different sense. Her proposal of "Nature which is"[19] as a term for God would seem apposite here, as will be seen. But, in one sense, "Nature which is" will bear little relation to "every tree is a nymph and every planet a god." It will fall short of a "rich and genial universe" in terms of ontology.

It may be that a definition of metaphor is a last bastion in the transfer "to the subjective side of the account." If this is so, the notion of metaphor merits close attention before such a transfer is irrevocably made. If we are to find a metaphor for how metaphor works in *The Wizard of Oz* there is another possible illustration. Etymologically, as noted above, "metaphor" comes from the Greek for "with" (*meta*) and "carry" (*phero*). The Silver Shoes are a means to carry Dorothy home.

---

18. Neumann, *The Great Mother*, 336.
19. See McFague, *Super, Natural Christians*, 173.

1

Two Kinds of Screen

In *The Wizard of Oz* Dorothy and her friends return from destroying the Wicked Witch of the West and demand audience with the Wizard. They expect to see the Wizard in one of his various shapes but this time they only hear a voice which appears to come from the throne in the middle of the room. In this guise the Wizard tries to avoid fulfilling his promises to them. The Lion roars. Dorothy's dog Toto jumps away in alarm and knocks over a screen in the corner. The real "wizard" is then revealed as a little old man who has been "making believe."[1]

In the Introduction I disclaimed the intention of discussing *The Wizard of Oz* as a narrative. But certain aspects of the story offer useful illustrations for a discussion of metaphor. The screen that conceals the old man prevents his audience from detecting who he really is. It is a device that screens out something. In her exploration of what is meant by "metaphor" McFague appeals to another kind of screen, the kind which has holes through which one may look. Here she follows the analogy for the operation of metaphor supplied by philosopher Max Black, as will be seen below. In spite of this McFague's notion of "screen" owes much to the kind of screen which blocks out what is really there. Her focus is consequently less on what the screen allows you to see and more on the screen itself, including what it may not allow you to see.

---

1. See Baum, *The Wizard of Oz*, chapter 15.

As noted in the Introduction, Colin Turbayne supplies the illustration of the Wizard's spectacles in relation to the concept of "metaphor." McFague writes:

> Colin Turbayne has listed three stages of metaphor. Initially, when newly coined, it seems inappropriate or unconventional; the response is often rejection. At a second stage, when it is a living metaphor, it has dual meaning—the literal and metaphorical—and is insightful. Finally, the metaphor becomes commonplace, either dead and/or literalized. At this stage, says Turbayne, we are no longer like the Wizard of Oz who knew green glasses made Oz green, but, like all the other inhabitants of Oz, we believe that Oz *is* green.[2]

McFague highlights the "literalized" stage:

> What has occurred, of course, is that similarity has become identity; the *tension* that is so critical in metaphor has been lost. This is an ever present danger in religious metaphors, though also in scientific ones, for in both cases models of reality, especially ones with long-term and widespread backing, are identified with reality.[3]

According to the above description, the Wizard's illusion is fulfilled in the third stage of the life of a metaphor. In this final stage, says McFague, we are in a similar position to that of the inhabitants of Oz, believing that the City is really green. In the same way, she continues, metaphors with long-term and widespread backing tend to be erroneously identified with reality.

In the third stage metaphors are said to deceive as the green glasses deceive. In one way the deception of the green glasses is unlike the deceptive appearances in the Wizard's Throne Room: Dorothy and her friends can still see the City through the glasses but cannot see the old man until the screen is knocked over. The point for McFague, however, is the false belief about the color of the City. In this sense the deception in both cases is the same. As appearances of the Wizard of Oz are erroneously identified with reality, the appearance of prevailing green is erroneously identified with the actual color of the City. But if the operation of metaphor is likened to the function of the glasses, how can it ever be described as

---

2. See McFague, *Metaphorical Theology*, 41–42 and 203 n. 25. McFague cites Turbayne, *The Myth of Metaphor*, 24–25 (McFague's italics).

3. McFague, *Metaphorical Theology*, 41. McFague's italics.

"insightful"? What is happening in the earlier stages? In order to understand what McFague means, I turn to Turbayne direct.

THE SCREEN THAT HIDES

Turbayne associates "metaphor" with Gilbert Ryle's definition of a category-mistake: "the presentation of the facts of one category in the idioms appropriate to another."[4] He states: "the use of metaphor involves both the awareness of a duality of sense and the pretense that the two different senses are one."[5] He indicates what he means by duality of sense in the following examples:[6]

Seeing the point of the needle and the joke

Smelling of musk and insolence

Clad only in her tiara and an embarrassed expression

A toast to general contentment and General de Gaulle

He takes the last example and illustrates how the two senses of "general" can be conceived as one and the same: "'Let us drink a toast to General Contentment' may start an allegory if we put the general on horseback or give him a uniform."[7]

The awareness of a duality of sense alongside the pretense of only one sense appears to operate as follows. General contentment is literally a state of mind. Such an emotional state, however, can take on the trappings of a real life general by means of an allegorical picture. A duality of sense is then discerned in the literal apprehension of the emotion "general contentment" and the allegorical apprehension of "General Contentment on horseback." The two senses can then be regarded as one in the pretense that General Contentment is in the same category as General de Gaulle. It is the pretense that constitutes what Turbayne means by metaphor. "Any trope can achieve full metaphorhood," he says, "but only for that user who fuses the two senses by making believe there is only one sense."[8]

---

4. See Turbayne, *The Myth of Metaphor*, 12. Turbayne cites Gilbert Ryle, *The Concept of Mind*, 8.

5. Turbayne, *The Myth of Metaphor*, 17.

6. Turbayne, *The Myth of Metaphor*, 15.

7. Turbayne, *The Myth of Metaphor*, 20.

8. Turbayne, *The Myth of Metaphor*, 18.

We may note at this point that "metaphor" is usually considered in the category of a figure of speech. The examples offered by Turbayne belong to figures of thought which have a rhetorical function rather than to figures of speech which extend or change the meaning of words. Linking "general contentment" and "General de Gaulle" is an example of "zeugma," the yoking of terms belonging to different categories. Turbayne does not offer a source for his examples but M. H. Abrams gives a similar example of this kind of yoking from Alexander Pope, "Or *stain* her honour, or her new brocade."[9]

Having drawn attention to the zeugma, Turbayne pursues the (on his terms) inappropriate usage of "general contentment." He refers again to Gilbert Ryle's definition of a category mistake: "It represents the facts . . . *as if* they belonged to one logical type or category (or range or types of categories), when they actually belong to another."[10] The rhetorical effect of Turbayne's examples relies on a juxtaposition of this kind. Whether this has anything to do with the operation of metaphor is another matter.

Put in the terms of the Throne Room in the *Wizard of Oz*, Turbayne's notion of "metaphor" will appear as something like this. In front of the screen is General Contentment, seen as an allegorical picture of a popular conception of a military general. Concealed behind the screen is the literal meaning of general contentment, as an emotional state. Apprehension of the "metaphor" involves awareness of the literal meaning (behind the screen) and the allegorical meaning (in front of the screen) alongside the pretense that "General Contentment" really is seated on his horse in full regalia.

As noted above, McFague describes the life of Turbayne's notion of metaphor from newly coined (first stage) to living metaphor (second stage) to commonplace usage (third stage). When newly coined, the metaphor is inappropriate in Turbayne's terms due to the association of

---

9. See Abrams, *A Glossary of Literary Terms*, 81–82 for the entry "Rhetorical figures" (Abrams' italics). McFague also cites Abrams. See *Speaking in Parables*, 43. (This book, published originally in 1975, is a prequel to her later series on "metaphorical theology.") McFague quotes Abrams, *The Mirror and the Lamp*, 31–32. Part of the quotation reads: "We tend to describe the nature of something in similes and metaphors, and the vehicles of these recurrent figures, when analyzed, often turn out to be the attributes of an implicit analogue through which we are viewing the object we describe." McFague comments that this is an "excellent description" of metaphor. At this point she seems to endorse Abram's notion of a figure of speech.

10. Turbayne, *The Myth of Metaphor*, 17. Turbayne cites *The Concept of Mind*, 16. Turbayne's italics.

disparate categories. In the living phase there is awareness of the duality of the categories alongside the pretense that the two are one and the same. In the third stage, McFague reports, "we are no longer like the Wizard of Oz who knew green glasses made Oz green, but, like all the other inhabitants of Oz, we believe that Oz *is* green."[11] In terms of the Throne Room, we no longer realize that the impressive appearances of the Wizard are a conjuring trick on the part of the old man in the corner. To use the illustration of general contentment and General de Gaulle, we forget that "General Contentment on horseback" is a mere allegory.

Having outlined Turbayne's notion of metaphor, McFague goes on to describe the effect of the third stage on religious and scientific metaphors. She states, "in both cases models of reality, especially ones with long-term and widespread backing, are identified with reality."[12] On this appropriation of Turbayne's terms, a religious (or scientific) metaphor would function as a conscious allegory until such time as the allegorizing process was forgotten. At this third stage, says McFague, similarity has become identity. To use Turbayne's example, General Contentment is mistaken for a real general. The kind of tension which results from awareness of the pretense has been lost.

The key factor in this kind of thinking is the sense of an intentional mistake which functions as make-believe. Turbayne states: "The use of metaphor involves the pretense that something is the case when it is not."[13] In the earlier stages the mistake may be recognized as such, as the Wizard knew that the glasses made the City look green. Later the pretense may be forgotten. What once was make-believe is now believed directly. The remedy for this kind of amnesia or false belief is to reveal "metaphor" for the allegory that it really is, to knock over the screen in the Throne Room as it were.

SCREEN OF THE PEEP-HOLE VIEW

How does this kind of thinking about the operation of metaphor relate to the usual understanding of how metaphor works? As noted above, I need to introduce another authority for the definition of metaphor, philosopher Max Black. Both Turbayne and McFague cite Black as offering

---

11. See McFague, *Metaphorical Theology*, 41–42 and 203 n. 25.
12. McFague, *Metaphorical Theology*, 41.
13. Turbayne, *The Myth of Metaphor*, 13.

support for their own ideas about metaphor. Black describes the operation of metaphor in terms of a screen. But Black does not mean the kind of screen that hides what is behind it. Rather, he means a screen that allows a partial view of what lies beyond. The claim to Black's imprimatur requires careful analysis. I will begin with a comparison of Black and Turbayne before going on to examine McFague's appeal to both Turbayne and Black.

Black describes what he means by screen in the following terms:

> Suppose I look at the night sky through a piece of heavily smoked glass on which certain lines have been left clear. Then I shall see only the stars that can be made to lie on the lines previously prepared upon the screen, and the stars I do see will be seen as organized by the screen's structure. We can think of metaphor as such a screen. We can say that the principal subject is "seen through" the metaphorical expression—or, if we prefer, that the principal subject is "projected upon" the field of the subsidiary subject. (In the latter analogy, the implication-system of the focal expression must be taken to determine the "law of projection.")[14]

Metaphor is described here in terms of a screen that allows a glimpse of what lies beyond it: "we can say that the principal subject is 'seen through' the metaphorical expression." In describing how metaphor works, McFague cites I. A. Richard's terms, "vehicle" (the means of description) and "tenor" (the referent described) as well as Black's terms "subsidiary subject" (for vehicle) and "principal subject" (for tenor).[15] In using the illustration of a screen, Black says that the subsidiary subject (or vehicle) allows a partial view of the principal subject (or tenor).

Black meticulously describes how his illustration of a screen may be said to apply to the operation of metaphor. His analogy of clear lines on a smoked screen indicates that some aspects of the referent (tenor or principal subject) are in view while others are not in view. It can be added that some aspects of the vehicle (subsidiary subject) are not in view either since the focus is on the lines which have been left clear. In Black's alternative analogy ("the principal subject is 'projected upon' the field of the subsidiary subject") he adds that the "implication-system of the focal expression must be taken to determine the 'law of projection'".

14. Black, *Models and Metaphors*, 41.
15. See McFague, *Metaphorical Theology*, 38. See also Introduction.

It is the implication-system that determines where the field of the tenor accords with the field of the vehicle.

Black spells out what this partial view means in connection with the particular metaphor "man is a wolf." He writes:

> The effect . . . of (metaphorically) calling a man a "wolf" is to evoke the wolf-system of related commonplaces. If the man is a wolf, he preys upon other animals, is fierce, hungry, engaged in constant struggle, a scavenger and so on. Each of these implied assertions has now to be made to fit the principal subject (the man) either in a normal or in abnormal senses. If the metaphor is at all appropriate, this can be done—up to a point at least. A suitable hearer will be led by the wolf-system of implications to construct a corresponding system of implications about the principal subject. But these implications will *not* be those comprised in the commonplaces *normally* implied by literal uses of "man". The new implications must be determined by the pattern of implications associated with literal uses of the word "wolf". Any human traits that can without undue strain be talked about in "wolf-language" will be rendered prominent, and any that cannot will be pushed into the background. The wolf-metaphor suppresses some details, emphasizes others—in short, *organizes* our old view of man.[16]

Here the human traits that can be talked about in "wolf-language" equate with the clear lines of the screen. Those traits that are pushed into the background equate with the non-visible aspects behind the smoked areas of the screen. In that sense "man" is seen through the lens of "wolf-language."

Turbayne draws attention to Black's example:

> To call a man a "wolf" metaphorically without specifying the wolf-properties implies that the "literal uses of the word normally commit the speaker to acceptance of a set of standard beliefs about wolves," for example, that they are fierce, hungry, scavengous [sic], and so on.[17]

But Turbayne does not go on to indicate that some traits of "man" will be rendered prominent while the "non-wolf" elements are pushed into the background. As seen above, Turbayne's kind of metaphor requires

---

16. Black, *Models and Metaphors*, 41. Black's italics.

17. Turbayne, *The Myth of Metaphor*, 18–19. Turbayne quotes Max Black, "Metaphor."

the user to hold two meanings together while making believe that there is only one meaning. Turbayne states that the metaphor relies on the pretense that humans are wolves in the literal sense: "It is as if the [sentence] 'Men and timber-wolves are wolves' which we know . . . to be absurd, were meaningful and true." In a way similar to the allegorical picture of General Contentment, "[w]e are aware of the duality of sense in . . . 'wolf,' but we make believe that [there is] only one sense—that there is no difference in kind, only in degree . . . between man-wolves and timber wolves."[18] Put in terms of the Wizard's Throne Room, the pretense operates as an appearance in front of the screen while the literal meanings of man and timber-wolves hide behind the screen.

If the key to the operation of metaphor for Turbayne is pretense, the key to the operation of metaphor for Black is a partial view. How then can Turbayne claim to follow Black? The answer to this appears in Turbayne's discussion of another metaphor supplied by Black, "war is a chess-game." "An effective metaphor," says Turbayne citing Black, "acts as a *screen* through which we look at the world; or it *filters* the facts, suppressing some and emphasizing others."[19] We might surmise that Turbayne entertains here the notion of a screen that allows a glimpse of what lies beyond it but if he does he abandons it in his next paragraph. The filtering process, says Turbayne, produces the attitude-shifts associated with the later stage of metaphor in which "what was before called a *screen* or *filter* is now called a *disguise* or *mask*."[20]

Let us be clear about what Turbayne is suggesting and how he appears to follow but actually differs from Black. Turbayne reports Black's example: "The chess metaphor . . . used to illustrate war, emphasizes the game-of-skill features while it suppresses the grimmer ones."[21] Black admits that we must not "neglect the shifts in attitude that regularly result from the use of metaphorical language."[22] As an example of this, he says, "to describe a battle as if it were a game of chess is to . . . exclude, by choice of language, all the more emotionally disturbing aspects of warfare." For Black, the grimmer features of war will be blocked out by the smoked areas of his kind of screen. The tenor (war) will only be partially described

---

18. Turbayne, *The Myth of Metaphor*, 17–18.
19. Turbayne, *The Myth of Metaphor*, 21. (Turbayne's italics.)
20. Turbayne, *The Myth of Metaphor*, 21–22. (Turbayne's italics.)
21. Turbayne, *The Myth of Metaphor*, 21.
22. See Black, *Models and Metaphors*, 42.

Two Kinds of Screen

by the vehicle (chess-game). To understand how Turbayne responds to the example, let us return to General Contentment on horseback. While not a chess piece, General Contentment also screens out the grimmer aspects of war. But the screen in question is not the same screen. The linked notions of a military general and an emotion of general contentment which gave birth to the allegorical picture will hide behind it. This kind of screen becomes a mask when the allegorical picture is confused with reality. For Black, the effect of a metaphor on attitude would seem a side-effect of obtaining a partial view of the referent, the *reality* of war. For Turbayne the metaphor "war is a chess-game" affects attitude in offering a potentially deceptive picture projected from the *concept* of war.

McFague also discusses the chess metaphor, put forward by Black, in terms of a screen. But which kind of screen does she have in mind? She states:

> Models, as is true of metaphors but in an organic, consistent and comprehensive manner, give us a way of thinking about the unknown in terms of the known. As Max Black says, a model gives us a "grid," "screen," or "filter" which helps us to organize our thoughts about a less familiar object by means of seeing it in terms of a more familiar one. He gives the example of seeing a military battle in terms of a chess game. The chess model will help to understand tactics and the movement of armies; as he shrewdly notes, however, it also "screens out" certain other aspects of battle—for instance we will not think of blood and death if we use only the chess analogy.[23]

Like Turbayne, McFague may appear to entertain the notion of the screen that allows a glimpse of what lies beyond it: "the chess model will help to understand tactics and the movement of armies." But in the same paragraph she moves to what the metaphor screens out. The language of "screens out" changes the emphasis of Black's illustration.

Black's illustration for the operation of metaphor focuses on what can be seen through the screen. Some irrelevancies are filtered out; this is intrinsic to the function of the metaphor. Black favors the positive insights afforded by metaphorical language over any possible literal paraphrase.[24] But McFague moves away from positive insight. She goes on to draw a moral about taking metaphors and models too seriously:

---

23. McFague, *Metaphorical Theology*, 23–24. See 200 n. 25 in which McFague refers to "Max Black's fine chapters 3 and 13 in his *Models and Metaphors*."

24. See Black, *Models and Metaphors*, 46.

> Models are necessary . . . for they give us something to think about when we do not know how to think, a way of talking when we do not know how to talk. But they are also dangerous, for they exclude other ways of thinking and talking, and in so doing they can easily become literalized, that is, identified as *the* one and only way of understanding a subject. This danger is more prevalent with models than with metaphors because models have a wider range and are more permanent; they tend to object to competition in ways that metaphors do not.[25]

At this point McFague abandons Black's type of screen. The focus is no longer on access to what lies beyond the metaphorical expression. Rather than offering partial access to the reality, metaphors or models seem, in her thinking, more in line with pictures illustrating a concept, as in the example of General Contentment on horseback.

How can we account for what appears a misuse by Turbayne (and McFague) of Black's usage of "screen"? I maintain that both Turbayne and McFague place their remarks about Black's screen in the context of introducing a different kind of screen. As seen above, Turbayne goes on to describe how a change in attitude is associated with changing a screen into a disguise which hides the juxtaposition of literal meanings behind it. McFague goes on to describe how the chess model screens out other ways of understanding the subject with a consequent risk of "literalizing" the model. As noted, McFague associates the danger of literalized metaphor with the situation of the duped inhabitants of the City of Oz who believe that Oz *is* green. The metaphor is seen to potentially disguise reality.

For the duped inhabitants what is screened out is the understanding that the color of the city is produced by the glasses. The duped inhabitants believe that the City is green. They also believe the appearances in the Throne Room really *are* the Wizard of Oz. Those in the secret might say that the appearances give us something to talk about when we do not know how to talk about this Wizard. Such talk is not to be identified with the actual Wizard. To do so would be the equivalent of "literalizing" the metaphor, identifying it with reality. The screen in this case, however, is not Black's but the screen of the Wizard's Throne Room. The Wizard's screen does not have the filtering function of Black's screen.

Black's examples are offered in the context of his careful description of the *modus operandi* of metaphor. By contrast, McFague's discussion of metaphor, including her appeal to Black's screen, has the wider context

---

25. McFague, *Metaphorical Theology*, 24.

of a discussion of undesirably dominant model-metaphors, especially that of "God the father." Her objection is not that the "God the father" metaphor screens out other aspects of the Godhead (as the chess model excludes other aspects of warfare). Rather, she says that the "God the father" metaphor excludes other models of God, for example that of "God the mother."[26] The focus here is not on the tenor (God) but on possible models of God and the concepts behind them.

KNOCKING OVER THE SCREEN

In *The Wizard of Oz*, the screen is in the corner of the Throne Room. The false pictures of the Wizard appear somewhere else in the room. For the sake of Turbayne's analogy of a screen becoming a mask, I will take the liberty of changing this. Let us imagine that, by a device of the Wizard, the make-believe is projected onto the screen for the view of those in front of it. In keeping with Turbayne's theory, let us suppose that the projection system operates from behind. The Wizard is naturally aware of this device. The screen is for him a cinematic screen. He knows how the projection system works. It is a mask for the inhabitants of Oz because they are not aware of the projection system. On the contrary, they have "literalized" the cinematic picture. For these duped citizens, the cinematic picture operates as a window with a view of the outside. They believe that the cinematic picture can be identified with reality.

Analyzed like this, the Wizard's screen does not appear to have much in common with Black's screen. Black's illustration of a smoked screen with clear lines is in accordance with the understanding of metaphor in standard usage, as described in the Introduction. Black's "suitable hearer" is able to apprehend both the smoked areas and clear lines of his kind of screen. The point of interaction between vehicle and tenor occurs along the lines of clear view. Those who take the metaphor literally will, according to Black's illustration, be mistaken in thinking that the vehicle allows unqualified, direct access to the tenor. In other words they will treat Black's partially smoked glass as a clear window. But, in terms of Black's illustration, they will still gaze at the stars. Viewers of the Wizard's screen are in a different case.

To appreciate the difference, we must bear in mind that what seems to operate as allegory also claims to be a metaphor. While allegory reverses

---

26. See McFague, *Metaphorical Theology*, 23–24.

vehicle and tenor such that the vehicle is projected from the underlying concept, the vehicle of metaphor looks outwards and tries to express something about the tenor which is separate from and usually greater than the vehicle. Using the method of allegory and calling the resulting picture "metaphor" complicates the issue. This kind of metaphor does not claim to refer to what lies beyond it but it does claim to *pretend* to do so. In these circumstances it would be more accurate to call it a notional metaphor. In this case the allegory has a dual function. It points backward to the literal meaning or meanings behind it and also pretends to point outwards to the notional tenor beyond it. Put in terms of the Throne Room, the picture on the Wizard's screen is the product of the projection system behind it; it also pretends to offer a view of an actual Wizard.

In this kind of notional metaphor the motif of a dual function predominates. We recall that for Turbayne, "the use of metaphor involves both the awareness of a duality of sense and the pretense that the two different senses are one."[27] The two different senses are the literal meaning or meanings and the allegorical picture projected by such meanings. Here we are dealing with simple allegory so let us call it the allegorical component. For Turbayne, the literal and allegorical meanings are fused in the pretense to refer to something. This secondary pretense may be termed the "metaphorical" component. But not only are there two components to this kind of metaphor; there are also two ways of looking at it. Some users of this kind of metaphor will recognize the pretense for what it is. Some will not.

Being unaffected by the supposed deception, McFague is anxious to alert others to the potential danger of "literalized" metaphor. At the same time she wishes to promote the use of metaphor. In this sense she plays the part of a Wizard who is anxious to reveal his own devices while at the same time continuing to employ them. This position on the part of the Wizard is something of a delicate balance. It is less than clear how supposed victims can be persuaded to adopt it. It is not just that the allegory must be unmasked. First the victims must be persuaded that "metaphor" is a picture rather than a window.

I find McFague's procedure for unmasking metaphor more a matter of assertion than nuanced explanation in linguistic terms. McFague denounces the "patriarchal model" in the context of outlining a history of Western society "rooted in 'God as transcendent Father'"; the corollary

---

27. Turbayne, *The Myth of Metaphor*, 17.

to this, she says, is a "subject-object dualism" with negative consequences for women.²⁸ She likens acceptance of the "patriarchal model" to the situation in the Emerald City:

> It remains only to remind ourselves that major models that become world views have subliminal, persuasive power to protect them against criticism. Such models constitute our "world" and their basic assumptions are buried deep within our consciousness, within our language. We, like the citizens of Oz who did not know that it was the glasses they wore that made Oz green, can see reality only "patriarchally."²⁹

Her remedy is to remove the patriarchal glasses through the agency of a feminist perspective.

Turbayne is more explicit, if not necessarily consistent, in describing how "metaphor" can be unmasked. His theory of metaphor hinges on *conscious* reallocation of "the facts" in which believed or hidden metaphor constitutes a trespass.³⁰ Once hidden metaphor is detected, the task is to "undress" it. The fancy dress so to speak must be removed. This can be done by "presenting the literal truth."³¹ In terms of the Wizard's Throne Room, the screen is knocked over. The appearances of the Wizard are shown to be nothing more than fancy dress. The literal meaning behind them is revealed. It was all a trick by a little man in the corner.

To illustrate the method, Turbayne cites David Hume's wish to dismantle the metaphor "God is a builder." According to Turbayne, Hume wishes to discredit "the argument for the nature of God from the order or design found in the world." Hume presents "the literal truth" by drawing attention to anthropomorphic characteristics of builders, including the possibility that the builder might be a woman. "This produces corollaries that [Hume] hopes are absurd," says Turbayne. He adds: "The notion that [God] is a builder is acceptable, but that He is a woman is absurd."³²

---

28. See McFague, *Metaphorical Theology*, 147–51. McFague cites Ruether, *New Woman-New Earth*, 74–75.

29. See McFague, *Metaphorical Theology*, 150–51.

30. Turbayne distinguishes between category-fusion (his theory of metaphor) and category-confusion (metaphor taken literally). He calls the former "sort-crossing" and the latter "sort-trespassing." See Turbayne, *The Myth of Metaphor*, 22.

31. See Turbayne, *The Myth of Metaphor*, 54–59.

32. Citing Hume, *Dialogues concerning Natural Religion*, Part V, Turbayne states that Hume extends the notion of "builder" to include propagator of the species, hence the inclusion of female "builders." He writes: "The burden of David Hume's refutation

Turbayne applies Hume's method to his own example:

> But what are the mechanics of this absurdity? Precisely the same sort of thing is done when the metaphor involved in 'Man is a wolf' is exposed.... We take 'wolf' literally and transfer properties such as *four-legged* and *tailed* to man. We then ask the victims to test the wolf-hypothesis. Any man they meet is now a disconfirming instance, and it is hoped that they will reject the hypothesis.[33]

Turbayne refers to the metaphor *involved* in "Man is a wolf." This would seem an admission that his notion of metaphor contains more than one component. He then confronts the "metaphor" with the literal truth. Victims are asked to test the "wolf-hypothesis" in terms of "any man they meet." The "metaphor" is disconfirmed. On literal terms it is absurd. The trick can be revealed. The man in the street does not have four legs and a tail.

It would seem an odd proceeding on Turbayne's part to hope that the absurdity of the "metaphor" would lead to its rejection. This is to repeat the method of producing the pretense in the first place: "It is as if the [sentence] 'Men and timber-wolves are wolves' which we know ... to be absurd, were meaningful and true."[34] In other words Turbayne unmasks the absurdity by drawing attention to the absurdity. The literal meanings were held together by pretense. Once exposed, the fusion of literal meanings which produced it is pulled apart. The test is then applied, not to the allegory but to a wholesale transfer of properties, from "wolf" (vehicle) to "man" (tenor). It is on Black's terms (without Black's screening function) that the absurdity of the "wolf-hypothesis" is asserted.

There is a step missing in this description of the unmasking process. Turbayne does not explain how victims of his method are persuaded that "metaphor" is really an allegory. For victims of the pretense, the

---

of the argument for the nature of God from the order or design found in the world amounts to the exposure of a metaphor, directly, by showing a weak analogy, and indirectly, by extending the metaphor" (*The Myth of Metaphor*, 57–58). As I understand this representation, Turbayne discerns a weak analogy between the literal meanings of human "builder" and God. Secondly, the weakness is further highlighted by extending "builder" to include (female) propagator, contrary to a literally masculine concept of God. This proceeding first reduces the metaphor to its underlying components (on Turbayne's terms) and secondly focuses on extended commonplaces normally implied by the literal uses of those components (contrary to Black's).

33. Turbayne, *The Myth of Metaphor*, 57–58. Turbayne's italics.
34. See Turbayne, *The Myth of Metaphor*, 17.

"wolf-hypothesis" is not a hypothesis but the literal truth. There is no screening function of Black's sort in this belief. On Turbayne's terms, reality is to be found in the "literal truth" which lurks behind the allegory. For confirmed inhabitants of Oz (as mooted in Turbayne's theory) reality is to be found in the "wolf-hypothesis." Turbayne states his hope to undeceive them by confronting them with the "literal truth" of any man they meet. But what is to distinguish belief in the "wolf-hypothesis" from belief in werewolves? Will the supposed victims of the hypothesis really find any man they meet to be a disconfirming instance? Will the absence of four legs and a tail reassure them when werewolves are known to only appear at certain phases of the moon?

But let us return to taking metaphor literally in its more standard meaning. Those who use Black's screen correctly will know where to place the literal aspect of metaphor. For suitable users, the literal aspect belongs to the smoked areas of the screen. Turbayne's argument will not unsettle *them*. But naïve users may treat Black's screen as a clear window. Let us suppose that Turbayne confronts such users with the "literal truth." For Turbayne, the literal truth resides in the concept which generates the allegorical picture. For naïve users of Black's screen, the literal truth resides in the unqualified view of the stars. Turbayne's argument tinkers with Black's peephole screen. One screen is exchanged for the other. The view of stars is no longer in question but naïve viewers, unaware of the exchange, may in their simplicity abandon the metaphor. They will be duped, not by the metaphor (albeit incorrectly apprehended) but by the method of unmasking (applied on quite different assumptions). This has particular application if the reason for unmasking is polemical, as in Hume's wish to discredit an argument for the nature of God or McFague's wish to discredit the patriarchal model.

For Turbayne, the literal truth accords with observable fact. The literal truth is verifiable: users of the metaphor "man is a wolf" have access to both humans and wolves. It is hardly likely, in fact, that anyone would take the metaphor "man is a wolf" literally: the example is something of a straw man in this respect. But, in unmasking the "wolf-hypothesis," Turbayne follows the method he attributes to Hume in which the properties of human builders are transferred (without any screening) to the concept of God. Hume, we are told, hopes that the "pretense" involved in "God is a builder" will be recognized as absurd. But will it? Unlike Turbayne's disconfirming instance for the metaphor "man is a wolf," there is no way of proving that God is not like a female builder. Hume's argument relies on the idea that God is literally masculine. The literal truth accords not with observable fact but with a metaphor for God taken literally. The patriarchal model is consequently a prerequisite for Hume's method. It is ironic that McFague would seem to rely on a somewhat similar method in dismantling the metaphor "God as transcendent Father."[35]

THE WIZARD'S PERSPECTIVE

I have said that the Wizard's position entails a delicate balance. Unlike the duped citizens of Oz, the Wizard knows that his kind of screen does not offer a view of the outside. His method of dismantling the metaphor will not deter those in the secret: for such users, the "metaphor" is not to be identified with reality. On such terms the notional view retains its currency. Turbayne suggests that Newton may have used the metaphor "God is a builder" from the Wizard's point of view (in contrast with that of the inhabitants of Oz):

> It may have been the case that . . . Sir Isaac [was] fully aware that [he was] speaking in metaphor. In which case, like any user of models, [he] would have rejected any extension beyond the para-designer' . . . hypothesis. Hume's method cuts no ice with those who are aware. It only reassures them.'[36]

A paraphrase may help to discern what Turbayne means:

> It may have been the case that . . . Sir Isaac [was] fully aware that [he was] speaking [in terms of *conscious pretense*]. In which case, like any user of [this *form of pretense*], [he] would have rejected any extension beyond the para-designer . . . hypothesis. Hume's method cuts no ice with those who are aware [of the potential *deception*]. It only reassures them.

In other words, if one is already disillusioned, one cannot be disillusioned further. The danger is to believe the "metaphor."

For both Turbayne and McFague, the danger is that the make-believe will be confused with the reality it purports to refer to. This does not deter either of them from using metaphor. McFague wishes to promote what she calls "metaphorical theology." One might ask what role

---

35. See McFague, *Metaphorical Theology*, 148. McFague cites Ruether, *New Woman-New Earth*, 74–75.

36. Turbayne, *The Myth of Metaphor*, 58–59.

an admitted form of pretense could usefully play in theology. In answer, let us consider Turbayne's explanation of the purpose of his method. He offers a linguistic model for the "events in nature" as an alternative to Newton's model:

> Let me extend the linguistic metaphor just as Newton extended the machine metaphor. Just as he believed that the "main business" of physics was to argue from the phenomena "till we come to the very first cause, which certainly is not mechanical," so I can argue from the signs, the things signified, and rules of grammar, to the conclusion that the events in nature are the language of the author of nature. In which case I have another *a posteriori argument* for the existence and nature of God. At least three courses are open to me. First, I could lose awareness of my metaphor, becoming so enthralled by the appealing picture . . . that I mistook the metaphor for the face of literal truth. Secondly, I could treat the Myth of Language as Plato treated the Myth of the Earth Born . . . : [treat] it as a modern allegory myself but offering it for literal consumption at a later time, knowing full well that the generation to whom it is first told cannot possibly believe it, but that the next may. If successful, I should attain to the full Wizardry of Oz, for the essence of full Wizardry consists in fooling others with our devices without being fooled by them ourselves. . . . The third course is to be fully aware of the presence of the disguise; aware that there are no proper sorts into which the facts must be allocated, but only better pictures or better metaphors . . . and then to treat the language metaphor as a myth, "a myth not to be taken literally, but to be dwelt on till the charm of it touches one deeply—so deeply that that when the 'initiated' say 'it is not true,' one is able to answer by acting *as if* it were true."[37]

The options presented here range from falling into the error of the inhabitants of Oz to steering clear of deception in one's own case (while fooling others) to looking around for new metaphors, some apparently better than others. The closest Turbayne comes to claiming validity for the metaphor is to "treat it as a modern allegory," with the Wizard remaining aware of the underlying concept behind the picture. The third option takes the allegory a step further. While aware of the deception, one could act as if the picture supplied by the "metaphor" were actually true while

---

37. Turbayne, *The Myth of Metaphor*, 216–17 (Turbayne's italics). Turbayne bases treating his language metaphor as a myth on Plato's Myth of the Earth Born. He cites Stewart, *The Myths of Plato*, 114.

at the same time looking for "better pictures" or "better metaphors." The question then arises as to what "better" means if "better" cannot mean closer approximation to reality on the part of the "metaphorical" picture.

In the Introduction I drew attention to the positivist assumption that metaphor belongs to the kind of language which expresses what is sensed within the subject. From a positivist perspective, such language is of less value than literal (or cognitive) language which refers beyond itself to the external world. I suggested that the linguistic Wizard would play the part of the positivist in detaching "metaphor" from its supposed referent. But there is more to his story. The Wizard can, if he so chooses, find a new use for metaphor. The imaginary vehicle projected from a reallocation of the "literal truth" can *become* the vehicle for a notional referent. But the referent has no external existence: it functions only "as if it were true." As such, it is an extension of the vehicle. The Wizard plays more than one double game here. If he does not wish to treat a particular picture (or model) as true, it is part of his stock in trade to knock over his screen and reveal the machinery behind it. If this proceeding consists of sleight of hand rather than solid process, we may expect no less from such a character.

Does McFague really subscribe to all these tactics? Where does she stand in relation to metaphorical reference? In her exploration of metaphor, McFague appeals to various authorities, Ricoeur and Lewis among them. We have seen that her appeal to Black may be less than reliable. Does she fare any better, with Ricoeur in particular? That is the burden of the next chapter.

2

"Is" and "Is Not"

IN *THE WIZARD OF OZ* Dorothy claps the heels of the Silver Shoes together three times and tells them where she wants to go. It only takes three steps to arrive at her destination. But something happens in transit. The Silver Shoes fall off and are lost for ever in the desert. Dorothy arrives at the farm in Kansas in her stocking feet.[1]

In standard usage, metaphor is not meant to be taken literally. Something is lost in transit, between vehicle and tenor as it were. The literal meaning drops away. The vehicle arrives in "stocking feet." Nevertheless, it reaches journey's end. In this sense the journey has two sides to it. To describe these two aspects, Sallie McFague uses Paul Ricoeur's terminology of "is" and "is not."[2] The "is not" refers to what is lost in transit, the "is" to what is carried over. Something is gained as well as lost. The illustration of stocking feet only goes so far. It does not do justice to the positive side of transformation. The "is" encapsulates new meaning as well as arrival. This is a home-coming with a difference.

I have said that McFague employs Ricoeur's terminology of "is" and "is not." But, to my mind, it is by no means certain that she means the same thing as he does. To the extent that she follows Turbayne, this cannot be the case. As noted in the previous chapter, the closest Turbayne comes to allowing metaphor to arrive anywhere is to suggest that his allegorical

---

1. See Baum, chapter 23.
2. McFague, *Metaphorical Theology*, 38.

pretense could be treated "*as if* it were true."³ This kind of journey would hardly satisfy Dorothy. I suspect, however, that it might satisfy McFague. But before engaging with what Ricoeur means by "is" and "is not" (and with where McFague might stand in relation to Ricoeur), I will turn to the kind of reference that can be attributed to literal language. Here we enter the territory of dead metaphor.

OSHTRANS

McFague claims to base her "metaphorical theology" on an amalgam of various theories about metaphor.⁴ She sums up the distinctive features of live metaphor as follows:

> A metaphor is an assertion or judgment of similarity and difference between two thoughts in permanent tension with one another, which redescribes reality in an open-ended way but has structural as well as affective power.⁵

To my mind, this summary fails to indicate the nature of the two thoughts, why they are in tension with one another and how metaphorical language differs from literal language.

We may compare McFague's summation with that of I. A. Richards:

> In the simplest formulation, when we use a metaphor we have two thoughts of different things active together and supported by a single word, or phrase, whose meaning is a resultant of their interaction.⁶

For McFague, the interaction is between two thoughts rather than between two thoughts about different *things*. The emphasis is different. McFague leaves out the "resultant" of the interaction, as already noted in the Introduction. For McFague, it is the *assertion* or judgment of similarity and difference, not the interaction and its consequence, which "redescribes" reality. In stating that metaphor redescribes reality, McFague

---

3. Turbayne, *The Myth of Metaphor*, 216–17. Turbayne cites Stewart, *The Myths of Plato*.

4. McFague, *Metaphorical Theology*, 37.

5. McFague, *Metaphorical Theology*, 42.

6. See Introduction for McFague's citation of Richards on the definition of metaphor.

follows Ricoeur. Whether the kind of structural power that she has in mind is in line with Ricoeur's will be seen below.

Let us consider firstly McFague's remarks about affective power. I turn here to a three-way comparison between McFague, Turbayne and Lewis. McFague links the affective power of metaphor with its stages of development. She cites Turbayne for the stages, as outlined in chapter 1. At the third stage, says McFague, "the metaphor becomes commonplace, either dead and/or literalized. At this stage . . . we are no longer like the Wizard of Oz who knew green glasses made Oz green, but, like all the other inhabitants of Oz, we believe that Oz *is* green."[7] A metaphor that is believed as the "thing itself," McFague goes on to say, "affects attitudes at profound levels."

Chapter 1 explored the fate of what McFague calls "literalized" metaphor. In the above quotation McFague implies a similar fate for dead metaphor. I suggest, however, that she misrepresents Turbayne at this point. Turbayne outlines the transition of metaphor from newly coined to the second and third stages as follows:

> The moments of inappropriateness and triumph are short compared to the infinitely long period when the metaphor is accepted as commonplace. The last two stages are sometimes described as the transition from a "live" metaphor to one "moribund" or "dead." But it is better to say that say that either the metaphor is now hidden or it ceases to be one. Within this long period the original metaphor may develop in various ways only one of which is a case of taking metaphor literally.[8]

The ways in which metaphor could be classed as hidden were examined in the previous chapter. According to Turbayne's theory, we are either aware of the literal meaning that is hidden behind the allegorical pretense (like the Wizard of Oz) or we are not aware of it (like the inhabitants of Oz). In this way of thinking, it is the inhabitants of Oz who are said to take metaphor literally. Apart from the two approaches to hidden metaphor, Turbayne refers to another possibility. Metaphor, he says, may cease to be one. This is dead metaphor.

As I understand Turbayne, dead or dormant metaphor is not to be considered in terms of his theory of live metaphor:

---

7. See McFague, *Metaphorical Theology*, 41–42.
8. Turbayne, *The Myth of Metaphor*, 25.

> In dead metaphors, such as "perceive," "comprehend," and "metaphor,"... the questions of homogeneity and likeness do not arise because, although the etymon overlaps its metaphorical meaning, these are overlooked by all but scholars. In dormant metaphors also, such as "high note," "to see meanings," and "to lay bare feelings," both meanings have become literal. There is some likeness between a high note and a high wall, but their common heights are not usually thought to be of the same kind.[9]

According to this evaluation of the dead metaphorical component in literal language, any comparison stemming from the original metaphor is ignored or forgotten, except by etymologists. Even in dormant metaphor, says Turbayne, the notion of height in a high note is not normally compared with the notion of height as in a wall. Without this kind of juxtaposition, the metaphor is not live; consequently the language is treated as literal or cognitive. The affective power attributed to live metaphor is no longer in question.

In stating that metaphor, in its third stage, becomes "either dead and/or literalized," McFague goes so far as to compare Turbayne's notion of hidden metaphor with Lewis's depiction of a "fossilized" metaphor:

> C. S. Lewis makes a somewhat similar point [to Turbayne] in a most engaging way when he insists that in order to avoid fossilized metaphors, one must use several metaphors as well as new ones. "If a man has seen ships and the sea, he may abandon the metaphor of a *sea-stallion* and call a boat a boat. But suppose a man has never seen the sea, or ships, yet who knows of them just as much as he can glean, say from the following list of Kenningar—sea-stallions, winged logs, wave riders, ocean trains. If he keeps all these together in his mind, and knows them for the metaphors they are, he will be able to think of ships, very imperfectly indeed, and under strict limits, but not wholly in vain. But if, instead of this he pins his faith on the particular kenning, *ocean trains*, because that kenning with its comfortable air of machinery, seems to him somehow more safely prosaic, less flighty and dangerous than its fellows, and if, contracting that to the form *oshtrans*, he proceeds to forget that it was a metaphor, then, while he talks grammatically, he has ceased to think of anything. It will not avail him to stamp his feet and swear that he is literal; to say 'An oshtran is an oshtran and there's an end!'"[10]

---

9. Turbayne, *The Myth of Metaphor*, 76.

10. See McFague, *Metaphorical Theology*, 42 cf. 203–4 n. 27. McFague cites Lewis, "Bluspels and Flalansferes," 47.

McFague introduces the comparison of Turbayne with Lewis by citing Turbayne's remark "a Dry-Martini health drink loses its flavor."[11] Turbayne, at this point, is describing the attitude shifts produced by metaphors that are believed as "facts." A new believed metaphor, says Turbayne, may lead to a change in "facts": "A rose by some other name might not smell as sweet. . . . A Dry-Martini health drink loses its flavor. . . . The human characteristics that Aesop pretended were owned by animals have become literally part of their equipment. We no longer make believe that foxes are cunning and lambs gentle. They are."[12]

Is McFague right in asserting that Lewis is making a "somewhat similar point" to Turbayne? Lewis is writing about the development of dead metaphor. As seen above, Turbayne remarks that the metaphorical origin of words, such as "perceive," "comprehend" and even "metaphor," is only of relevance to etymologists. Lewis disagrees. His hypothetical man will need to have some idea about the meaning of *oshtrans* if he is to think about what he means when he says it. Turbayne dissociates literal language from its metaphorical origin. In this he could be said to be making a somewhat similar point to the stamping insistence of Lewis's hypothetical man.

The illustration of *oshtrans*, quoted by McFague, is part of an essay by Lewis entitled "Bluspels and Flalansferes" on the contribution of metaphorical language to language in general. *Bluspels*, a contraction of blue spectacles, is a reference to Kant's philosophy of perception resulting in a subjectivist approach to reality, similar to that cited in the Introduction. *Flalansferes* is a contraction of Flatlanders' sphere. Lewis offers it as a metaphorical explanation by means of which space might be perceived as finite:

> Imagine a race of people who knew only two dimensions—like the Flatlanders. And suppose they were living on a globe. They would have no conception, of course, that the globe was curved—for it is curved round that third dimension of which they have no inkling. They will therefore imagine that they are living on a plane; but they will soon find out that it is a plane which nowhere comes to an end; there are no edges to it. Nor would they be able even to imagine an edge. For an edge would mean that, after a certain point, there would be nothing to walk on; nothing below their feet. But that *below* and *above*

---

11. See McFague, *Metaphorical Theology*, 41–42.
12. See Turbayne, *The Myth of Metaphor*, 22.

> dimension is just what their minds have not got; they have only backwards and forwards, and left and right. They would thus be forced to assert that their globe, which they could not see as a globe, was infinite. You can see perfectly well that it is finite. And now, can you not conceive that as these Flatlanders are to you, so you might be to a creature that intuited four dimensions? Can you not conceive how that which seems necessarily infinite to your three-dimensional consciousness might none the less be really finite?[13]

The purpose of the Flatlander example is to provide access to a possible truth (a proposed fourth dimension) which would otherwise be unavailable (to a non-mathematician). Lewis suggests that the metaphor "Flatlanders' sphere" might in a later contracted form (*Flalansfere*) be employed in a literal sense. He makes the point that language, apart from that referring to the world of our senses, relies on metaphor.

While Turbayne and Lewis agree that literal language relies etymologically on metaphor, they differ about the effect such a relationship has on thinking about language. Lewis goes so far as to suggest that forgetting the meaning supplied by metaphor, as it contributes to literal language, may have profound affective consequences. To a non-mathematician, the imagery of the Flatlanders' sphere was the only access to the concept of finite space. Later usage of the contracted form (*Flalansfere*) without memory of its metaphorical import may result in grammatical, but meaningless, usage of the term. In such a case, says Lewis:

> I am only talking, not thinking when I use the word. But this fact will be long concealed from me, because, *Flalansfere*, being a noun, can be endlessly fitted into various contexts, so as to conform to syntactical usage and to give the appearance of meaning. . . . And what *affective* overtones the word may have taken on by that time, it is dangerous to predict. It had an air of mystery from the first: before the end I shall probably be building temples to it, an exhorting my countrymen to fight and die for the *Flalansfere*.[14]

Despite McFague's observation about a somewhat similar point being made by Lewis, Turbayne and Lewis have quite different concerns about the affective power of metaphor. Turbayne is concerned about the effect of taking metaphor literally (in the sense of believing the allegorical

---

13. Lewis, "Bluspels and Flalansferes," 38–39. Lewis's italics.
14. Lewis, "Bluspels and Flalansferes," 42–43. Lewis's italics.

pretense); he appears to detach dead metaphor (and consequently literal language) from this kind of effect. Lewis is concerned about the possible loss of meaning and the consequences of such a vacuum in dead metaphors which have become part of literal language.

The differences between Turbayne and Lewis stem from radically different approaches both to live metaphor and to the dead metaphor of literal language. As already seen, Turbayne believes in access to "facts" while judging metaphor to constitute a "mistake" about "facts." Lewis, on the other hand, asserts that a metaphor may have access to reality which is "not wholly in vain" and that literal language (in the form of dead metaphor) also relies on this kind of access. Meaning for Turbayne comes from literal language. Meaning for Lewis, apart from direct language for the world of our senses, comes from metaphor.

In linking dead and "literalized" metaphor, McFague takes her concern about the affective power of metaphor to its logical conclusion: dead metaphor can deceive in the same way that "literalized" metaphor can deceive. She writes: "Religion is obviously a prime candidate for housing familiar and submerged metaphors, since religious images—through tradition and ritual—seldom change and become accepted as ordinary language."[15] She does not appear to take the consequence that all literal language insofar as it relies on dead metaphor is potentially deceptive. Lewis's understanding of metaphor (live or dead) leads in the opposite direction.

THREE STEPS TO HOME

I turn now to considering the "structural power" of metaphor, how it operates in other words. According to the positivist distinction, "metaphor" belongs to language that is sensed within the subject whereas literal language can claim to point reliably to the external world. Contrary to this kind of thinking, Max Black takes the line that metaphorical language has its own kind of external reference. His illustration of a screen enables a view of what lies beyond it. Similarly, Lewis argues that live metaphor allows for apprehension of the referent that is "not wholly in vain." This section considers Paul Ricoeur's position on live metaphor.

In her remarks about the "structural, organizational power of metaphor," McFague states that Ricoeur insists on a tension "between a literal

---

15. McFague, *Metaphorical Theology*, 41.

or conventional interpretation which self-destructs and an extended new interpretation which is recognized as plausible or possible."[16] She goes on to qualify this by saying, that when "Ricoeur says that metaphor redescribes reality, at one level he is only saying that in metaphor old views of reality are traded for new ones." McFague claims more than once that her position is similar to Ricoeur's. She writes, "Metaphor always has the character of 'is' and 'is not': an assertion is made but as a likely account rather than a definition."[17] In her attached footnote, she adds: "My position here is very close to that of Ricoeur, as found in his *The Rule of Metaphor* and elsewhere." She also states:

> The heart of metaphorical reference, as Ricoeur insists, is summarized in the aphorism "is" and "is not." Models do not refer directly to reality; they are not copies of it. Yet they do refer indirectly through their own interpretive glasses, and the reality to which they refer is concerned with relationship, with ways of being in the world.[18]

In associating herself with Ricoeur, McFague describes the metaphorical expression as an assertion, as in her summation above. The kind of reference that can be attributed to metaphors or models is said to be that of "a likely account." But does this "assertion" through "interpretive glasses" encompass the kind of "is" and "is not" that Ricoeur has in mind?

McFague quotes Ricoeur's complex description of metaphorical tension which gives rise to what Ricoeur calls "the paradoxical character of metaphorical truth":

> The paradox consists in the fact that there is no other way to do justice to the notion of metaphorical truth than to include the critical incision of the (literal) "is not" within the ontological vehemence of the (metaphorical) "is." In doing so, the thesis merely draws the most extreme consequences of the theory of tension. In the same way that logical distance is preserved in metaphorical proximity, and in the same way as the impossible literal interpretation is not simply abolished by the metaphorical interpretation but submits to it while resisting, so the ontological affirmation obeys the principle of tension and the law of "stereo-scopic vision." It is this tensional constitution of the verb

---

16. See McFague, *Metaphorical Theology*, 38–40.

17. McFague, *Models of God*, 33. See also her appended footnote (194 n. 6) for the additional comment.

18. McFague, *Metaphorical Theology*, 134–35.

to be that receives its grammatical mark in the "to be like" of metaphor elaborated into simile, at the same time as the tension between *same* and *other* is marked in the relational copula.[19]

Ricoeur states that the "ontological affirmation obeys the principle of tension and the law of 'stereoscopic vision.'" He appears to share Lewis's assumption about the possibility of metaphorical reference. For this kind of thinking to operate as intended, the user must, in Lewis's words, know the metaphors for what they are.

As I understand him, Ricoeur states that the "relational copula" (the "is" that links vehicle and tenor) relies on paradox (the "is" includes "is not") at various levels: at the level of the expression itself, at the level of the journey from vehicle to tenor, and finally at the level of external reference. In simpler parlance, the paradoxical tension occurs firstly in terms of the smoked areas and clear lines of Black's screen, secondly (to change the analogy) in terms of the loss of the Silver Shoes and arrival in stocking feet and thirdly in terms of Dorothy's homecoming with its memory of her journey (she rolls over several times before she realizes where she is).[20] In each of these three levels (or steps to make use of Dorothy's flight across the desert), there is awareness of two things at once: in Ricoeur's terminology, "stereoscopic vision."

The passage cited by McFague comes in Ricoeur's conclusion to his study on metaphor and reference. What McFague leaves out is Ricoeur's critique of Turbayne that immediately precedes it. Given her endorsement of Turbayne's theory this would seem a significant omission. Before engaging with Ricoeur's critique of Turbayne, it would seem helpful to focus once again on different ways of thinking or frames of reference. In this regard, Ricoeur gives specific guidelines for apprehension of metaphor. I believe that Ricoeur and Lewis are at one in their approach to live metaphor: the "is" of acknowledged access to the referent alongside the qualification of "is not" or "very imperfectly indeed and under strict limits." I will call this the approach of the Silver Shoes. The shoes that carry Dorothy across the desert to her home in Kansas illustrate the "is" and "is not" quality of metaphor. They are effective in carrying her to her destination. That is the "is." But they also fall off in transit. That is the "is

---

19. McFague, *Metaphorical Theology*, 214 n. 45. McFague cites *The Rule of Metaphor*, 255–56.

20. See Baum, *The Wizard of Oz*, chapter 23.

not." The Silver Shoes frame of reference is very different from that of the Wizard's perspective, critiqued by Ricoeur below.

LOSING THE "IS"

In his study on metaphor and reference, Ricoeur places his threefold concept of the "is" and "is not" in a context of dissociation from what he sees as two incorrect approaches. He announces that he will proceed on the following lines:

> In order to demonstrate this "tensional" conception of metaphorical truth, I will proceed dialectically. First, I will point out the inadequacy of interpretation that gives in to ontological *naïveté* in the evaluation of metaphorical truth because it ignores the implicit "is not". I will then portray the inadequacy of an inverse interpretation that, under the critical pressure of the "is not", loses the "is" by reducing it to the "as-if" of a reflective judgement.[21]

By ontological naïveté, Ricoeur would appear to mean the kind of reference associated with a naïve version of Black's screen. He states that the "myth," denounced by Turbayne, scarcely differs from ontological naïveté. (Ricoeur says that he would call it "believed poetry" or "metaphor taken literally.")[22] Ricoeur then goes on to use Turbayne's theory of metaphor as his example of what he terms "an inverse interpretation that, under the critical pressure of the 'is not,' loses the 'is' by reducing it to the 'as-if' of a reflective judgement."

Let us pause here to compare this analysis with the conclusions of Chapter 1. Ricoeur states that Turbayne denounces the "myth" produced by metaphor taken literally. Chapter 1 distinguished between believed allegory (on Turbayne's terms) and a naïve approach to metaphor (on Black's) but also suggested that Turbayne's method of dismantling "metaphor" might target metaphor taken literally on Black's terms rather than his own. Ricoeur takes issue with the kind of interpretation that, "under critical pressure of the 'is not,' loses the 'is' by reducing it to the 'as-if' of a reflective judgement." Chapter 1 engaged with "metaphor" (on Turbayne's

---

21. Ricoeur, *The Rule of Metaphor*, 248–49.

22. See Ricoeur, *The Rule of Metaphor*, 251. See also 249–50. Ricoeur detects "ontological naiveté" in Philip Wheelwright's theory of metaphor. From Ricoeur's description, the theory seems to claim a kind of reference attributed to poetic ecstasy in Romantic union with nature.

terms) in which a juxtaposition of concepts produces an allegorical pretense, only appearing to refer beyond itself in the realm of the "as-if."

In conversation with Turbayne's theory, Ricoeur describes Turbayne's choice of scientific models as epistemological "myths." Ricoeur states, "Turbayne discusses at length the reification of mechanical models in Descartes and Newton, that is, their immediate ontological interpretation. The tension between metaphorical and literal, therefore, is absent from the very start."[23] (Chapter 1 noted that the Wizard's screen does not have the filtering function of Black's screen. The point at issue for Turbayne is naïve or enlightened ontological interpretation, not what Ricoeur calls the "stereoscopic vision" of metaphorical tension.)

Ricoeur distances his method from Turbayne's for three key reasons:

> In the first place, [Turbayne] installs himself in an order of reality homogeneous with that of the positivism criticized by his thesis. The concern is always with "facts" and therefore also with truth in a verificationist sense, and this is not fundamentally altered. There is no escaping this ultimately neo-empiricist character of the thesis, if we consider that the examples of model-metaphors are borrowed not from restricted areas of physics but from the order of meta-scientific world views, where the border between model and scientific myth tends to be erased.... Furthermore, the author speaks of a mastery of models that is not to be found in poetic experience, where something other than the poet speaks even as he speaks, and where, beyond the control of the poet, a reality comes to language.... The problem afflicting Turbayne is that of demythologized myth: does it still have its power as speech? Is there something like metaphor-faith beyond demythologization? A second *naïveté* beyond iconoclasm? The question requires different replies for epistemology and for poetry. A lucid, mastered, concerted employment of models may be conceivable, even though it seems difficult to maintain the ontological abstinence of the "as-if" without believing in the descriptive and representative value of the model.... Can one create metaphors without believing them and without believing that, in a certain way, "that is"?[24]

---

23. Ricoeur, *The Rule of Metaphor*, 253.

24. Ricoeur, *The Rule of Metaphor*, 253–54. Ricoeur uses the term "epistemology" for scientific epistemology. He raises the possibility of a "mastered" employment of scientific models but also queries it.

Ricoeur's critique of Turbayne may be summarized in the following way. Firstly, Turbayne's model-metaphors are situated in an order of reality that denies their truth since the criterion for truth is verification. Secondly, the models are unmasked. On what basis do they then claim validity? Thirdly, a demythologized approach to models, while conceivable, may be unsustainable. Here Ricoeur suggests an alternative approach.

Taking his critique point by point, Ricoeur states firstly that Turbayne's concern is "always with 'facts' and therefore also with truth in a [positivist] sense." I have referred already to Ricoeur's remarks about the positivist position. Here is what he says in full:

> Critics shaped by the school of logical positivism state that all language that is not *descriptive*, in the sense of giving information about *facts*, must be *emotional*. Furthermore, the suggestion is that what is 'emotional' is sensed purely 'within' the subject. Emotion is an affect which has only an inside, and not an outside.[25]

The models chosen by Turbayne belong to an area of science that is not closely related to facts. As I understand him, Ricoeur says that these models pose no challenge to the assumptions of positivism.

Ricoeur queries the positivist dichotomy about ontological reference. He goes on to say that what Turbayne has to say about models does not tally with literary usage of metaphor, where "beyond the control of the poet, a reality comes to language." The question then becomes: where do scientific models in general stand in relation to facts? While allowing for the possibility of difference between scientific theory and poetry, Ricoeur questions whether the operation of scientific model is in practice distinct from that of poetic metaphor. McFague states that there are two different schools of thought about this. She describes the two approaches as the "low-view" and "high-view" of scientific models.[26]

The scientific low-view of models, says McFague, "treats a model 'as if' it pertained to the principal subject but one need not make a commitment that it really does."[27] She compares this view with "C. S. Lewis's description of a 'Master's' metaphor in which one knows what one wants to say and illustrates it for others, as contrasted with a 'Pupil's' metaphor in which the speaker is in the position of learner and has no means other

---

25. Ricoeur, *The Rule of Metaphor*, 227. Ricoeur's italics.
26. See McFague, *Metaphorical Theology*, 84.
27. McFague, *Metaphorical Theology*, 87.

than the metaphor to express the subject."[28] On McFague's terms, Lewis's master has a low-view of models. He has access to the facts by an alternative (possibly mathematical) route. But the pupil is not a mathematician. Consequently the master offers a metaphor as the only way of explaining the concept. (The Flatlanders' Sphere analogy considered above is an example of a Pupil's metaphor offered by the master to help his non-mathematical student understand the concept that space might be finite.)

In terms of Lewis's master and pupil, however, McFague's distinction between low-view and high-view leaves something out. Lewis makes the point that the model is offered and received differently. The non-mathematician receives it in the spirit of an indispensable Pupil's metaphor. In this case the pupil is in the position of taking what McFague calls a high-view of the model by necessity. For Lewis's master, access to the facts via the metaphor is technically dispensable. Nevertheless, the intention is to offer access to what is described. The master's endorsement of the model seems to go further than the uncommitted low-view approach.[29]

But if not applicable to Lewis's master, McFague's description of the low-view of models accords with Ricoeur's appraisal of Turbayne's approach. Ricoeur describes this approach as "the ontological abstinence of the 'as-if.'" Both Lewis and Ricoeur dissociate themselves from this kind of approach. In practice Lewis thinks the master will also make use of his own metaphor. "Purely magistral metaphor may never occur," he says.[30] Ricoeur agrees. He states, "a lucid, mastered concerted employment of models may be conceivable, even though it seems difficult to maintain the ontological abstinence of the 'as-if' without believing in the descriptive and representative value of the model." For Lewis, as for Ricoeur, such a master would be an oddity.

To my mind, a mastery of models accords with what I term the Wizard's perspective. As noted in chapter 1, Turbayne considers the possibility that Newton shared the Wizard's attitude of conscious pretense towards his own models. Turbayne describes the approach of full wizardry towards the linguistic model-metaphor for the events of nature:

> The third course is to be fully aware of the presence of the disguise; aware that there are no proper sorts into which the

---

28. McFague, *Metaphorical Theology*, 87–88. McFague cites Lewis, "Bluspels and Flalansferes," 38–39.

29. See Lewis, "Bluspels and Flalansferes," 38–44.

30. Lewis, "Bluspels and Flalansferes," 41.

> facts must be allocated, but only better pictures or better metaphors ... and then to treat the language metaphor as a myth ... [so that] when the "initiated" say "it is not true," one is able to answer by acting *as if* it were true.³¹

For Turbayne, the "as if it were true" is the positive side to the negative "it is not true."

While the low-view approach seems to accord with the Wizard's perspective, the high-view approach would appear more closely aligned with what I term the perspective of the Silver Shoes. McFague describes the high-view school of thought as follows:

> Metaphor has a positive as well as a negative pole and the positive pole is an assertion, albeit an indirect one, of reference to reality. That reference is, however, not only indirect but redescriptive; that is, metaphorical construction refers to reality both in the sense of creation as well as discovery. The epistemology that lies behind this statement is, of course, "critical realism," and it is ... the view not only of high-view supporters of models in science but also of ... Paul Ricoeur.³²

Here McFague aligns Ricoeur with the epistemology of high-view supporters of models in science. The high-view of the model also entails positive and negative poles. But the poles play a different role in the high view school of thought. Ontological abstinence of the "as if it were *true*," while it is the positive pole for Turbayne, would seem to accord with the *negative* pole of metaphor for Ricoeur. On the positive side, for Ricoeur, is the descriptive and representative value of the model.³³

If Ricoeur and Turbayne exemplify respectively high view and low-view approaches to scientific models, it is difficult to see how McFague can endorse both. To my mind, her approach is much closer to Turbayne's than Ricoeur's, even though she claims otherwise. She writes: "To the extent that I think that there is something, someone to which our metaphors refer, my belief falls into Ricoeur's notion of a wager.... Yet how the metaphor refers we do not know—or indeed even if it does. At the most one wagers it does and lives as if it does."³⁴ In other words, McFague

---

31. Turbayne, *The Myth of Metaphor*, 216–17. Turbayne cites Stewart, *The Myths of Plato*.

32. McFague, *Metaphorical Theology*, 132.

33. See Ricoeur, *The Rule of Metaphor*, 255–56.

34. McFague, *Models of God*, 195–96 n. 13. Cf. her discussion in *Metaphorical Theology*, 90–102.

does not espouse "the descriptive and representative value of the model." As with Turbayne, the *as if it were true* appears to represent the *positive* "is" for McFague.

Turbayne's program for unmasking "literalized" scientific metaphors accords closely with McFague's program for unmasking "literalized" religious metaphors. Ricoeur does not share this approach to religious metaphor. In her outline of Ricoeur's hermeneutical approach, McFague states:

> Ricoeur's devotion to a "hermeneutics of recollection or restoration" versus a "hermeneutics of suspicion" means that, like Gadamer, he is principally interested in what language says to us, not its possible false consciousness or the oppressive cultural structures it may mask as absolutes. What both Ricoeur and Gadamer do very well is show us how we can become integrated into a tradition, appropriate it as our own, overcome our initial alienation to it, allow its poetic universality to speak to us and our concerns.[35]

McFague comments: "The difficulty with this view, of course, is that many... experience tradition as alien and here we must part company with Gadamer."[36] McFague aligns herself with a "hermeneutics of suspicion." Ricoeur stresses the side of a "hermeneutics of restoration" but McFague is not happy with this.[37] Her plea for a "remythologization of Christianity"[38] is on a different footing to Ricoeur's "hermeneutics of restoration."

This brings me to Ricoeur's second point: if metaphor (or model) is demythologized, can the method still claim validity? The problem afflicting Turbayne is that of demythologized myth, says Ricoeur. He asks: "does it still have its power as speech?" If we apply the question to McFague, we may ask if her proposed alternative models have the same

---

35. McFague, *Metaphorical Theology*, 63. She refers to Ricoeur, *Freud and Philosophy* and Gadamer, *Philosophical Hermeneutics* and *Truth and Method*.

36. McFague, *Metaphorical Theology*, 63–64. McFague goes so far as to refer to "Marxist hermeneuts such as Jürgen Habermas [who] have clearly contended that the hegemony of linguisticality makes criticism of a tradition impossible." She cites Habermas, "A Review of Gadamer's Truth and Method."

37. McFague goes on to contrast Ricoeur's position with Gadamer's (*Metaphorical Theology*, 64). She states here that she supports "a modified hermeneutics of restoration" but at the same time she indicates that this modified stance is in line with the position of Ricoeur "who introduces a distinctly negative note." She does not acknowledge here that, for Ricoeur, the positive outweighs the negative.

38. McFague, *Models of God*, xi.

power of assertion as the metaphor "God the father" which she critiques. She writes:

> Metaphors and models relate to reality not in imitating it but in being productive of it. There are only versions, hypotheses or models of reality (or God): the most one can say of any construct, then, is that it is illuminating, fruitful, can deal with anomalies, has relatively comprehensive explanatory ability, is relatively consistent, has humane consequences etc. This is largely a functional, pragmatic view of truth, with heavy stress on what the implications of certain ways of seeing things (certain models) are for the quality of both human and nonhuman life (since the initial assumption or belief is that God is on the side of life and its fulfillment).[39]

McFague denies that the models she constructs "illustrate a concept of love (that is basically an allegorical direction)."[40] Turbayne, on the other hand, states that his linguistic model can function as a "modern allegory."[41] Despite her denial, I would class what McFague calls metaphor as a form of allegory. In her case the allegorical construct would illustrate the concept that God is on the side of life and its fulfillment. What marks its *modern* character is perhaps the ontological disclaimer in the form of "as if it were true." Demythologized myth in this "modern" sense carries with it the hallmarks of what Ricoeur terms "ontological abstinence." If all that you ever have are interpretive glasses ("ways of seeing things" that are "productive" of reality), becoming aware of various sets of glasses (and wearing them anyway) is no substitute for what Ricoeur calls "metaphor-faith beyond demythologization."

Nevertheless, as noted above, McFague enlists Ricoeur in describing her position as an ontological wager:

> I do not *know* who God is, but I find some models better than others for constructing an image of God commensurate with my trust in a God as on the side of life. God is and remains a mystery. We really do not know: the hints and clues we have of the way things are—whether we call them experiences, revelation, or whatever—are too fragile, too little (and more often than not, too negative) for much more than a hypothesis . . . that, although it can be comprehensive and illuminating, may

---

39. McFague, *Models of God*, 192 n. 37.
40. McFague, *Models of God*, 192 n. 37.
41. Turbayne, *The Myth of Metaphor*, 217.

not be true. We can believe it is and act as if it were, but it is, to use Ricoeur's term, a "wager."[42]

Anthony Thistelton's survey of recent thinking about language has a more positive view of Ricoeur's notion of "wager," linking it with the "hermeneutics of retrieval." He draws attention to Ricoeur's remark towards the end of *Symbolism of Evil*:

> How shall we get beyond the "circle of hermeneutics"? By transforming it into a *wager*. I wager that I shall have a better understanding of man and of all beings if I follow the *indication* of symbolic thought. That wager then becomes the task of *verifying* my wager and saturating it, so to speak, with intelligibility.[43]

Not content with acting as if it were true, Ricoeur follows the direction of symbolic thought.

For Ricoeur, symbols are "non-linguistic bonds uniting us with the cosmos," as McFague herself notes.[44] She states that, for Ricoeur, the "hermeneut's task" is "to interpret the multivalent, rich, ambiguous metaphors arising from the symbolic base of a tradition so that those symbols will once again speak to our existential situation." It is, however, this kind of retrieval and integration to a tradition that McFague's "metaphorical theology" disclaims.

METAPHORICAL TRUTH

We now come to Ricoeur's third point, an alternative approach to that of the disillusioned allegorist. Ricoeur asks: "Is there something like metaphor-faith beyond demythologization? A second *naïveté* beyond iconoclasm?" In his critique of Turbayne, Ricoeur acknowledges a debt to Douglas Berggren:

> Berggren tries to arbitrate (as I do) between ontological *naïveté* and the critique of mythified metaphor. Thus he carries the tensional theory of the internal semantics of the statement forward to the subject of truth and dares to speak of the tension between metaphorical truth and literal truth.[45]

---

42. McFague, *Models of God*, 192–93, n. 37. McFague's italics.
43. See Thiselton, *New Horizons in Hermeneutics*, 369.
44. See McFague, *Metaphorical Theology*, 120.
45. See Ricoeur, *The Rule of Metaphor*, 254–55. Ricoeur refers to Berggren, "The

Ricoeur goes on to conclude:

> The convergence of the two internal critiques, that of ontological and that of demythologization, culminates in a reiteration of the thesis of the "tensional" character of metaphorical truth and of the "is" that carries the affirmation. . . . [T]here is no other way to do justice the notion of metaphorical truth than to include the critical incision of the (literal) "is not" within the ontological vehemence of (metaphorical) "is".[46]

For Ricoeur, metaphor has a part to play at the level of truth, contrary to positivist thinking. But what part, we may ask.

Let us remind ourselves again of the dichotomy of "orders of reality" in Ricoeur's representation of positivism. "Critics shaped by the school of logical positivism state that all language that is not *descriptive*, in the sense of giving information about *facts*, must be *emotional*," says Ricoeur.[47] For positivists, the "emotional" side lacks what Ricoeur terms "ontological vehemence." Ricoeur indicates that Turbayne's metaphors "maintain the ontological abstinence of the 'as if' without believing in the descriptive and representative value of the model." The "as if" is fictional in the sense of belonging to the realm of "ontological abstinence." As I understand him, Ricoeur *spans* the two realms of ontological abstinence and ontological vehemence with an orientation towards the latter. Verification is not confined to "literal truth" since "the indication of symbolic thought" can be saturated with "intelligibility." Such intelligibility comes from the outside. "A mastery of models," says Ricoeur, "is not to be found in poetic experience, where something other than the poet speaks even as he speaks, and where, beyond the control of the poet, a reality comes to language."[48] (He implies doubt about whether the scientific experience of model-making is any different from this poetic experience.) The thrust of the experience is towards ontological vehemence, notwithstanding the fictional element from the realm of ontological abstinence. The net result of this description of poetic discourse is discovery as well as creation: beyond the control of the poet, a reality comes to language.

If Ricoeur appears to accept the ontological distinction between the fictional "as if" and the descriptive "is," Lewis, writing about metaphor

---

Use and Abuse of Metaphor."

46. See Ricoeur, *The Rule of Metaphor*, 255.
47. Ricoeur, *The Rule of Metaphor*, 227.
48. See Ricoeur, *The Rule of Metaphor*, 253–54.

from a different angle, may have a more positive conception of the "as if." As seen above, Lewis emphasizes the metaphorical base of cognitive language. Ricoeur shies away from this interest in dead metaphor, stating that he "leans towards the position that dead metaphors are no longer metaphors, but instead are associated with literal meaning, extending its polysemy."[49] Here Ricoeur agrees with Turbayne. For Ricoeur, a deterrent to focus on dead metaphor is the deconstructionist argument of an infinite regress of metaphoricity.[50] But Lewis avoids this difficulty. The regress is not infinite because it is grounded in language which points to the world of our senses. Here language is not metaphorical (or not necessarily metaphorical).

But Lewis goes on to say that, beyond the direct level, language is sourced by imaginative use of metaphor. "When we pass beyond pointing to individual sensible objects," he writes, "when we begin to think of causes, relations, of mental states or acts, we become incurably metaphorical":

> But it must not be supposed that I am in any sense putting forward the imagination as the organ of truth. We are not talking of truth, but of meaning: meaning which is the antecedent condition of both truth and falsehood, whose antithesis is not error but nonsense. I am a rationalist. For me, reason is the natural organ of truth; but imagination is the organ of meaning. Imagination, producing new metaphors or revivifying old, is not the cause of truth but its condition. It is, I confess, undeniable that such a view indirectly implies a kind of truth or rightness in the imagination itself.[51]

Unlike Ricoeur, Lewis does not go so far as to speak of "metaphorical truth"; rather, metaphor provides the requisite language for access to truth. Poets, says Lewis, can be expected to have a leading role in this activity. Ricoeur's indication of his distance from a positivist rejection of an "outside" to non-cognitive thinking may move in the direction of rapprochement to Lewis's suggestion.

Where then does McFague sit with this? She asks: "what is the relationship between our construct of God and *God*, or in our postmodern, deconstructionist era is that distinction even appropriate? That is, do our constructions refer to anything, anyone?"[52] In answer, she states:

49. Ricoeur, *The Rule of Metaphor*, 290.
50. See Ricoeur, *The Rule of Metaphor*, 287.
51. Lewis, "Bluspels and Flalansferes," 49–50.
52. See McFague, *Models of God*, 195–96 n. 13.

> Metaphorical theology applied to the "being of God" agrees with the tradition of the *via negativa* and the deconstructionists in stressing the absence of God over our presumptuous insistence in Western religious thought on the presence of the divine. . . . To affirm all this, however, does not mean there is not a reality (nor does it mean there is), though the presumption of metaphorical discourse . . . is that these metaphors, these versions, are of something, or there would be no point in arguing for one rather than another.[53]

McFague, it seems, leans towards what Ricoeur calls "ontological abstinence" while still leaving the door open to a vague possibility of a referent for her theological metaphors.

But a vague possibility of the existence of God is not the driving force of McFague's theology. She states that what can be said with assurance about "the character of Christian faith is very little."[54] On the other hand, what can be said about contemporary assumptions that necessitate a change from previous religious imagery is much less tentative. McFague lists some assumptions suitable for "the postmodern sensibility":

> a greater appreciation of nature . . . the recognition of the importance of language . . . the acceptance of the challenge that other religious options present to the Judeo-Christian tradition; a sense of the displacement of the white, Western male and the rise of those dispossessed because of gender, race, or class; an apocalyptic sensibility, fueled in part by the awareness that we exist between two holocausts, the Jewish and the nuclear; and . . . a growing appreciation of the thoroughgoing, radical interdependence of life at all levels and in every imaginable way.[55]

The term "postmodern sensibility" would seem to accord with the positivist notion of "emotional" language that is sensed purely within the subject. If what can be said about Christianity is very little, one may surmise that "metaphors" arising from such sensibility will not claim ontological reference beyond the Wizard's "as if."

As seen above, McFague claims to base her "metaphorical theology" on "an amalgam" of various theories about metaphor.[56] Here is her summation again:

---

53. McFague, *Models of God*, 196 n. 13.
54. McFague, *Models of God*, x.
55. See McFague, *Models of God*, ix–x.
56. McFague, *Metaphorical Theology*, 37.

> A metaphor is an assertion or judgment of similarity and difference between two thoughts in permanent tension with one another, which redescribes reality in an open-ended way but has structural as well as affective power.[57]

To my mind, metaphor represented as an assertion or judgment is reminiscent of the reflective judgment in Ricoeur's depiction of Turbayne. A judgment of similarity and difference may take us back to Turbayne's example of General De Gaulle and general contentment giving rise to the allegorical figure on horseback, cited in chapter 1.

As an illustration of metaphor, the green glasses in *The Wizard of Oz* do not contribute towards an actual view of the City. Rather they impose their own assertion of greenness on the City. The assertion is confined to the green glasses. How then could the green glasses be said to "redescribe" the City in an open-ended way? As noted above, McFague says that her metaphorical theology "applied to the 'being of God' agrees with the tradition of the *via negativa* and the deconstructionists in stressing the absence of God." The next chapter will compare the approaches of the *via negativa* and deconstruction and consider where McFague stands in relation to both.

---

57. McFague, *Metaphorical Theology*, 42.

3

The *Via Negativa*

In *The Wizard of Oz*, the old man who pretends to be the Wizard finally offers Dorothy a way to cross the desert as the first step to finding her home in Kansas. He decides to go with her, being tired of living under false pretenses. The two of them make a balloon which is filled with hot air. A crowd watches the process wonderingly. At the last minute Dorothy misses the flight. The ropes that tether the balloon to the ground snap apart. The balloon sails away without her. That is the last that is seen of the Wizard. No one knows whether his flight across the desert is successful or not.[1]

McFague describes the kind of effectiveness that she attributes to "metaphorical theology" in terms that to my mind are reminiscent of this flight by the Wizard. As noted in chapter 2, she asks about the relationship between our construct of God and *God*, in our postmodern, deconstructionist era. The quotation is part of a very long footnote. Here it is again. This time I have quoted the relevant section in full:

> Metaphorical theology applied to the "being of God" agrees with the tradition of the *via negativa* and the deconstructionists in stressing the absence of God over our presumptuous insistence in Western religious thought on the presence of the divine. God *is not*, not just in the sense of being unavailable to us or absent from our experience but as a basic aspect of the being of God. I think something like this is necessary both to include the very

---

1. See Baum, *The Wizard of Oz*, chapter 17.

different notions of other major religious traditions and to preserve a sense of the mystery of the divine, whatever our hopes, beliefs, or wagers might be. It is a recognition of the "privacy" of God, of the dark side of the divine that the mystics speak of and that a phrase of Robert Scharlemann's points to: "the being of God when God is not being God" (see the essay by that title in Thomas J. Altizer et al., *Deconstruction and Theology* [New York: Crossroad, 1982]). To affirm all this, however, does not mean there is not a reality (nor does it mean there is), though the presumption of metaphorical discourse—as evidenced by the conflict of metaphors, the competing "versions" of reality that metaphors project—is that these metaphors, these versions, are of something, or there would be no point in arguing for one rather than another.[2]

According to this description, users of "metaphorical theology" are by no means certain that there is a reality beyond theology or whether versions of reality that metaphors project express that reality. Such users are in a position that in some way resembles that of the witnesses to the Wizard's flight. Apart from Dorothy, the witnesses do not know anything about what lies beyond the Land of Oz. From their point of view, something is launched on the surmise that it travels in the right direction to reach something.

In general, narrative details in *The Wizard of Oz* cannot be pressed too far as illustrations but in this case it may be helpful to look at some of these more closely. Dorothy knows that Kansas exists and also the old man's home town, Omaha. The other witnesses do not know of either. The inhabitants of Oz are told that the supposed Wizard is going to make a visit to a great brother Wizard who lives in the clouds. The old man preserves his role of "Wizard" by describing his proposed journey in terms of what a wizard might popularly be supposed to do. In other words, he appeals to a *construct* of a wizard. Such a construct does not tell us all there is to be known; in fact it is misleading. McFague seems to claim no more than this for the relationship between our construct of God and *God*.

"God *is not*," says McFague, "not just in the sense of being unavailable to us or absent from our experience but as a basic aspect of the being of God. I think something like this is necessary both to include the very different notions of other major religious traditions and to preserve a sense of the mystery of the divine, whatever our hopes, beliefs, or wagers might be." Put in terms of the balloon flight in *The Wizard of Oz*, the old

---

2. McFague, *Models of God*, 195–96 n. 13. McFague's italics.

man *is not* a wizard nor is he making a visit to a brother wizard, whatever the surmises of the inhabitants of Oz. Nevertheless, his disappearance into the clouds could include such notions. In fact, McFague would seem to say, it is necessary that such notions are included in order to preserve the mystery of wizards. McFague detects some resemblance here to the non-referential ontology of deconstructionist thinking as well as to the tradition of the *via negativa*. To my mind, however, the traditional *via negativa* is more like the position of Dorothy. Although she knows something of what the flight is about, she is unable to communicate it, not least because the other witnesses would not understand her if she did.

THE WIZARD'S CINEMA

In continuing to draw comparisons from *The Wizard of Oz*, I follow the assumption, initiated by McFague, that she operates from what I call the Wizard's perspective. In a certain tongue in cheek sense the Wizard shares the perspective of the inhabitants of Oz. The inhabitants believe that the old man is going to visit a brother wizard in the clouds. The old man is aware that this is not the case. Nevertheless, he plays the part of the Wizard. In terms of reference, the Wizard's perspective accords with the "low-view" of models, noted in the last chapter. McFague states that the scientific low-view of models "treats a model 'as if' it pertained to the principal subject but one need not make a commitment that it really does."[3] Her description of religious metaphors seems in keeping with this view. Such metaphors offer competing versions of the reality they project. One may treat them as if they pertain to reality. One need not make a commitment that they really do.

The suggestion that metaphors project versions of reality takes us back to the Wizard's throne room, explored in chapter 1. Turbayne states that the analogy of "screen" for the function of metaphor, could at a later stage of development, more appropriately be described as a mask. For the sake of the analogy, I suggested that the screen in the corner of the Throne Room could be understood in terms of a cinematic screen. It is a mask for the inhabitants of Oz because they believe that the projected versions really do pertain to reality. While the Wizard treats the cinematic picture as if it pertains to reality he does not make a commitment that it really

---

3. See McFague, *Metaphorical Theology*, 87.

does. Unlike the other inhabitants of Oz, he is aware of the projection system that produces the picture on the screen.

Something similar appears to be happening with "metaphorical theology." "As remythologization," says McFague, "[metaphorical] theology acknowledges that it is, as it were, painting a picture." The ontological disclaimer is accompanied by an endorsement of the method:

> The picture may be full and rich, but it *is* a picture. What this sort of enterprise makes clear is that theology is *mostly* fiction: it is the elaboration of key metaphors and models. It insists that we do not know very much and that we should not camouflage our ignorance by either petrifying our metaphors or forgetting that our concepts derive from metaphors. We must not forget the crack in the foundation beneath all our imaginings and the conceptual schemes we build upon them. That crack is exemplified by the "is not" of metaphor which denies any identity in its assertions. Nonetheless, admitting that theology is mainly fiction, mainly elaboration, we claim some fictions are better than others, both for human habitation and as expressions of the gospel of Christian faith at a particular time.[4]

McFague does not acknowledge a debt to Turbayne here but I find echoes of his "linguistic metaphor" for the events of nature. Turbayne outlines the function of such a metaphor, once one is aware that it is a "picture":

> The third course is to be fully aware of the presence of the disguise; aware that there are no proper sorts into which the facts must be allocated, but only better pictures or better metaphors . . . and then to treat the language metaphor as a myth . . . [so that] when the "initiated" say "it is not true," one is able to answer by acting *as if* it were true.[5]

For McFague, as for Turbayne, some pictures are better than others. We must not petrify our metaphors, says McFague. Our "pictures" must be open to review. At the same time "some fictions are better than others." These pictures or models are not better in the sense of ontological reference but better in what is judged to assist "human habitation" and accord with [the constructs of] a particular time.

The Wizard's perspective allows one to discard some pictures while looking for better pictures. The search for better pictures or fictions is the

---

4. McFague, *Models of God*, xi–xii. McFague's italics.

5. Turbayne, *The Myth of Metaphor*, 216–17 (Turbayne's italics). He bases his remark on a quotation from Stewart, *The Myths of Plato*.

driving force of McFague's theology. She states that "theology, as constructive and metaphorical, does not 'demythologize' but 'remythologizes.'"[6] It is the loss of "myth" in the tradition of demythologizing that McFague seeks to rectify: "What our time lacks, and hence a task that theology must address, is an imaginative construal of the God-world relationship that is credible to us." I will explore the status of such a "myth" below.

The task of "remythologizing" is accompanied by a caveat. McFague's theology is constructed on a crack in the foundation: "the 'is not' of metaphor which denies any identity in its assertions." Despite her apparently positive emphasis, McFague retains the demythologizing component. Without it her kind of metaphors would not be open to review. The assumption of non-reference or non-commitment about reference precludes external measurement; hence the review is a subjective one, based on a judgment about what is "better" for a particular time. McFague links her ontological disclaimer with the tradition of the *via negativa*. Where then does this tradition stand in relation to what I call the Wizard's cinema?

As an example of demythologizing, Lewis cites Catholic modernist, George Tyrrell:

> It was put long ago by Tyrrell. As man progresses he revolts against 'earlier and inadequate expressions of the religious idea. . . . Taken literally, and not symbolically, they do not meet his need. And as long as he demands to picture to himself distinctly the term and satisfaction of that need he is doomed to doubt, for his picturings will necessarily be drawn from the world of his present experience'.[7]

Lewis responds:

> In one way of course Tyrrell was saying nothing new. The Negative Theology of Pseudo-Dionysius had said as much, but it drew no such conclusions as Tyrrell. Perhaps this is because the older tradition found our conceptions inadequate to God whereas Tyrrell finds it inadequate to 'the religious idea'.

The traditions of demythologizing and the old-style *via negativa* may appear similar but the assumptions are different.

---

6. McFague, *Models of Theology*, 32.

7. Lewis, "Fern-seed and Elephants," 122. Lewis quotes from Tyrrell, *Christianity at the Cross-Roads*, 125.

The Via Negativa

Let us now turn to Tyrrell direct and compare his thinking with McFague's. Tyrrell detaches biblical language from what it appears to describe. Such language is said to be an expression of "the religious idea." Nevertheless Tyrell regrets the loss entailed in discarding earlier expressions. In *Christianity at the Cross-Roads,* he writes: "I feel sure that the apocalyptic Heaven with its colour and music and light and happiness is a truer symbol of man's spiritual aspirations than the cold constructions of intellectualism."[8] While the language used to describe "the apocalyptic Heaven" cannot be taken literally, Tyrrell states that it can be taken "symbolically." But for Tyrrell, "symbol" refers to the expression of "man's spiritual aspirations," not to a glimpse of what heaven is like. As with the Wizard's cinema, the picture of heaven is a projection of human aspiration. There is no commitment that it pertains to reality.

Tyrrell intimates that this kind of symbolic language is less adequate to contemporary spiritual aspirations than to those of the biblical era. Nevertheless, it is more adequate, says Tyrrell, than "the cold constructions of intellectualism." This statement may offer a precursor to McFague's desire to replace biblical metaphors with new "metaphors," said to express "the salvific love of God" in a contemporary way.[9] McFague does not question the assumption that human picturing of "the religious idea" must be drawn from present experience (and apparently nothing else). What she does question is whether this dooms humanity to doubt. Given the assumptions expressed by Tyrrell, McFague looks for imaginative expression of "the religious idea" in a way that *will* satisfy current human need

This method belongs to what Ricoeur calls "demythologized myth." Chapter 2 cited his question on this point: if metaphor is detached from its referent, does it still have its power as speech?[10] What happens, one may ask, if it does not? To some degree McFague seems to acknowledge a consequent loss of speech. The lack of claimed reference for her models, she says, agrees with the tradition of the *via negativa.* According to Lewis, however, a claim of inadequacy in religious expression is unlike the older *via negativa* in being called inadequate to "the religious idea" rather than inadequate to God.[11] In Tyrrell's way of thinking, biblical descriptions of the things of God are no longer inadequate to express what God is really

---

8. George Tyrrell, *Christianity at the Cross-Roads,* 207.
9. See McFague, *Models of God,* 30.
10. Ricoeur, *The Rule of Metaphor,* 253–54.
11. Lewis, "Fern-seed and Elephants," 122–23.

like; they are inadequate to express a human idea of what God ought to be like. Similarly, McFague states that something like her description of what "God *is not*" is "necessary" to accord—not with what cannot be said about God—but with "the very different notions of other major religious traditions and to preserve a sense of the mystery of the divine." This also is a construct of what God ought to be like.

THE FRAME OF NON-REFERENCE

As noted above, McFague writes: "Metaphorical theology applied to the 'being of God' agrees with the tradition of the *via negativa* and the deconstructionists in stressing the absence of God over our presumptuous insistence in Western religious thought on the presence of the divine." Lewis's remarks about Tyrrell may serve to cast doubt on her claim to follow in the footsteps of the traditional *via negativa*. But what of her appeal to similarity between "metaphorical theology" and a deconstructionist stress on the absence of God?

McFague's kind of picturing, derived from the world of present experience, while seeming to point to a world beyond it, does not claim to actually do so. This, as has been seen, is to use the term "metaphor" in a sense that denies its power to carry a transferred sense of meaning. Deconstructionist theory uses a similar way of thinking to deny the carrying power of *any* language: "there is nothing outside the text" because language does not point to the world outside it.[12] Words point to other words. George Steiner refers to this loss of linguistic carrying power to the world outside as "the break of the covenant between word and world."[13] He dates this way of thinking to a movement among French poets in the nineteenth century. According to Steiner, the effect was to "splinter the foundations of the Hebraic-Hellenic-Cartesian edifice in which the *ratio* and psychology of the Western communicative tradition had lodged."[14]

Steiner outlines the "disjunction of language from external reference" in the poetic writings of French poet, Stéphane Mallarmé. Steiner comments that Mallarmé's preferred epithet for external reference is "impure": "to ascribe to words a correspondence to 'things out there,' to see

---

12. See Smith, *Jacques Derrida: Live Theory*, 56.
13. Steiner, *Real Presences*, 93.
14. Steiner, *Real Presences*, 95.

and use them as somehow representational of 'reality' in the world, is not only a vulgar illusion. It makes of language a lie":

> To use the word *rose* as if it was, in any way, like what we conceive to be some botanical phenomenon, to ask of any word that it stand in lieu of, as a surrogate for, the perfectly inaccessible 'truths' of substance, is to abuse and demean it. It is to encrust language with falsehood.[15]

Steiner indicates the ensuing disconnection between word and world: "That which endows the word *rose*, that arbitrary assemblage to two vowels and two consonants, with its sole legitimacy and life force is . . . '*l'absence de toute rose.*'"[16] Steiner calls this kind of approach the "linguistics of 'real absence.'"[17]

The movement of which Mallarmé was a part had a momentous effect on the understanding of the role of language and human access to reality. Steiner reports of this kind of thinking:

> Only when we realize that what words refer to are other words . . . can we return to a true freedom. It is within the language system alone that we possess liberties of construction and deconstruction, of remembrance and futurity, so boundless, so dynamic, so proper to the evident uniqueness of human thought and imagining that, in comparison, external reality, whatever that might or might not be, is little more than brute intractability and deprivation.[18]

In this approach, the break of the covenant between word and world is accompanied by a negative view of external reality along with indifference to whether or not the world of language corresponds to reality. Steiner goes on to observe that, for Mallarmé, "the self-referential, self-regulating and transformative cosmos of discourse is neither like the world, nor unlike it (how would we know?)."

Steiner describes this disjunction between word and world as the breakpoint of the *Logos*-order, leading to the replacement of "a central supposition of 'real presence' by one of 'real absence.'"[19] It is clear, how-

---

15. Steiner, *Real Presences*, 95–96.
16. Steiner, *Real Presences*, 95.
17. Steiner, *Real Presences*, 97.
18. Steiner, *Real Presences*, 97.
19. See Steiner, *Real Presences*, 96.

ever, that Steiner is not claiming that the previous *Logos*-order was necessarily a biblical one. He writes:

> Western theology and the metaphysics, epistemology and aesthetics which have been its major footnotes, are 'logocentric'. This is to say they axiomatize as fundamental and pre-eminent the concept of a 'presence'. It can be that of God (ultimately, it *must* be); of Platonic 'Ideas'; of Aristotelian and Thomist essence. It can be that of a Cartesian self-consciousness; of Kant's transcendent logic or of Heidegger's 'Being'. It is to these pivots that the spokes of meaning finally lead. They ensure its plenitude. That presence, theological, ontological or metaphysical, makes credible the assertion that there 'is something *in* what we say'.[20]

But if the historical *Logos*-order is not necessarily biblical, it is, at least ultimately, theist. The pivot to which the spokes of meaning finally lead is ultimately God. According to Steiner, deconstructionist writer, Jacques Derrida concedes the point. "Derrida's formulation is beautifully incisive: 'the intelligible face of the sign remains turned to the word and the face of God.'" Steiner goes on to remark:

> A semantics, a poetics of correspondence, of decipherability and truth-values arrived at across time and consensus, are strictly inseparable from the postulate of theological-metaphysical transcendence. Thus the origin of the axiom of meaning and of the God-concept is a shared one.[21]

For deconstructionists, however, the sign is no longer "intelligible" in the old sense and God is no longer the pivot to which the spokes of meaning lead.

Despite claiming similarity to this negative way of thinking, McFague distances herself from full acceptance of the deconstructionist position. In her presentation, the "is not" of metaphor that denies *any* identity in its assertions is said to be accompanied by the "is" of metaphor. But what does she mean by "is"? This is how McFague describes her understanding of the relationship between human constructions and reality:

> There is indeed no way behind our constructions to test them for their correspondence with the reality they presume to represent, but the constructions do, I believe, have a twofold relationship with reality which deconstruction ignores. First, they are

---

20. Steiner, *Real Presences*, 121. Steiner's italics.
21. Steiner, *Real Presences*, 119.

> productive of reality. . . . In this sense we create the reality in which we live; we do not copy it, or to put it more pointedly, there are no copies, only creations. The assumption here, however, is that there is a reality to which our constructions refer, even though the only way we have of reaching it is by creating versions of it. This is altogether different from the deconstructionist's position that there is nothing to which the text refers.[22]

Contrary to Mallarmé's disinterest, McFague expresses an interest in "a reality to which our constructions refer." On the other hand, the kind of reference she has in mind falls short of what Steiner calls "a semantics . . . of correspondence." This is the "is not" of her project. Her second point expresses the positive "is":

> Second our constructions are intended to be better than the ones they refute or replace. This of course a very difficult issue, because if one admits that all are readings, with the new replacing the old, on what basis can some be better than others? The certainly cannot claim to be better absolutely, or from all perspectives, or for all time. At the most they might be better relatively (to other constructions) from a particular perspective, and for a particular time.[23]

Better perspectives are what McFague's project is all about.

McFague's notion of "God" lacks the kind of solidity required for what Steiner calls "a central supposition of 'real presence'" in language.[24] As seen above, McFague states that metaphorical theology "applied to the 'being of God' agrees with the tradition of the *via negativa* and the deconstructionists in stressing the absence of God over our presumptuous insistence in Western religious thought on the presence of the divine." That said, her method is premised on what she terms the inextricable and symbiotic connection of metaphor and concept in relation to theology.[25] She states: "I do not *know* who God is, but I find some models better than others for constructing an image of God commensurate with my

---

22. McFague, *Models of God*, 26. McFague claims that her assumption (that there is a reality to which constructions refer, even though the only way we have of reaching it is by creating versions of it) accords with critical realism (see 193 n. 43). This leaves out the "discovery" aspect of critical realism, (cf. McFague, *Metaphorical Theology*, 132).

23. McFague, *Models of God*, 26–27.

24. See Steiner, *Real Presences*, 96.

25. See McFague, *Models of God*, xi.

trust in a God as on the side of life."[26] Models of God representing the concept of God "as on the side of life" can be used as the building blocks for constructing a further image of God.

For building purposes how deep is the crack in the foundation? Despite the term "theology," God has nothing to do with the way language works in McFague's depiction of it. God does not ensure its plenitude. The spokes of meaning do not lead, even indirectly, to God but rather to humanity. The only way we have of reaching the reality, according to McFague, is by creating versions of it and the resulting constructions are verified from a particular (human) perspective.

THE POWER OF SPEECH

What I call the Wizard's perspective allows for a certain amount of equivocation. One does not have to commit oneself about ontological reference. One may, so to speak, believe, with the inhabitants of Oz, that the Wizard really has gone to visit a brother wizard in the clouds. At the same time one is aware of the "is not" that qualifies one's belief. Ricoeur calls this kind of thinking "ontological abstinence"[27] and questions whether such demythologized metaphor still has its power of speech. One may surmise that it only functions *as if* it had the power of speech; one need not make a commitment that it really does.

McFague admits to drawing close to the deconstructionist position on the efficacy of language. She parts company, however, with the "purity" of its early exponent, Mallarmé. This kind of purity would put the question of reference beyond bounds. According to Mallarmé, it is *within* the language system alone that we possess liberties of construction and deconstruction. By comparison, external reality (whatever that might or might not be) is "little more than brute intractability and deprivation."[28] According to McFague, there is a reality to which our constructions refer (although she is less than committed about this in the case of constructions about God). But it is not clear how constructions can be said to refer to reality if all they ever do is create versions of it. She also states that some constructions are better than others from a particular perspective

---

26. McFague, *Models of God*, 192–93 n. 37.
27. See Ricoeur, *The Rule of Metaphor*, 253–54.
28. Steiner, *Real Presences*, 97.

The Via Negativa

for a particular time. Can anything be said, particularly about theology, on such a basis?

McFague herself is in no doubt on this point (although the kind of speech she has in mind differs in terms of substance to that envisaged by Ricoeur). At the end of her first chapter in *Models of God* she writes:

> In this chapter, I have been searching for a standpoint from which to do Christian theology in our time. I have suggested that a new sensibility is required, one characterized by the felt awareness of our intrinsic interdependence with all that lives, a holistic, evolutionary, ecological vision that overcomes ancient and oppressive dualisms and hierarchies, that encourages change and novelty, and that promotes an ethic of justice and care; one characterized as well by a profound acceptance of human responsibility for the fate of the earth, especially in view of a possible nuclear holocaust, and therefore by the willingness to think differently, to think in metaphors and models that support a unified, interdependent understanding of God-world and human-world relationships; and finally, one characterized by the recognition that although all constructive thought is metaphorical and hence necessarily risky, partial and uncertain, implying an end to dogmatism and absolutism, it is not thereby fantasy, illusion or play.[29]

Christian theology is not illusion, says McFague. But her linguistic assertions about the object of faith are at best tenuous and shadowy. What is not illusory appears to be the "sensibility" behind them.

There are certain difficulties in basing theology or even ethics on relativism and doubt about linguistic reference. McFague seems to admit this because she goes on to say:

> A person who is starving, imprisoned, discriminated against, tortured, or homeless can scarcely be expected to believe that the ideology that permits such oppression is a mere [language] game, no worse than any other. Nor would such a person believe that language is the totality of reality: hunger, fear and suffering unite beings, both human and nonhuman, in a wordless community where a cry of pain is the universal word.[30]

Here McFague falls back on non-speech as a way of testing ideology. Apart from the cry of pain, it would appear that "there is indeed no way behind

---

29. McFague, *Models of God*, 27.
30. McFague, *Models of God*, 28.

our constructions to test them for their correspondence with the reality they presume to represent."[31] This kind of thinking would seem a long way from the correspondences, discerned by Black's "suitable hearer," between the subsidiary subject (or vehicle) and principal subject (or tenor).[32] It would seem a long way from Lewis's statement that various metaphors will enable his hypothetical man "to think of ships, very imperfectly indeed and under strict limits, but not wholly in vain."[33] McFague's metaphorical constructions do not allow for the sense of "not wholly in vain" which both affirms and qualifies ontological reference. As I judge, she operates in a space that does not take cognizance of such criteria.

Let us pause here and consider the scope of McFague's way of thinking. Her kind of theology is "risky, partial and uncertain." Nevertheless, the method retains the wish to communicate and even to "make sense" as will be considered in chapter 7. How does she accommodate these factors? As noted, McFague has a respect for reality which is not characteristic of deconstructionist writers. But her protest against certainty militates against this; her theory of metaphor endorses a relativist subjectivism. Nevertheless, an appeal to the epistemological reality of a wordless cry of pain indicates the need for an ontological context to her standpoint. Further, "metaphorical theology" (along with the ability to write about it) relies on the validity of conceptual truth. We may recall here Ricoeur's remark about Turbayne. Ricoeur writes that Turbayne "installs himself in an order of reality homogeneous with that of the positivism criticized by his thesis. The concern is always with 'facts' and therefore also with truth in a verificationist sense, and this is not fundamentally altered."[34] As I judge, McFague does not query the positivist dichotomy with regard to orders of reality. At the same time she critiques the loss of "myth." Here she follows Turbayne in pursuing the subjectivist aspect of the dichotomy while at the same time drawing attention to its ontological limitation. This is the Wizard's perspective.

Such thinking, as Ricoeur says, will concern itself with truth in a factual sense. Contrary to the nuanced test of metaphor in standard usage, positivism applies a laboratory kind of test to metaphorical construction. In a positivistic way of thinking, the facts of the comparison do not

---

31. McFague, *Models of God*, 26.
32. See Black, *Models and Metaphors*, 41.
33. See McFague, *Metaphorical Theology*, 42 and 203–4 n. 27.
34. Ricoeur, *The Rule of Metaphor*, 253–54.

match; hence comparing one with the other is, as Turbayne would say, a kind of category mistake. Such a "mistake" does not pass the test in terms of positivist verification. But the Wizard's perspective adds something to this: the "mistake" may not pass the test of positivism but it does not fail it either as long as its terms are restricted to the sensibility behind the comparison. Because this is the domain of both the "is" (in the guise of "as if") and the "is not" of her conception, McFague is able, without overt absurdity, to include "the very different notions of other major religious traditions and to preserve a sense of the mystery of the divine, whatever our hopes, beliefs, or wagers might be."[35] But it also means that she cannot say very much either. The fact that she does say a great deal from her subjectivist standpoint is somewhat inconsequent.

McFague links the mystery of the divine with the absence of God. Here she finds common ground with deconstructionist thought. But can the same thing be said about her claim to accord with the traditional *via negativa*? In the concluding chapter of *The Body of God*, McFague quotes from a reflection, by the medieval mystic Julian of Norwich, on the creation:

> . . . a little thing, the size of a hazelnut, in the palm of my hand, and it was as round as a ball. I looked at it with my mind's eye and I thought, 'What can this be?' And the answer came, 'It is all that is made.' I marvelled that it could last, for I thought it might have crumbled to nothing, it was so small. And the answer came to my mind, 'It lasts and ever shall because God loves it.' And all things have being through the love of God. In this little thing I see three truths. The first is that God made it. The second is that God loves it. The third is that God looks after it. What is God indeed that is maker and lover and keeper? I cannot find words to tell.[36]

McFague links "the dark side of the divine that the mystics speak of" with the phrase "the being of God when God is not being God."[37] But if God is not being God what, according to Julian of Norwich, will be the fate of all that is made?

The presence of God and the power of speech are eschewed by deconstructionists. The presence of God is queried by McFague in a space

---

35. See McFague, *Models of God*, 196 n. 13. McFague's italics.

36. See McFague, *The Body of God*, 212 and 262 n. 9. McFague quotes from the modernized text of Julian of Norwich in Glasscoe, *The Revelation of Love*, chapter 5.

37. See McFague, *Models of God*, 196 n. 13. McFague's italics.

where the non-spoken cry of pain is the universal word. But the tradition of the *via negativa* does not deny reference and access to truth. On the contrary, it affirms both while acknowledging that some things are beyond the reach of language. The presence of God is the source of everything for Julian of Norwich, in a way that words cannot express.

MOSTLY FICTION

"Metaphorical theology" paints a picture, says McFague. She adds, "What this sort of enterprise makes clear is that theology is *mostly* fiction."[38] From a positivist point of view, fiction belongs to an order of reality that is sensed within the subject. McFague seems to claim little more, in terms of reference, for her models. This kind of approach not only says something about her notion of theology; it also says something about her notion of fiction. By contrast, Lewis finds a kind of truth or rightness in imagination itself[39] and Ricoeur states that "beyond the control of the poet, a reality comes to language."[40]

This chapter has considered the road negative, to use a more neutral term than *via negativa*. McFague finds a similarity between her approach and those of the traditional mysticism and the deconstructionist movement. In order to assess the validity of her claim, I have tried to sketch both. Despite its admission of a limited power of expression, the traditional *via negativa* is wholly oriented towards the living God. It is this external orientation which limits its power of speech. Deconstructionist thinking, on the other hand, is oriented towards internal reference. In my judgment, McFague does not enter the domain of the *via negativa* (except in the redefined sense, attributed above to Tyrrell). Her picture, one might say, is not oriented towards its subject. Similarity between the deconstructionist position and hers is clearer: a picture which does not claim to represent anything beyond itself brings her into the orbit of internal reference.

But McFague's method belongs to the tradition of demythologizing, not deconstruction. The flavor is different: the "myth" is deconstructed but not the concept behind it. McFague takes the method a step further in her project to "remythologize" the Christian faith. She endows the

---

38. McFague, *Models of God*, x. McFague's italics.
39. Lewis, "Bluspels and Flalansferes," 49–50.
40. Ricoeur, *The Rule of Metaphor*, 254.

demythologized kind of myth with new cogency. This takes her "myth" into the realm of the "as if." Since McFague's kind of "as if" claims the imprimatur of metaphor, its orientation might more appropriately be discussed in terms of the *via analogia* which is the topic of the next chapter. But, as already seen, the imprimatur may give a false impression. This is where McFague's understanding of metaphor is at issue.

Before moving on to the *via analogia*, I wish to be as clear as possible about what McFague means by fiction. As I judge, McFague does not step outside the positivist demarcation: her kind of fictional "as if" belongs within the realm of the feeling subject. Here she parts company with Ricoeur, as is explored further in the next chapter. McFague states a wish to bring a literary approach to theology. Whether her concept of fiction makes this a legitimate enterprise remains to be seen. An appeal to a literary approach would seem to take her beyond the road negative. But does it? While this chapter has already touched on some of the issues involved, I believe a little more needs to be said about the part played by the "as if" in her notion of metaphor.

The status of the fictional "as if" is perhaps most easily discernable in considering the status of scientific hypothesis. This chapter has already recalled a distinction, made in chapter 2, between the "low view" and "high view" of scientific models. Ricoeur holds to the equivalent of the "high view," endorsing the fictional "as if" as the negative pole of metaphor while maintaining the positive pole in its descriptive orientation.[41] For Turbayne, however, the fictional "as if it were true" is the positive pole of the negative "it is not true."[42] I suggested that Ricoeur understands metaphor to span the realms of ontological abstinence and ontological reference. Lewis stresses a further role for the imaginative use of metaphor. "All our truth, or all but a few fragments," he says, "is won by metaphor."[43] But this cannot be the case if the "as if" of metaphor lacks an orientation to external reality.

While the scientific notion of model differs in certain respects from the literary use of metaphor, there is sufficient overlap in terms of external reference for a parity of conclusions between the two. The next chapter will engage with McFague's endorsement of a literary approach. Here I will draw attention to a contrast of ideas between Turbayne and

41. See McFague, *Metaphorical Theology*, 87 and 132.

42. See Turbayne, *The Myth of Metaphor*, 217. Turbayne quotes Stewart, *The Myths of Plato*.

43. Lewis, "Bluspels and Flalanferes," 50.

Lewis on the "as if" of science. One needs to attend closely on this point because, while some terms may be similar, the differing contexts alter their meaning.

In describing his notion of metaphor, Turbayne cites Francis Bacon on the status of the scientific enterprise: "in my judgment all the received systems are but so many stage-plays representing worlds of their own creation . . . neither only of entire systems but also of many principles and axioms in science which by tradition, credulity, and negligence have come to be received".[44] Turbayne applies this subjectivist understanding to model-metaphors: he claims that metaphor also represents no more than a world of its own creation. Given this assumption, he takes it a step further. "I shall show how the 'stage-plays' may be re-performed, or the 'masks' put back," continues Turbayne, "but with this crucial difference, with awareness that they are only 'stage-plays' or only 'masks.'"

Chapter 1 noted Turbayne's surmise that Newton may have made use of model-metaphor on the understanding that it constituted no more than a "mask":

> It may have been the case that . . . Sir Isaac [was] fully aware that [he was] speaking in metaphor. . . . In which case, like any user of models, [he] would have rejected any extension beyond the para-designer . . . hypothesis.[45]

Let us now compare Turbayne with what Lewis has to say in a similar area. Lewis states that Newton must have recognized the provisional nature of a scientific theory if "he wrote not 'the attraction varies inversely as the square of the distance', but 'all happens as if' it so varied."[46] Moving on to Galileo, Turbayne states his intention of following the advice of Galileo's inquisitor, Cardinal Bellarmine: "Galileo will act prudently if he will speak hypothetically (*ex suppositione*)."[47] Lewis observes: "The real reason why Copernicus raised no ripple and Galileo raised a storm, may well be that whereas the one offered a new supposal about celestial motion, the other insisted on treating this supposal as fact."[48] This may sound as if Lewis and Turbayne agree about the lack of ontological status for scientific theory.

---

44. Turbayne, *The Myth of Metaphor*, 29. Turbayne cites *Novum Organum*, 1.44.
45. Turbayne, *The Myth of Metaphor*, 58–59.
46. Lewis, *The Discarded Image*, 16.
47. Turbayne, *The Myth of Metaphor*, 40 cf. 53.
48. Lewis, *The Discarded Image*, 16.

But let us look a little deeper. Lewis writes about *two* principles held by medieval scientists. Suppositions about their concept of the universe were expressed in terms of "saving the appearances." This is to say that a scientific theory "must 'save' or 'preserve' the appearances, the phenomena, it deals with, in the sense of getting them all in, doing justice to them."[49] But, since "a lively inventive faculty could devise a good many different supposals which could equally save the phenomena," Lewis cites another principle, "first perhaps, formulated with full clarity by Occam" in which "we must accept (provisionally) not any theory which saves the phenomena but that theory which does so with the fewest possible assumptions."

Lewis believes these principles are still applicable:

> In every age it will be apparent to accurate thinkers that scientific theories, being arrived at in the way I have described, are never statements of fact. That stars appear to move in such and such ways, or that substances behaved thus and thus in the laboratory—these are statements of fact. The anatomical or chemical theory can never be more than provisional. It will have to be abandoned if a more ingenious person thinks of a supposal which would 'save' the observed phenomena with still fewer assumptions, or if we discover new phenomena which it cannot save at all.[50]

As represented by Lewis, new phenomena have the power to falsify scientific theory. In other words, the "stage-plays" so-called are subject to an ontological test. They may have to be replaced.

For Lewis, the scientific "as if" is the negative pole while openness to an ontological test is the positive pole of scientific modeling. But, as noted, the fictional "as if it were true" is the positive pole for Turbayne. Ricoeur states that Turbayne's examples of "model-metaphors" come from the "order of meta-scientific world views where the border between model and scientific myth tends to be erased."[51] As I understand it, scientific myth would be less exposed than a model to the rigor of the scientific method. Turbayne applies the conclusions drawn from his meta-scientific examples to his notion of metaphor. In the process of "undressing" a metaphor, Turbayne purports to confront the "mask" with the "literal truth."[52] But the purpose is to expose rather than test since

---

49. Lewis, *The Discarded Image*, 14–15.
50. Lewis, *The Discarded Image*, 15–16.
51. Paul Ricoeur, *The Rule of Metaphor*, 253–54.
52. See Turbayne, *The Myth of Metaphor*, 54–59. See discussion of Turbayne's

his kind of metaphor already carries the assumption that it does not correspond to reality. The "stage-plays" of Turbayne's method can never be tested in an ontological way. They can only be unmasked.

Where does McFague stand with this? She finds a similarity between the reference of metaphor and that of a scientific hypothesis. "The criteria of truth for a hypothesis in science," she says, "are not unlike criteria applied to metaphors in poetry and religion." In terms of "hypothesis," she cites Nelson Goodman, "Truth of a hypothesis . . . is a matter of fit—fit with a body of theory, and fit of hypothesis and theory to the data at hand and the facts to be encountered."[53] But I find that, in her application, McFague leaves out the data at hand and the facts to be encountered. She continues:

> One speaks of metaphor as apt or appropriate because it fits into the assumptions of a poem or into a system of doctrines or to life as lived. The hypothesis or metaphor may well transform or even revolutionize the conventional theory or set of expectations, but in either case it is not considered true because it corresponds with some uninterpreted reality but because it gives us a more apt, fitting way of interpreting reality than did the traditional view.[54]

McFague does not explain here how metaphor can have the power to transform or revolutionize conventional theory without access to reality outside pre-existing assumptions. As she describes it, the fictional "as if" of scientific hypothesis (and of poetry and the meaning of a life) is confined to its underlying construct.

In wishing to "remythologize" Christianity, McFague moves away from what Tyrrell calls "the cold constructions of intellectualism."[55] Her literary impulse is perhaps at its clearest in a prequel to *Metaphorical Theology*, before, that is, she embarks on her hermeneutic of suspicion towards the metaphor "God the father." She writes:

> If theology becomes overly abstract, conceptual and systematic, it separates thought and life, belief and practice, words and their embodiment, making it more difficult if not impossible for us to believe in our hearts what we confess with our lips. There is a way to do theology, a way that runs from the gospels and Paul

---

rationale for "undressing" a metaphor in chapter 1 "Knocking over the screen."

53. McFague, *Metaphorical Theology*, 40 and 203 n. 22. McFague quotes Goodman, *Languages and Art*, 79, 80.

54. McFague, *Metaphorical Theology*, 40–41.

55. Tyrrell, *Christianity at the Cross-Roads*, 207.

The Via Negativa 59

through Augustine and Luther to Teilhard and the Berrigans, that one would call intermediary or parabolic theology, theology which relies on various literary forms—parables, stories, poems, confessions—as a way from religious experience to systematic theology.[56]

But if the fictional "as if" of poetry and the meaning of a life is confined to its underlying construct what is to distinguish it from illustration of concepts? Does this amount to an allegorical use of literary resources?

McFague tends to disown the suggestion that her method produces allegory. In her Introduction to *Speaking in Parables* she writes that metaphor "is not just ... a useful (or even a necessary) means of communicating something we already know":

> This would be allegory, not metaphor. Rather metaphor is a way of *knowing*, not just a way of communicating. In metaphor knowledge and its expression are one and the same; there is no way *around* the metaphor, it is not expendable. One can insist that certain metaphors are incorrect or inappropriate or do not "fit," but then all one can do is suggest other metaphors that are preferable. One cannot do without *any* metaphors.[57]

It is not clear how metaphor can move beyond communicating something we already know if it must fit into "the assumptions of a poem or into a system of doctrines or to life as lived." Let us recall once again. McFague's definition of metaphor:

> A metaphor is an assertion or judgment of similarity and difference between two thoughts in permanent tension with one another, which redescribes reality in an open-ended way but has structural as well as affective power.[58]

Can metaphor be a way of knowing reality if it does not have the capacity to correspond to "some uninterpreted reality"?

Steiner says of Mallarmé's position, "to ascribe to words a correspondence to 'things out there,' to see and use them as somehow representational of 'reality' in the world, is not only a vulgar illusion. It makes of language a lie."[59] By contrast, McFague maintains that "there is a reality to which our constructions refer." But she qualifies this: "even though

56. McFague, *Speaking in Parables*, 1–2.
57. McFague, *Speaking in Parables*, 4.
58. McFague, *Metaphorical Theology*, 42.
59. Steiner, *Real Presences*, 95–96.

the only way we have of reaching [reality] is by creating versions of it."[60] Such versions are not open to an ontological test. How then can the versions be distinguished from illusion?

But McFague would deny that her kind of "as if" leads to illusion. She states a wish to find a standpoint for Christian theology: "one characterized by the recognition that although all constructive thought is metaphorical and hence necessarily risky, partial and uncertain . . . it is not thereby fantasy, illusion or play."[61] She also says that her kind of theology is mostly fiction and that her enterprise "insists that we do not know very much."[62] Like Turbayne's Wizard, she seems to want to have it both ways: although metaphors are "masks" or "stage-plays," some are better than others. Can it be that the denial of allegory and illusion in her method is, in itself, an illusion? Does she sometimes forget her green glasses and, in a more than tongue in cheek sense, step into the shoes of the inhabitants of Oz? This is a large question and one which I will continue to ask. My next chapter will consider metaphor as a way of knowing.

---

60. McFague, *Models of God*, 26.
61. McFague, *Models of God*, 27.
62. McFague, *Models of God*, xi–xii.

4

The *Via Analogia*

ONE OF THE REASONS why Dorothy's journey in the Land of Oz reaches its goals is because she follows the Yellow Brick Road. On one occasion she and her companions have to cross a river. The current takes them downstream. When they finally reach the far side of the river, they find themselves at some distance from the Road. The journey back to the Road is hazardous. To return to it they must cross a field of deadly poppies.[1]

Chapter 3 drew attention to what Steiner calls the break in the covenant between the word and the world: the old idea that there is something in what we say is open to dispute. There is more than one way to respond to this situation. One may, in terms of *The Wizard of Oz*, cross the river and find the Road on the other side. Ricoeur seems to belong to this category. "Beyond the control of the poet," he says, "a reality comes to language."[2] Alternatively, one may travel downstream with the deconstructionists. I think it would be fair to say that McFague does not quite do either. But if she is trying to find a way that lies somewhere between the two, one might ask if her road of the "as if" will not offer a deceptive kind of attractiveness like that of the Deadly Poppy Field.

To enter the discussion requires taking cognizance of different frames of reference. Deconstruction, in the pure form espoused by its early exponent Mallarmé, is strictly what I term the frame of non-reference.

---

1. See Baum, *The Wizard of Oz*, chapters 7 and 8.
2. Ricoeur, *The Rule of Metaphor*, 254.

Language does not refer to what is outside it or, if it does, it is demeaned. This applies not only to live metaphor but to all language. Beyond this, I have distinguished two other frames of reference which I call the Wizard's perspective and the frame of the Silver Shoes. I argue that only the frame of the Silver Shoes allows for the reassertion of the covenant between word and world.

There is a delicate balance to be maintained in this. What I call the frame of the Silver Shoes admits the tentative nature of reference. I have expressed this in terms of Dorothy's home-coming in stocking feet. Lewis writes about the provisional nature of scientific modeling and also attributes to metaphor the kind of reference which is at best "not wholly in vain." Reference in this understanding is by no means absolute but nevertheless assured. By contrast, the Wizard's home-coming is wholly uncertain. (He could be lost in the desert for all we know.) The difference in the two ways of thinking seems to me one of focus. In the frame of the Silver Shoes the focus is on arrival. In the Wizard's perspective the focus is on the vehicle itself as a carrier of human aspiration.

It is the contention of this book that much hangs on what is meant by metaphor. Ricoeur asks in relation to Turbayne, "Can one create metaphors without believing them and without believing that, in a certain way, 'that is'?"[3] In other words, can one sustain the neutral stance about reference demanded by the Wizard's perspective? As already seen, what is termed "metaphor" in such thinking tends to refer back to the construct behind it.[4] Yet McFague professes a kind of wager on belief in a God who is "on the side of life."[5] Her "metaphorical theology" is then faced with the question posed by Ricoeur. To my mind, McFague moves in the direction of believing in the truth of one of her models at least. She recommends an ecological "subject-subjects" model in place of a rationalist "subject-object" model.[6] But does she invoke the "subject-subjects" model by abandoning the neutral stance (entering the frame of the Silver Shoes) or by forgetting the neutral stance (adopting the perspective of the inhabitants of Oz)? I will explore this model and the kind of truth it professes in chapter 5.

---

3. See Ricoeur, *The Rule of Metaphor*, 253–54.
4. See McFague, *Models of God*, chapter 1.
5. McFague, *Models of God*, 192 n. 37.
6. See McFague, *Super, Natural Christians*, 36–39.

The Via Analogia 63

In the Silver Shoes frame of transfer, God in some sense underpins thinking and language as a whole. The role of God in underpinning linguistic transfer can be put in various ways. Ricoeur links metaphorical reference with a sense of belonging, as will be explored in the fourth section of this chapter. As seen in chapter 3, Steiner distinguishes "a central supposition of 'real presence' in language" from one of "real absence."[7] By contrast, McFague goes so far as to say that "metaphorical theology" stresses "the absence of God over our presumptuous insistence in Western thought on the presence of the divine."[8] If stressing the presence of the divine in our thinking is presumptuous, what, one may ask, is the status of her wager regarding a God who is "on the side of life"?[9] The answer, as we have already seen, is to believe and act as if such beliefs were true without commitment that they really are. A lack of commitment, it seems, is understood to guard against presumption.

But McFague also describes metaphor as a way of knowing.[10] She expresses a desire to engage in theology by means of various literary genres: parables, stories, poems, confessions. She indicates that this method will assist us "to believe in our hearts what we confess with our lips."[11] Can it be done on her terms? What kind of belief can occur through a medium that relies on her notion of metaphor? Put another way, what effect does her search for belief have on her linguistic approach? To my mind, such questions confront McFague's attempt to reach the *via analogia*. Before exploring that road and its surroundings, however, I will first consider the deconstructionist river that cuts across it, the source of the current, some strange counter-currents mid-stream as well as how the river might be crossed.

THE LOST COVENANT

In chapter 3, I cited a quotation by McFague of the medieval mystic, Julian of Norwich. Some things can be said about what God does as maker, lover and keeper, says the mystic, but some things about who God is are

---

7. Steiner, *Real Presences*, 96.
8. McFague, *Models of God*, 195–96 n. 13.
9. McFague, *Models of God*, 192 n. 37.
10. McFague, *Speaking in Parables*, 4
11. McFague, *Speaking in Parables*, 1–2.

beyond human words to tell.¹² What cannot be said marks the tradition of the *via negativa*. Michael Christensen describes another tradition of knowing something of God:

> The great medieval theologian Thomas Aquinas related to ultimate reality in the intuitive as well as in the rational sense, and concluded that human beings can know what God *is* and that he is his own essence, but we cannot know in any precise, affirmative sense *what* God's essence is. The attributes of the Infinite cannot be contained in finite language and thought. Aquinas also asserted, however, that mankind was not destined to silence about the Source of his religious experience. We can speak of God in two ways. We can say what God is not (*via negativa*). . . . We can also approximate the nature of God by employing useful analogies (what can be termed *via analogia*).¹³

The *via analogia* is a term which is usually confined to an approach to language about God. But such an approach presupposes the efficacy in general of analogical or metaphorical reference. This kind of understanding encompasses Black's glimpse of stars as well as Steiner's covenant between the word and the world and Ricoeur's emphasis on truth in the metaphorical "is."

Chapter 3 noted the kind of thinking which underpins this kind of reference. Steiner writes:

> Western theology and the metaphysics, epistemology and aesthetics which have been its major footnotes, are 'logocentric'. This is to say they axiomatize as fundamental and pre-eminent the concept of a 'presence'. It can be that of God (ultimately, it *must* be); of Platonic 'Ideas'; of Aristotelian and Thomist essence. It can be that of a Cartesian self-consciousness; of Kant's transcendent logic or of Heidegger's 'Being'. It is to these pivots that the spokes of meaning finally lead. They ensure its plenitude. That presence, theological, ontological or metaphysical, makes credible the assertion that there 'is something *in* what we say'.¹⁴

I will briefly consider the Thomist doctrine of analogy as well as a potential development in Cartesian self-consciousness below. McFague distances herself from the doctrine of analogy, as will be seen.

---

12. See McFague, *The Body of God*, 212.
13. Christensen, "We see through a glass darkly," 57–58. Christensen's italics.
14. Steiner, *Real Presences*, 121.

Is there something in what we say? This is not the place for a restatement of the doctrine of analogy so much as a restatement of the terms on which the doctrine is proposed. E. L. Mascall writes:

> We are not merely concerned with the question "How can an infinite, necessary and immutable Being be described in terms that are derived from the finite, contingent and mutable world?" but with a question that is anterior to this and without which this cannot be properly discussed at all, namely "How is the possibility of our applying to the infinite Being terms that are derived from the finite order conditioned by the fact that the finite order is dependent for its very existence on the fiat of the infinite and self-existing Being?"[15]

The dependence of the finite order upon the infinite and self-existing Being would seem to bring us to the heart of what Steiner means by "presence" in language.

McFague, however, critiques "a traditional, Thomistic view of analogy":

> It is sometimes asserted that the so-called transcendentals can be predicated properly of God whereas metaphors are always improper. Thus, in the analogy of proper proportionality, one can assert that human goodness is to human being as God's goodness is to God's being. To this I would respond with two points:(1) Since we do not know *what* God's being is, we have no corollary for asserting [sic] "goodness" to God. (2) "Goodness" can *only* be a metaphor when asserted of God (if it is to mean anything at all); that is, we use the associations of human goodness as a grid or screen to say something about God.[16]

Leaving aside the distinction between "transcendentals" and "metaphors," let us ask what McFague means by "*only*" a metaphor. Her assertion that "we do not know *what* God's being is" would seem to overstate Thomist thinking regarding our ignorance of God. As seen, Christensen represents the Thomist view in the following terms: "we cannot know in any precise, affirmative sense *what* God's essence is." McFague's assertion would imply complete ignorance rather than tentative knowledge of God.

Christensen reports that we can "approximate the nature of God by employing useful analogies": this is the *via analogia*. By contrast,

---

15. Mascall, *Existence and Analogy*, 116.
16. McFague, *Models of God*, 194 n. 10. McFague's italics.

McFague's notion of metaphor only allows for assertion as a projection from human traits. Contrary to Mascall's representation, McFague leaves out the dependence of the finite order on the infinite and self-existing Being. She uses the language of "screen" to illustrate what she means by "*only* a metaphor." That this is not the kind of screen of Black's illustration is evident in her denial of the view of "stars" (in this case the referent, God) which can be seen through it.[17] Mascall indicates that the dependence of the finite order *on* God is relevant to the possibility of speech *about* God. Steiner broadens the application to language on general. This is what he means by "presence" in language: if "presence" is absent, linguistic correspondence is denied.

What process has led to the loss of a sense of "presence" in language? In her engagement with deconstructionist thinking, McFague outlines the history of Western linguistics as seen through deconstructionist eyes. She describes a kind of linguistic "sacramentalism," understood to link the visible and transcendent worlds in the Western world prior to the modern era:

> Michel Foucault has written a fascinating study of the decline of the complex system of "resemblances" or "signs" between the visible and invisible worlds which until the sixteenth century served as a kind of linguistic sacramentalism, linking all dimensions of reality.... The assumption was that there was an original Text that all the signs pointed to and interpreted, albeit mostly in an oblique fashion.[18]

McFague goes on to say: "This linguistic 'sacramentalism' ended with the loss of faith in an original Text to which the signs referred, and one is left with 'mere' words that refer to nothing outside themselves."

The original Text, reports McFague, had supplied a "metaphysics of presence" giving a sense of cogency to linguistic meaning. She writes: "Western theology claims also to have assurance of this Presence in the Book, the Text of texts, in which human words truly refer to the Word itself."[19] Such a statement might give the impression that the historical

---

17. Black, *Models and Metaphors*, 41. See also chapter 1.

18. McFague, *Models of God*, 212 n. 17. McFague cites Michel Foucault, *The Order of Things*, 33. Cf. also *Models of God* 193 n. 44 for McFague's remarks about Foucault's contribution "to the demise of the metaphysics of presence."

19. McFague, *Models of God*, 24. McFague attributes this statement to "deconstruction." For her own emphasis on the lack of transcendent biblical meaning, see 22–23.

The Via Analogia

loss of faith in linguistic "presence" arose from a historical loss of faith in Christianity. But the Text to which the previous "sacramentalism" referred was not the biblical text. McFague indicates elsewhere that the so-called original Text was the medieval "book of nature."[20] What was this "book of nature"? The background to linguistic "sacramentalism" was a popularized cosmological model of reality. It would be more accurate to describe the model as pre-modern rather than specifically medieval, since it had begun to develop in late antiquity. Lewis writes:

> In the last age of antiquity many writers . . . were, perhaps half-consciously, gathering together and harmonising views of very different origin: building a syncretistic Model not only out of Platonic, Aristotelian and Stoical, but out of Pagan and Christian elements. This Model the Middle Ages adopted and perfected.[21]

Mascall reports that, according to this older view, the external world is to be perceived in a trans-sensory sense, offering access to a transcendent "intelligible object of which it is the manifestation." In recent centuries the visible world has become detached from such transcendent meaning. For Kant, notes Mascall, perception of externals is reduced to sensation requiring "categories of understanding" in order to be perceived.[22]

Although the *loss* of a "metaphysic of presence" may date from the sixteenth century, Steiner has a broad view of the origins of linguistic cogency. As noted in chapter 3, he writes of the "Hebraic-Hellenic-Cartesian edifice in which the *ratio* and psychology of the Western communicative tradition [has] lodged."[23] He states that the various sources of meaning are validated by God, their ultimate source. In this respect, Cartesian self-consciousness (as similarly with Kantian "categories of understanding") retains the source of meaning.

But the Cartesian or Kantian source has tended to become internalized. McFague writes that René Descartes was "the father of the modern notion of objectivity." She states, however, that the source of knowledge for Descartes was not metaphysical but subjectivist: "For Descartes, knowledge was not to be found through a return to the gods, but by a

---

20. McFague, *Super, Natural Christians*, 54.
21. Lewis, *The Discarded Image*, 12.
22. Mascall, *Words and Images*, 36–38. Mascall cites Kant, *Critique of Pure Reason*.
23. See Steiner, *Real Presences*, 94–95.

turn inward, to the individual's internal thoughts: 'I think therefore I am.'"[24] McFague quotes feminist philosopher, Lorraine Code:

> For each knower, the Cartesian route to knowledge is through private abstract thought, through the efforts of reason unaided either by the senses or consultation with other knowers. It is this individualistic, self-reliant private aspect of Descartes' philosophy that has been influential in shaping subsequent epistemological ideals.[25]

The father of the modern notion of objectivity is also said to be the father of individualistic epistemology.

Without going so far as to attribute it to Descartes directly, one may detect the seeds of the positivist dichotomy in the Cartesian legacy. Epistemology (how we know what we know) has become detached from its external source of validation. At the same time the realm of objectivity has tended to become detached from its subjectivist epistemological source. Such validity as it possesses has become the search for verification. I suspect that we have yet to see the full effect of this dichotomy in terms of its effect on the *ratio* and psychology of our Western tradition.

THE LOST COIN

A traditional assumption that there "is something *in* what we say" is in dispute. As Steiner puts it, deconstructionist thinking "challenges this presumption of insured content, of cognitive ballast."[26] At the same time the loss of ballast or epistemology has not found easy acceptance: the departure of meaning seems to have become a search for meaning. This search takes various guises. I have entitled this section "the lost coin," which comes from an analogy promoted by the deconstructionist movement. As indicated above, deconstructionist theory denies "presence" in language but retains the memory of it. I will explore this below. A further source of meaning finds a shadowy existence in the subconscious mind. This kind of epistemology does not constitute a return to the *via analogia* but it may appear to operate in a similar locality.

---

24. McFague, *Super, Natural Christians*, 74

25. McFague is quoting Code, *What Can She Know?*, 5. (See McFague, *Super, Natural Christians*, 188 n. 10.)

26. Steiner, *Real Presences*, 121.

I believe McFague's project finds common ground with such tendencies. As seen, McFague distances herself from the doctrine of analogy and in the process parts company with its traditional epistemology. In the last book of her series she promotes an ecological subject-subjects model of the self and world in place of a rationalist subject-object model. Here she invokes the priority of the sub-rational self, constituted through contact with the natural world. There is a deconstructionist precursor to such thinking. I will consider this development and possible parallels with McFague in the next chapter but a short description may be helpful here.

The Introduction drew attention to two nineteenth century French poets, Stéphane Mallarmé and Arthur Rimbaud.[27] Mallarmé's theory of linguistic non-reference was considered in the last chapter. Rimbaud is known for the saying: "*Je est un autre*." This saying challenges the notion of a unitary self which thinks and therefore is, in a Cartesian sense. Steiner writes: "Rimbaud posits at the now vacant heart of consciousness the splintered images of other and momentary 'selves.'"[28] Douglas Parmée describes Rimbaud's theory of the *voyant* or poet as seer and prophet, expressed in "two disjointed and rhapsodic letters" written to two friends in May 1871:

> *On a tort de dire; je pense. On devrait dire; on me pense. Car Je est un autre*. As soon as one examines oneself closely, one realises that one's personality contains depths of which one is normally unaware . . . our thoughts which we take to be our own, spring from something within us which we cannot control because we do not know what it is.[29]

Parmée goes on to comment that "colours, scents, shapes that occur to [Rimbaud] in his exploration of these depths . . . seem very similar to the unconscious of psychologists."[30] Chapter 5 will suggest a similarity in McFague's notion of an inner life or "deepest, most basic sense of self" which governs the thinking self.[31]

The possibility of a subjectivist epistemology has not only situated a search for meaning in the self but has promoted a separation between the conscious self and something other than the conscious self. But what

---

27. Steiner, *Real Presences*, 94.
28. Steiner, *Real Pesences*, 99.
29. Parmée, *Twelve French Poets*, liii.
30. Parmée, liv.
31. McFague, *Super, Natural Christians*, 92.

exactly is this other self and what function does it have? Carl Jung finds a parallel to pre-modern metaphysics in the subconscious mind:

> Significantly enough, it is Kant's doctrine of categories, more than anything else, that destroys in embryo every attempt to revive metaphysics in the old sense of the word but at the same time paves the way for a rebirth of the Platonic spirit.[32]

The pre-modern model assimilated and adapted Plato's notion of an invisible world of forms, ideas or archetypes. Jung argues that something like this invisible world has since become part of the *inner* world, archetypes residing in the subconscious mind:

> [T]here are present in every psyche forms which are unconscious but nonetheless active—living dispositions, ideas in the Platonic sense that perform and continually influence our thoughts and feelings and actions.[33]

In this regard, we may recall Neumann's remarks about the location of feminine archetypes in the subconscious mind, as cited in the Introduction.[34]

In sum, two linguistic tendencies appear to have operated in recent Western history. Firstly, there is a shift of focus: attention has moved from the external world providing access to a transcendent world to the conceptual world providing access to the external world. More recently deconstructionist theory has cast doubt on conceptual access to the external world. Secondly, the old sacramental view has given way to a new source of meaning in the world of the subconscious. Jung terms this the rebirth of the Platonic spirit. Such thinking will not offer a return to the *via analogia* but it may look as if it does. In terms of the *Wizard of Oz*, it comes near the Yellow Brick Road. But this is deceptive, perhaps perilously so. Close to the Road lies a source of hallucination, the Deadly Poppy Field.

The deconstructionist movement has a foot in the territory of the sub-rational "other." At the same time, awareness of what has been lost is a strong theme for the movement. A key image associated with the loss of truth and meaning is that of a coin that has been ground down to a mere disc of metal. McFague cites Friedrich Nietzsche in this respect:

---

32. Jung, *Aspects of the Feminine*, 119.
33. Jung, *Aspects of the Feminine*, 122.
34. Neumann, *The Great Mother*, 336.

The Via Analogia

> What then is truth? A mobile army of metaphors, metonymics, anthropomorphisms: in short a sum of human relations which become poetically and rhetorically intensified, metamorphosed, adorned, and after long usage, seem to a nation fixed, canonic and binding; truths are illusions of which one has forgotten that they *are* illusions, worn-out metaphors which have become powerless to affect the senses, coins which have their obverse effaced and now are no longer of account as coins but merely as metal.[35]

In his image of a rubbed coin, we may note that Nietzsche links metaphor with illusion. Derrida also uses the image of the coin in referring to philosophical amnesia about its dependence on "metaphor." Derrida likens metaphysicians to "knife-grinders, who instead of knives and scissors should put medals and coins to the grindstone to efface the exergue, the value and the head."[36]

James K. A. Smith reports that Derrida replaces the old idea of cogency supplied by a metaphysic of "presence" with a "presence-in-absence":

> In the place of a metaphysics of presence is a quasi-ontology of the trace (or presence-in-absence), and instead of an isolated, self-conscious subject fully present to itself in the interiority of a pure consciousness, Derrida sketches a subject who is constituted by a relation to an exteriority—the alterity of the Other in the communal networks of signification.[37]

This is to bring the strands of the lost sense of presence and the loss of Cartesian self-consciousness together and to supply an alternative to them. Given the deconstructionist emphasis on lack of access to external reality, the sense in which a subject could be said to be constituted by a relation to an exteriority might be difficult to determine. The door would seem open to the kind of "exteriority" located within "splintered images of other and momentary 'selves'" in the subconscious mind.

---

35. See McFague, *Models of God*, 5. McFague cites Nietzsche, "On Truth and Falsity in Their Ultramoral Sense." The italics are in the text as cited.

36. See Smith, *Jacques Derrida: Live Theory*, 54–57. Smith states that Derrida cites Nietzsche about metaphor as a rubbed coin in *Margins of Philosophy*, 211.

37. Smith, *Jacques Derrida: Live Theory*, 45.

THE TOWER OF BABEL

Disenchantment with Cartesian subjectivity and a denial of linguistic reference might be supposed to spell the end for philosophy in deconstructionist thinking. But this is not the case. As noted above, McFague draws attention to deconstructionist interest in "linguistic sacramentalism," a system that was abandoned due to the loss of faith in medieval cosmology. In this section I consider a deconstructionist appeal to linguistic validation in the memory of "presence" as well as its deferral. Secondly, I indicate a possible reversal of direction, implicit in a reading by Derrida of the biblical story of the Tower of Babel.

The positive effect residing in the memory of linguistic cogency appears to be in view in a remark made by Derrida about Walter Benjamin who in turn quotes Mallarmé. Benjamin, as cited by Derrida, writes:

> Philosophy and translation are not futile. . . . For there exists a philosophical genius, whose most proper characteristic is the nostalgia for that language which manifests itself in translation.[38]

Derrida then goes on to quote from Benjamin's citation of Mallarmé, the philosophical genius that Benjamin appears to have in mind. "The diversity of terrestrial idioms," says Mallarmé, "prevents anyone from uttering words in which there would otherwise be a unique mintage, itself the substance of the truth."[39] Here the notion of mintage (or coinage) is linked with the notion of truth.

Chapter 3 cited Mallarmé's aversion to linguistic correspondence:

> To use the word *rose* as if it was, in any way, like what we conceive to be some botanical phenomenon, to ask of any word that

---

38. See Derrida, "Des Tours de Babel," 112–13. Derrida quotes from Benjamin, "On Language as Such and on the Language of Man" (1916). Derrida writes that reference to Babel is "explicit there" but that he does not deal with that aspect of Benjamin's writing in "Des Tours de Babel" (see 111).

39. Derrida does not supply the original source for the quotation from Mallarmé which remained untranslated from the French in Benjamin's work and is not translated (into English) by Joseph F. Graham, Derrida's translator. The above is my attempt to render part of the quotation from Mallarmé, which reads poetically in the French. (Here is the untranslated quotation in full: "Les langues imparfaites en cela que plusieurs, manque la suprême: penser étant écrire sans accessoires ni chuchotement, mais tacite encore l'immortelle parole, la diversité, sur terre, des idiomes empêche personne de proférer les mots qui, sinon, se trouveraient, par une frappe unique, elle même matériellement la vérité.")

it stand in lieu of, as a surrogate for, the perfectly inaccessible 'truths' of substance, is to abuse and demean it. It is to encrust language with falsehood.[40]

But, according to Derrida's citation, Mallarmé associates this denial of linguistic efficacy with the diversity of terrestrial idioms. Translation of languages, Benjamin indicates, provides access to a kind of nostalgia which offers a basis for philosophy.

The term "nostalgia" suggests an earlier state in which language did have access for "the perfectly inaccessible 'truths' of substance." As I understand him, Mallarmé goes so far as to say that were it not for the diversity of languages, words in themselves would offer "a unique mintage" of such "truths." One may detect here a Romantic quality of longing for a truth which is at the same time tragically unobtainable.

Derrida explores this loss of linguistic correspondence in the context of the biblical story of the Tower of Babel. As such, he locates the break in the *Logos*-order in the "mythical" past. Deconstructionist philosophy cannot be said to have a history of supporting the biblical God. Nevertheless Smith reports that "by calling into question the linguistic ideal of immediacy and one (univocal) language . . . deconstruction has sided with Yahweh at Babel":[41]

> In seeking to 'make a name for themselves', to found at the same time a universal tongue and a unique genealogy, the Semites want to bring the world to reason, and this reason can signify simultaneously a colonial violence (since they would thus universalise their idiom) and a peaceful transparency of the human community. Inversely, when God imposes and opposes his name, he ruptures the rational transparency but interrupts also the colonial violence of linguistic imperialism.[42]

40. Steiner, *Real Presences*, 95–96.
41. See Smith, *Jacques Derrida: Live Theory*, 51–52.
42. Smith, *Jacques Derrida: Live Theory*, 51–52. Smith quotes Derrida, "Des Tours de Babel." As I understand the essay, Smith's statement that deconstruction has sided with Yahweh at Babel could also be phrased as Yahweh has sided with deconstruction at Babel. See 118: "in giving his name, God also appealed to translation, not only between the tongues that had suddenly become multiple and confused, but first *of his name*, of the name he had proclaimed, given, and which should be translated as confusion to be understood, hence to let it be understood that it is difficult to translate and so to understand. . . . For Babel is untranslatable. God weeps over his name." Derrida's italics. Derrida regards this association of God's name with confusion as disempowering correspondence between languages (see 117) and calls the Babel story "archetypal" and "allegorical" of the "so-called theoretical problems of translation"(111). He also

Deconstruction, it may be observed, sides with Yahweh to the extent that the critique is not directed against "the linguistic ideal of immediacy" *as such*, since it is God who "imposes and opposes his name" with the result that humanity disperses over the earth in forced implementation of the commandment of Genesis 1:28. Rather, the critique is directed against a *specific kind* of "linguistic ideal of immediacy" reminiscent of Cartesian self-consciousness, "the sphere of the knowing subject" in which what is to be known is subject to the conditions of the knower.[43] Making a name for *oneself* imposes conditions on the world. The Semites are said to want to universalize *their* idiom.

For Derrida, however, there is poignancy in the imposition of God's name: this is at once the supreme example of "the linguistic ideal of immediacy" and the supreme example of the loss of "the linguistic ideal of immediacy." God, on deconstructionist terms, imposes and opposes his name *at the cost of* Babel, which signifies confusion. In other words, God's linguistic interference in imposing the meaning of his name initiates the tragic necessity of translation in which pure transfer of meaning, including the meaning of God's name, is forever out of reach.

As noted above, Derrida replaces the old idea of cogency supplied by a metaphysic of "presence" with a "quasi-ontology" of the "trace" (or presence-in-absence). In my view, the twin poles of erstwhile purity of language and current messianic "trace" haunt the deconstructionist conception in a Romantic trajectory.[44] There is something Wagnerian in the picture of Yahweh as the hero who rises to the tragic heights of willing his own downfall.[45] Whether this trajectory accords with the

---

appears to treat the story as a metaphor of deconstruction: "from abyss to abyss [the Babelian text] deconstructs the tower, and every turn, twists and turns of every sort, in a rhythm" (133).

43. See McFague, *Super, Natural Christians*, 188 n. 10. Cf. Smith, *Jacques Derrida: Live Theory*, 31. Smith writes that, for Derrida, the "metaphysics of presence" is "a kind of shorthand for naming the ontological xenophobia that has characterized Western philosophy."

44. See Smith, *Jacques Derrida: Live Theory*, 76–80. Smith states that Derrida, influenced by Emmanuel Levinas, picks up the notion of the "trace" which "permits the possibility of thinking beyond the binary opposition of presence and absence" about "the enigma of absolute alterity, that is, the Other" (76). Derrida's thinking here seems to be summed up as follows: "Deconstruction is a kind of minion to the haunting ghost of the 'to come'" (see 80); "Deconstruction is the prophet of a new kingdom of ends, seeking to make straight the way for the other to arrive" (see 90); "this is a messianicity without messiah, a religion without religion" (see 115).

45. Cf. Lewis, "The Funeral of a Great Myth," 112.

biblical writings is another matter. Derrida bases the association of God's name with that of Babel on Voltaire's statement that "*Ba* signifies father in the Oriental tongues, and *Bel* signifies God."[46] This can be compared with the statement by Derek Kidner that Babel "called itself Bab-ili or 'gate of God', but by a play of words Scripture superimposes the truer label *bālal* ('he confused')."[47] Despite his persistent play on "confusion," there is perhaps more confusion than Derrida admits in his premise of the supposed identification of God's name with the name of Babel. But the *tour de force* style of his essay tends to preclude exegetical critique. What it does not preclude, admittedly figuratively, is interaction between Yahweh and creation.

Deconstruction, says Steiner, is anti-God as the Father of meaning.[48] Derrida posits an ironic twist to this, attributing the deconstruction of meaning to the self-deconstruction of Yahweh at Babel. But, as I judge, the irony rebounds upon itself. Even on deconstructionist terms the memory of meaning sustains its philosophical pursuit. Steiner maintains:

> The deconstructive discourse is *itself* rhetorical, referential and altogether generated and governed by normal modes of causality, of logic and of sequence. The deconstructive denial of 'logocentrism' is expounded in wholly logocentric terms.[49]

The deconstructive discourse critiques Cartesian self-consciousness but does not abandon it. One might add that in one sense it accentuates it. According to Steiner, the "logocentrism" of Cartesian self-consciousness retains an external sense of "presence" as the source of meaning. In discarding an external sense of "presence," the deconstructive critique becomes all the more reliant for its validity on "the sphere of the knowing subject" in which what is to be known is subject to the conditions of the knower.[50] It is the knowing subject who retains the memory of meaning. In critiquing the knowing subject the deconstructive discourse undermines the validity of its own critique.

---

46. See Derrida, "Des Tours de Babel," 105. Derrida quotes Voltaire, *Dictionnaire philosophique*.

47. Kidner, *Genesis: Introduction and Commentary*, 110.

48. Steiner, *Real Presences*, 127.

49. Steiner, *Real Presences*, 129.

50. See McFague, *Super, Natural Christians*, 188 n. 10. Cf. Smith, *Jacques Derrida: Live Theory*, 31.

Even within deconstructionist ranks are hints of a desire for a source of truth and meaning of some kind. In one breath deconstructionist writers denounce the "coin" of truth that underpins language. In another breath, a memory of the old "mintage" appears to sustain their philosophical endeavor. Derrida's interpretation of the Tower of Babel undermines a Cartesian source of language. It does not undermine the original power of language since without it Yahweh would not have been able to impose and oppose his name. One might ask whether all the deconstructionists have done is to critique the Cartesian or Kantian legacy of subjectivity. In siding with Yahweh at Babel, does deconstruction point the way out of its own impasse?

THE YELLOW BRICK ROAD

We touch on complex issues in an apparently simple question: is there something *in* what we say? I agree with McFague when she says that metaphor is a way of knowing. But it depends what is meant by "metaphor" and "way of knowing." McFague posits two kinds of metaphor, as will be seen below. The introduction to this chapter drew attention to what I call the Silver Shoes frame of transfer in which God in some sense underpins thinking and language as a whole. Steiner refers to this anchoring process as "cognitive ballast." Epistemologically, it is an established way with solid brick underfoot. McFague detaches "modern consciousness" from this known thoroughfare. But does the trajectory of modern consciousness necessarily support her conclusions? Have we really lost touch with the Yellow Brick Road?

Too much, it seems, has been discarded with the loss of faith in a historical *Logos*-order. Deconstructionist nostalgia for a vanished "mintage" of linguistic cogency bears witness to the resultant vacuum. At the same time the Romantic expression of that loss is misleading. It is fanciful to link the loss of linguistic cogency with the biblical story of the Tower of Babel. The diversity of terrestrial idioms did not historically militate against "linguistic sacramentalism" linking all dimensions of reality; it persisted until the sixteenth century. Further, Mallarmé's nostalgia for access to "'truths' of substance" overstates the historical understanding of linguistic transfer. In terms of *The Wizard of Oz*, Mallarmé mourns the loss of the Silver Shoes: if Dorothy does not arrive with the Shoes, she may not arrive at all. But, according to Steiner, the notions of semantic trust and semantic inadequacy have gone hand in hand: "Not even the purest tautologist . . . has ever held the total sum of essence to be convertible into the currency of the word and sentence."[51] Dorothy has always arrived in stocking feet.

If too much has been discarded with the medieval universe with the result that too much has been attributed to a subjectivist substitute, where then can meaning be found? Is there a way of crossing the deconstructionist river with the old transcendence intact? If we abandon medieval cosmology and Cartesian subjectivity, we need not abandon the historical *Logos*-order nor the biblical God. If deconstruction sides with Yahweh at Babel against subjectivism, Yahweh may survive the crossing where subjectivism would be swept aside. This is not to say that the Yahweh of the Tower of Babel bears much resemblance to the unmoved mover of medieval "sacramentalism." Chapter 9 will consider the possibility of a sacramental universe which moves away from medieval syncretistic accretions.

In differing ways, Steiner, Jung, deconstructionist writers and McFague, bear witness to a loss of "myth" that validates language. But if Jung is right, the only source of the Platonic spirit now comes from within. If so, the new source of meaning is at odds with the positivist suspicion of what is sensed within the subject. What kind of credibility can be supplied on such terms? Put in terms of *The Wizard of Oz*, if it is possible to cross the deconstructionist river on some sort of positivist raft, where does one arrive? One cannot rejoin the Yellow Brick Road on the old terms and McFague does not try. At best one can act as if the old transcendence were true. One may "believe" without external commitment.[52] One may come close to the Yellow Brick Road. That is the domain of the Deadly Poppy Field.

What has brought us to this pass? The loss of "myth" and the loss of faith in the carrying power of metaphor go hand in hand. Both Nietzsche and Lewis draw attention to the relationship between metaphor and truth but their conclusions are very different. As seen above, Nietzsche deconstructs truth on the ground that it is dependent on metaphor. As seen in Chapter 2, Lewis states that, beyond the world of the senses, linguistic reference relies on metaphor and that "all our truth, or all but a

---

51. See Steiner, *Real Presences*, 91–92.
52. McFague, *Models of God*, 192–93 n. 37.

few fragments, is won by metaphor."[53] Lewis makes a positive statement, Nietzsche a negative one. It depends what is meant by metaphor. McFague's remarks about two types of metaphor are revealing in this respect.

Chapter 3 noted McFague's endorsement of a literary approach to theology as a way to unite thought and life.[54] On the face of it, there is much to be said for making theological use of literary sources. Contrary to her stated aim, however, McFague seems to reject the kind of metaphor which claims to unite thought and life. She writes:

> Philip Wheelwright makes a very useful distinction between two kinds of metaphor—metaphor of association or transference (epiphor) and metaphor of juxtaposition (diaphor). The former is the classical type: the transference of a word from what it usually means to some other object, as in "the milk of human kindness" or "God the Father." The ability to employ this sort of metaphor, however, seems to rest on a confidence that things really *are* associated, that the centre holds, that the web is not broken—that, in other words, the universe is in some sense sacramental, that God is somehow the true and original father, that all things are connected among themselves because they are connected in God. It depends, as C. Day-Lewis says, on believing that the human mind can claim "kinship with everything that lives or has lived," or, as Paul Ricoeur puts it, "it is an index of the situation of man at the heart of the being in which he moves, exists and wills, that the symbol speaks to us." In significant ways, this sense of unity of the human with all that is, is still part of our culture, and heightened ecological and mystical awareness has increased it for many. But it is not, I believe, the dominant sensibility in Christian circles, at least among those attempting to create new contexts for Christian symbols and stories.[55]

McFague admits here the "classical" type of metaphor which allows for transfer in the metaphor "God the Father" (with a capital F for Father which later becomes lower case when subject to demythologizing). She admits that Ricoeur supports "a confidence that things really *are* associated" and that "the universe is in some sense sacramental." But McFague herself queries this kind of sacramental understanding.

---

53. See Lewis, "Bluspels and Flalansferes," 47–50.

54. See McFague, *Speaking in Parables*, 1–2.

55. McFague, *Speaking in Parables*, 106. McFague refers to Wheelwright, *Metaphor and Reality*, 72–91.

The Via Analogia

Apart from the "classical" type of metaphor, McFague describes another kind:

> The other kind of metaphor, juxtaposition, is particularly pertinent to modern consciousness, for, alienated and disbelieving as we are, we respond to the ambiguity, irony, and covert cynicism of metaphorical juxtaposition. Wheelwright quotes the following extreme examples of new meaning by juxtaposition.
>
> My country 'tis of thee
> Sweet land of liberty
> Higgledy-piggledy my black hen.
>
> The apparition of these faces in the crowd;
> Petals on a wet black bough.
>
> The connections are not spelled out; two images are simply juxtaposed and the reader is left to make his or her own connections, though the choice of images juxtaposed of course delimits meaning in a certain direction.[56]

McFague distinguishes between "metaphor of association or transference" and "metaphor of juxtaposition" as if they are two different types of metaphor. She adds: "it seems to me that contemporary Christian attempts [to create new contexts for Christian symbols and stories] rely heavily on metaphor by juxtaposition."[57] Here the metaphorical reference is said to be manufactured by the reader. The method would seem conducive to allegorical picturing stemming from arbitrary associations. Two images in juxtaposition generating an idea or picture by connotation is reminiscent of Turbayne's example of General De Gaulle juxtaposed with general contentment producing the allegorical picture of General Contentment on horseback.

In fact, McFagues does not sustain her distinction between the two different types of metaphor. She also says that "most successful metaphors . . . are an indissoluble blend of both."[58] At this point I turn to Ricoeur's comments on Wheelwright's theory. Ricoeur detects the paradox of metaphor ("is" and "is not") in Wheelwright's distinction between epiphor and diaphor. "Epiphora," says Ricoeur, "is Aristotle's term for

---

56. McFague, *Speaking in Parables*, 107.
57. See McFague, *Speaking in Parables*, 106–8.
58. McFague, *Speaking in Parables*, 107.

'transference as such, that is, the unitive process, the sort of assimilation that occurs between alien ideas, ideas distant from each other.'" He goes on to say:

> But there is no epiphor without diaphor, no intuition without construction. Indeed, the intuitive process, bringing together what is disparate, contains an irreducibly discursive moment. . . . Max Black captures this discursive moment . . . in another metaphor, that of screen, filter, or lens, in order to express the way the predicate chooses and organizes certain aspects of the principal subject.[59]

Ricoeur associates "diaphor" with Black's organizing process in which the "suitable hearer" takes a system of implications about the vehicle (or subsidiary subject) and constructs a corresponding system of implications about the tenor (or principal subject).[60] Black's organizing process facilitates transfer from one to the other. This is the point of his illustration of a view of stars which can be seen through the mesh of a screen.

Despite her assertion that most successful metaphors are a blend of both "epiphor" and "diaphor," McFague appears to endow "diaphor" with an independent (and contrary) existence. She finds that contemporary Christian forays in "metaphorical theology" rely heavily on metaphor by juxtaposition, as if Black's organizing process could occur on its own without metaphorical transfer. Juxtaposition on its own would not involve a subsidiary and principal subject. Reducing the method to a simple matter of juxtaposition would explain what I see as its allegorical effect.

McFague's distinction between "epiphor" and "diaphor" amounts to a distinction between different kinds of epistemology. By her own admission, the metaphor of transference relies on the notion that "all things are connected among themselves because they are connected in God." But the so-called metaphor of juxtaposition relies on the reader. This is to omit a level of meaning which Ricoeur attributes to poetic language.

---

59. Ricoeur, *The Rule of Metaphor*, 195. Ricoeur refers here to Philip Wheelwright, *Metaphor and Reality*. Cf. Ricoeur's later remark that Wheelwright comes "quite close to a tensional conception of truth itself by his semantic conception of the tension between diaphor and epiphor" but that the "dialectical inclination of his theory is dissipated by the intuitionist and vitalist tendency" (*The Rule of Metaphor*, 250–51). Far from discerning the seed of disbelief in Wheelwright's theory, Ricoeur associates it with ontological naïveté. Wheelwright's theory functions for Ricoeur as the counter-example to Turbayne's theory of metaphor.

60. Black, *Models and Metaphors*, 41. See chapter 1 on Black's "screen."

Michel Philibert sums up Ricoeur's thinking about metaphorical reference in relation to "ordinary reference":

> Poetic language is no less *about* reality than any other use of language but refers to it by the means of a complex strategy. This strategy implies a suspension and seemingly an abolition of the ordinary reference attached to descriptive language. This suspension, however, is only the negative condition of a second-order reference, an indirect reference built on the ruins of direct reference. But this second-order reference appears as such only with respect to the primacy of reference of ordinary language, which obeys our interest for control, manipulation, pragmatic activities. This "second-order" reference is actually our fundamental, first-order reference, and expresses our ontological belonging to life, to beings, to the world, to Being.[61]

It is this "second-order" reference (or actually our fundamental, first-order reference) which McFague's notion of metaphor disclaims.

McFague's endorsement of a literary approach to theology as a way to unite thought and life runs counter to her theory of linguistic disempowerment in this respect. "Metaphorical theology," she says, "is a tentative affair and can advance few solid claims in its own behalf. In this sense it is . . . in the tradition of the *via negativa*: finding little to say of God with certainty, it boldly makes its case hypothetically and lets it rest."[62] There is a certain irony in a *metaphorical* theology which does not claim the referential function of the *via analogia*. By contrast, Ricoeur's notion that poetic language supplies a kind of verbal link with the universe finds an echo in Steiner who detects evidence of "presence" in the arts as will be seen.

Despite expressing her distance from a sacramental universe, McFague retains a degree of nostalgia for it. In her own way she wants to revive it. I will explore this further in chapter 9. But her parameters, as already noted, remain positivist and relativist while she also finds some common ground with the deconstructionist movement. In a sense Steiner begins at a similar point to McFague but he does not draw the same conclusions. He writes: "We must ask of ourselves and of our culture whether a secular, in essence positivist, model of understanding and of the experience of meaningful form (the aesthetic) is tenable in the light

---

61. Philibert, "Ricoeur as the Singer of Ruins," 133. Philibert's italics.

62. Cf. McFague, *Models of God*, 40. Cf. 182: "metaphorical, heuristic theology . . . is mostly fiction."

of, or if you will the dark of the nihilistic alternative."[63] This is to stand on the brink of the deconstructionist river.

Nevertheless, Steiner says of the late twentieth century, "No period since the early Renaissance has been more concerned with, has addressed itself more insistently to, the nature of the mythical than our own."[64] He adds prophetically, "Remythologization in a time which has found agnostic secularism more or less unendurable may, in future, be seen as defining the spirit of the age." This is to search for a way to cross the river.

But what does Steiner mean by "remythologization"? He argues that the arts offer a clue to regaining a sense of "presence" in language. In this the *via negativa* plays alongside the *via analogia*:

> So very much in Western art and literature enlists the proposal that we are close neighbours to the unknown, that we move among orders of pragmatic substance themselves permeable to that which lies on the other side, which acts from beyond the 'shadow line'.[65]

For Steiner, "remythologization" offers a glimpse of what is otherwise unknown:

> The artist and poet and musician translate this insight into living and lived form. Theirs is the metaphysical assumption, where the metaphysical also extends to the religious. The "verification transcendence" which this entails is a discipline of unknowing. Be it in a specifically religious, for us Judaeo-Christian sense, or in the more general Platonic-mythological guise, the aesthetic is the making formal of epiphany. There is a "shining through".[66]

This is to cross the river and find the Yellow Brick Road on the other side.

---

63. Steiner, *Real Presences*, 134.
64. Steiner, *Real Presences*, 221.
65. Steiner, *Real Presences*, 225.
66. Steiner, *Real Presences*, 226. Steiner seems to take "a more general Platonic mythological guise" in a non-subjectivist sense.

5

"Beam Me Up, Scotty"

IN *THE WIZARD OF OZ*, the little man who purports to be the Wizard makes a balloon with Dorothy's help. The supposed Wizard hopes to cross the desert and to find his home town on the other side of it. But the inhabitants of Oz do not know this. They watch in curiosity as the balloon fills with hot air. The basket of the balloon just touches the ground while the balloon itself rides above it. At this point the supposed Wizard addresses the people, commanding them to obey the Wise Scarecrow as their ruler until his return.[1]

So far this book has considered McFague's notion of metaphor in relation to external reality. This chapter focuses on a particular model-metaphor, an "ecological model of self and world."[2] At times McFague's focus narrows to an understanding that would seem parallel to the experience of the Wizard's audience. At other times the perspective moves to that of the Wizard. While this chapter considers McFague's use of the term "model" in a way that impinges on "science," I distinguish between McFague's usage of these terms and the usage of hard science. McFague engages with "science" in its ethical implications, as will be explored more fully in chapter 10. The vantage point of a balloon only just in touch with the ground may serve to illustrate the tentative nature of her frame of reference and any consequent ethic.

---

1. See Baum, *The Wizard of Oz*, chapter 17.
2. See McFague, *Super, Natural Christians*, 98.

In the last book of her series, *Super, Natural Christians*, McFague contrasts two very different ways of seeing the world. Her first example is evidenced in a piece of "nature writing" by Annie Dillard about a goldfish named Ellery. "This fish," writes Dillard, "has a coiled gut, a spine radiating fine bones, and a brain. Just before I sprinkle his food flakes into his bowl, I rap three times on the bowl's edge; now he is conditioned, and swims to the surface when I rap. And, he has a heart." The second example, says McFague, is "epitomized in the now famous whole earth picture of our planet from the NASA files—the photograph of the earth as a blue and white marble floating in black empty space, lonely and vulnerable. Unlike the subject-subjects kind of knowing in nature writing, it can be seen as an example of subject-object knowing."[3]

McFague wishes to distinguish between the kind of knowing which treats the natural world as a "subject" in a way similar to an intimate person to person encounter and a detached kind of knowing that treats the natural world as an "object." She advocates what she calls the "subject-subjects" model of approach to the natural world as distinct from that of a "subject-object" model. My question is: does McFague's linguistic theory allow for the kind of intimate personal encounter that she advocates? In chapter 3, I queried her claim that her "metaphorical theology" operated in accordance with the traditional *via negativa*. Similarly, I will query her claim that her "subject-subjects" model operates in accordance with the kind of thinking associated with "nature writing."

McFague advocates "a Christian nature spirituality."[4] She factors God into her picture. As has been seen, however, the claim to speak of God is non-committal. This does not stop her from using language for God. McFague writes:

> How the metaphor [for God] refers we do not know—or indeed, even if it does. At the most one wagers it does and lives as if it does, which means that the main criterion for a "true" theology is pragmatic, preferring those models of God that are most helpful in the praxis of bringing about fulfillment for living beings.[5]

Despite her preference for intimate encounter, this representation does not reflect a person to person encounter with God, except *within* the model.

---

3. See McFague, *Super, Natural Christians*, 30–32. McFague cites Dillard, *Pilgrim at Tinker Creek*, 126.

4. McFague, *Super, Natural Christians*, 2.

5. See McFague, *Models of God*, 195–96 n. 13.

McFague's linguistic method precludes the kind of spirituality she has in mind; her models are detached from what they purport to describe. But her advocacy of a "subject-subjects" model entails living as if the model actually does refer to reality. The proviso of the "as if" consciously maintained would preclude a direct relationship with the other party but living the "as if" would have the likely effect of suspension of disbelief. In effect, one could live within the model.[6] One might do so with the best of motives. McFague justifies living in this kind of model on the grounds that it is "helpful in the praxis of bringing about fulfillment for living beings." In the same way the old man in *The Wizard of Oz* lives in his own model by acting as if he is a real Wizard in order to promote the wellbeing of the inhabitants of Oz. But the motive for the model does not alter its orientation to reality.

"Christian nature spirituality," says McFague, "should be based on a subject-subjects model of being, knowing and doing in place of the subject-object model of Western culture."[7] McFague's objection to the subject-object view is that it promotes an attitude of control over nature. She writes:

> The whole-earth view simplifies and objectifies the earth: it is the outsider's view, the spectator view. . . . We can do what we want with this earth for, in the astronaut's view, there are other possibilities, other planets, as we read on the *Star Trek* bumper sticker: "Beam me up, Scotty, this planet sucks."[8]

I suggest, however, that her "Christian nature spirituality" does not avoid the "Beam me up, Scotty" orientation. Rather it adds to it. To detachment is added pretense, whether conscious or less than conscious. The Wizard rides above the world in a balloon-shaped model, so to speak.

McFague goes so far as to associate her "Christian nature spirituality" with the attitude to nature pioneered by Francis of Assisi. By contrast, I suggest that her method has affinities with the vision advocated by nineteenth century French poet, Arthur Rimbaud. Rimbaud's vision was introduced in chapter 4. In this chapter I will engage further with his method and compare it with McFague's. I will then go on to assess the legitimacy or otherwise of McFague's appeal to Francis of Assisi.

---

6. See McFague, *Models of God*, 27.
7. McFague, *Super, Natural Christians*, 2.
8. McFague, *Super, Natural Christians*, 32.

IDENTITY AND EXTERIORITY

Chapters 3 and 4 drew attention to various aspects to deconstructionist thinking. Firstly, there is a deconstruction of linguistic reference to the external world. Steiner sums this up as a loss of covenant between word and world, espoused by nineteenth century French poet, Mallarmé. Further, there is a deconstruction of truth or meaning, summed up in Nietzsche's image of a coin without value or validity. Added to this is Rimbaud's notion of the deconstructed subject. Smith draws these elements together in his observation that Derrida replaces the old idea of "presence" in linguistic meaning with "a quasi-ontology of the trace (or presence-in-absence)."[9] Linguistic reference and meaning gives way to a shadowy substitute. The subject is also deconstructed. Smith adds: "instead of an isolated, self-conscious subject fully present to itself in the interiority of a pure consciousness, Derrida sketches a subject who is constituted by a relation to an exteriority—the alterity of the Other in the communal networks of signification."

Derrida deconstructs the thinking subject and looks elsewhere for a vantage point for human operation. But if doubt is already cast on the validity of access to what is outside the subject, one must then go on to ask what is meant by an "exteriority" that constitutes the subject. Likewise, if doubt is cast on meaning itself, one may ask what is meant by the "communal networks of signification." In this regard, McFague postulates an "exteriority" that is not, strictly speaking, outside the subject. What she refers to as a "sense of self" appears to operate at a pre-cognitive level which she builds into a *constructed model* of the external world.[10] Her somewhat complex proposal is considered below.

As indicated in chapter 4, the idea of relation to an "exteriority" as a source of identity stems from Mallarmé's contemporary, Rimbaud. The context for Rimbaud's statement, "Je est un autre" comes from letters to friends written in May 1871. Rimbaud writes that one is wrong to say "I think." One ought to say I am thought. For "I" is an "other."[11] The real identity comes, apparently, from the outside: it is the "other" that

---

9. Smith, *Jacques Derrida: Live Theory*, 45.

10. See McFague, *Super, Natural Christian*, chapter 5.

11. Parmée, *Twelve French Poets*, liii. My translation. Cf. John Martis, "The Self Found Elsewhere", 204. Martis cites "Rimbaud's celebrated formulation, 'I is an other (Je est un autre).'"

constitutes the "I." But the "other" is not apprehended directly from the external world. Rather it is mediated though the inner life of the poet.

Douglas Parmée describes how Rimbaud attempts to get in touch with his inner life by a course of experiments with drugs, alcohol and "every possible exploitation and mortification of the senses of smell and touch and hearing."[12] In this regard, Steiner remarks:

> Rimbaud posits at the now vacant heart of consciousness the splintered images of other and momentary 'selves'. And he does so in ways and in contexts which render almost inescapable the intuition that those other selves are not some neutral or parallel alterity, but parodistic, nihilistic anti-matter, radically subversive of order and creation.[13]

Rimbaud would have agreed that these contacts with the other selves had an infernal character, since he himself recounted his experiences in *Une Saison en Enfer*.[14] But Steiner omits the motive for the experiments. Parmée writes:

> Rimbaud's purpose is not only artistic but moral: if and when we can recognise and understand all the hitherto unknown and neglected aspects of humanity, if we can come to terms with reality in all its complexity, if we can accept all the monstrous discoveries of the poet as something natural, then the poet will have become a *mutiplicateur de progrès*. Mind and body will achieve a harmony unknown since the Greeks, for despite the apparently subjective nature of his experiences, Rimbaud believed that the poet is merely a more privileged and richer personality than normal people, so that in spite of the individual nature of his methods, he will be discovering truths of universal validity.[15]

While Rimbaud's method is subjectivist, it stems not from the thinking subject but from what Steiner calls "the vacant heart of consciousness." The gateway to the new vision of the poet is not conscious subjectivity but "the non-rational, sensorial aspect of the poet's imagination."[16]

Further, it is the poet's duty to convey this radically new vision to the world. Parmée reports:

---

12. Parmée, *Twelve French Poets*, liv.
13. Steiner, *Real Presences*, 99.
14. Parmée, *Twelve French Poets*, lvi. *Saison en Enfer* was published in 1874.
15. Parmée, *Twelve French Poets*, lv.
16. Parmée, *Twelve French Poets*, liv.

> This supreme revolt, not only against the organisation of society but against any normal conception of life, is being undertaken not as a mere destruction but as a destruction that will lead to a new and better conception of mankind. . . . Rimbaud is always conscious of his social responsibility as a poet and of his duty to communicate his findings to others.[17]

While apparently individualistic, the new vision has an alleged communal function. A new identity is bound up with a new exteriority.

In a context in which discourse claims no reliable access to external reality and consequent appeals to truth are illusory, the poet is somehow said to offer new access to reality, providing new "truths" of "universal validity." In a context in which the consciousness of the subject is deconstructed, a new form of subjectivity comes to the fore. The focus of identity shifts from the rational, conscious self to the sensory, imaginative and possibly monstrous, sub-rational self. All this must be conveyed to the world for the good of society, a moral goal that ignores the question of how it is to be communicated in the absence of linguistic efficacy. A philosophical frame of linguistic non-reference takes on the character of self-reference explored through the inner world. I will compare this kind of thinking with McFague's "subject-subjects" model outlined below.

IN SEARCH OF THE SUBJECT

Steiner describes Rimbaud's relationship to an exteriority as occurring through "splintered images of other and momentary 'selves,'" while "the heart of consciousness" is vacant and deconstructed.[18] In McFague's proposal, the possibility that the natural world will become an extension of the self or multiple selves is perhaps not far away. In an attempt to dissociate herself from an arrogant subject-object viewer, she posits a "sense of self coming from touch rather than from sight" as the vantage point of connection with the natural world.[19] But the heart of consciousness is not entirely vacant for McFague. Her ecological model is built into her project to consciously "remythologize" the relationship between God and the world, as will be seen below. To my mind the status of the subject as

---

17. Parmée, *Twelve French Poets*, lv.
18. See Steiner, *Real Presences*, 99.
19. McFague, *Super, Natural Christians*, 92.

it refers to self, world or God tends to be elusive. This is a consequence of her method.

McFague's relation to her models is twofold. On the one hand she does not know how or if her model-metaphors refer to God. On the other hand she offers the possibility of living as if her theological models refer to reality. The twofold nature of her method spans a series of four books. In the opening pages of the last book, McFague offers an overview of all four books:

> *Super, Natural Christians* is the last in a series of four books on religious language. *Metaphorical Theology* laid the groundwork with the claim that since all religious language is metaphorical, alternatives to traditional metaphors are possible. *Models of God* experimented with several alternative models: God as mother, lover and friend and the world as God's body. *The Body of God* attempted a systematic theology through the lens of one of these models. The present book suggests that a Christian nature spirituality should be based on a subject-subjects model of being, knowing, and doing in place of the subject-object model of Western culture.[20]

We may note a progression of method in the series, from a more detached approach to the operation of metaphor in her earlier books to an approach that looks through the lens of a particular model as the source of an ethical framework.

Using an illustration from *The Wizard of Oz*, I have compared the two aspects of McFague's approach to the situation of the Wizard addressing the inhabitants of Oz from the vantage point of a tethered balloon where the tether can break at any moment. In one sense the Wizard is the detached outsider, free to depart at will. In another sense, his address to the inhabitants involves him in his own pretense. To operate as if he is a true wizard is to look through the lens of his own model. Similarly, while the subject-subjects model, described in McFague's last book, moves from detachment to an appearance of lived experience, it is still a model in McFague's sense. As such, it does not claim to be grounded in external reality; that is the difference between living in a model and actual lived experience.

I have drawn attention to Rimbaud's way of coming to terms with reality in order to compare it with the method adopted by McFague. Rimbaud stresses the social responsibility of the poet. McFague lays equal

---

20. McFague, *Super, Natural, Christians*, 2.

stress on the social responsibility of the theologian.[21] But McFague takes a step towards the office of the poet in her plea for a "remythologizing" of the relationship between God and the world.[22] Her project is imaginative and sensory, deriving impetus from the inner life. But, unlike Rimbaud, she does not appear to find any demons in the inner world. She pursues what she calls an "ecological model of self and world"[23] with a sense of self or identity constituted through contact with nature. She writes:

> Our assumption is that how we see the world, whether with an arrogant or a loving eye, depends upon our deepest, most basic sense of self in relation to the world. Our thesis is that a sense of self coming from touch rather than from sight gives us a way to think about ourselves as profoundly embodied, relational, responsive beings, as created to love others, not to control them.[24]

This sense of self is part of "a way to think about ourselves," that is, part of the model. Within the model, the process is circular. The deepest sense of self derives from being in touch with the natural world.[25] This sense of self then acts upon the conscious, perceiving self to encourage a sense of social responsibility and embodiment that feeds into the inner life.

Rimbaud seems to assume a connection between the "hitherto unknown and neglected aspects of humanity" and "reality in all its complexity."[26] McFague states that the "in touch model [of being and knowing] . . . insists on a continuum" between humanity and the natural world.[27] This is in accordance with her project of producing a new sensibility towards the natural world in which the self can be related to the world on equal terms. As part of a way to think about ourselves and the world, her model goes so far as to endow nature with subject-hood: "In [the ecological] model the self is not just related to nature; rather nature is constitutive of the self . . . not only are we body but nature is spirit (or

---

21. See Preface to McFague, *Models of God*.

22. McFague writes that, as understood in "metaphorical theology," theologians "are poets insofar as they must be sensitive to the metaphors and models that are at once consonant with the Christian faith and appropriate for expressing that faith in their own time (*Models of God*, 32)."

23. McFague, *Super, Natural Christians*, 98.

24. McFague, *Super, Natural Christians*, 92.

25. See McFague, *Super, Natural Christians*, 103–8.

26. Parmée, *Twelve French Poets*, lv.

27. See McFague, *Super, Natural Christians*, 118–19.

subject, soul—whatever we call that part of ourselves that we consider 'more than' nature)."[28]

I have suggested that Rimbaud's method constitutes a philosophical frame of linguistic non-reference which takes on the character of self-reference explored through the inner world. As already seen, McFague contends that "the only way we have of reaching [external reality] is by creating versions of it" and that there is "no way behind our constructions to test them for their correspondence with the reality they presume to represent."[29] Nevertheless, McFague posits a relationship with the world which hinges on "our deepest, most basic sense of self." Rimbaud sees his method offering a harmony of mind and body unknown since the Greeks. McFague maintains that her method will "give us a way to think about ourselves as profoundly embodied, relational, responsive beings, created to love others, not to control them." Such methods may appear to allow for interaction with others and the natural world. But do they actually do so?

McFague goes so far as to link her "metaphorical theology" with contemporary science. She describes "the human self's relation to the world as one instance of ecological interrelationship and interdependence."[30] In her appeal to the genre of "nature writing" she states that "a combination of scientific knowledge, empathy, and aesthetic distance can join to produce sketches of natural subjects in their own worlds that are closer to these worlds than would be works of either imagination or science."[31] But the prior philosophical claim that models cannot be tested for correspondence to external reality is not retracted. A model that purports to produce sketches which are closer to the natural world than other models might give the impression of offering a benchmark for other models. But, on McFague's terms, such sketches are still part of the model. What then does she mean by "closer"?

Let us return to McFague's examples representing "subject-subjects" and "subject-object" knowing. In the description of a goldfish called Ellery, offered by McFague above, the nature writer observes *and* interacts with the goldfish. If "nature writing" offers a clue towards treating the world as subject, it does so not by abandoning the subject-object model

---

28. McFague, *Super, Natural Christians*, 104.
29. McFague, *Models of God*, 26.
30. McFague, *Super, Natural Christians*, 107.
31. McFague, *Super, Natural Christians*, 115.

of scientific observation but by combining it with personal encounter. As such, the description of the goldfish moves towards a more relational view of the world than that illustrated by the NASA picture.

But one must bear in mind that the subject-object model, illustrated by the NASA picture of the planet, is less equivocal than McFague's models in terms of orientation to reality. As I attempted to outline in chapter 3, scientific models are always open to new data. By contrast, the wizardly detachment of McFague's method does not reach this point. The hermeneutic of suspicion is most evident in her remarks about God. But her aim to "remythologize" the relationship of God and the world affects the world. Contrary to her stated aim, her hermeneutic of suspicion towards God drives a wedge between her and the world. As such, the natural world which she wishes to treat as "subject" becomes part of her self-contained model: what she means by a "closer" sketch of the natural world is confined to the model. Any testing of other models would then occur *within* the preferred model. But this kind of model is *more* of an "object" than the scientific object of the "subject-object" method.

An antithesis of subject-object versus subject-subjects models oversimplifies what is going on in terms of subject and object. In McFague's proposed subject-subjects model, there is an external subject ("we" who see the world) producing a model (that is, an object). *Within* the model, the subject relates to the natural world in being constituted by nature through a deep sense of self. *Within* the model the process is such that the subject confers subject-hood (or a spiritual persona) on the natural world. *Within* the model, the human subject relates to the natural world as subject. But the external subject is still not in relation with the external world *unless* there is a method of ensuring that the model accords to some degree with external reality. McFague's method does not allow this.

I have ventured to draw a diagram of McFague's subject-subjects model (see below). The solid lines of the box around, and of the wide arrows in, the diagram are my attempt to indicate a lack of relationship between the model and external reality:

"Beam Me Up, Scotty"

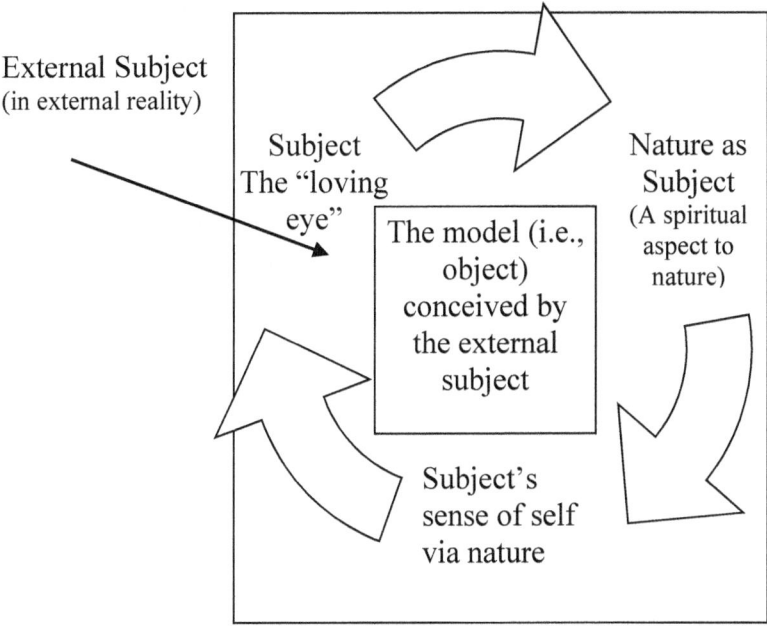

McFague's Ecological Model of Self and World

McFague's advocates what she terms the "subjectification of the world."[32] But, on her terms, the subjectification occurs within the model. The model provides the locus of subject-subjects encounter. While a sense of self is prominent in the model, there is a disjunction of identity between the model-maker who consciously controls the model and the self within the model. *Within* the model, the process by which contact with nature feeds into the sense of self supports a sense of self that is received rather than controlling. This raises the possibility of *two* sources of identity: an externally *constructing* identity and an internally *constructed* identity, both of human origin.

Who or what, one may ask, is the subject in this kind of thinking? There is, as I have tried to indicate, an external subject who conceives the model of the external world. There is also an internal subject (the subject within the model) in encounter with an internal world (the world within the model). The subject within the model is conceived to relate, in a seemingly idealized way, with a "subjectified" natural world. The actual

---

32. See McFague, *Super, Natural Christians*, 112.

subject and the real natural world stand outside the model which is only a version of the external world without means of verification.

McFague describes her approach as "largely a functional, pragmatic view of truth, with a heavy stress on what the implications of certain ways of seeing things (certain models) are for the quality of both human and non-human life."[33] This focus centres on the *way of seeing* rather than on *what is seen* of the external reality. McFague proposes that humanity has a moral duty to see things in a particular way, one that will promote the quality of both human and non-human life. But if the method disclaims access to external reality, the possibility of promoting the quality of life is lessened in real terms. On the assumption that the only way we have of reaching external reality is by creating versions of it, the proposed moral duty will be exercised towards created versions or models of reality rather than towards external reality itself.

In one sense McFague detaches herself from her models. They are "mostly fiction."[34] Nevertheless, living within the "ecological model of self and world" seems to allow for "a way to think about ourselves" which offers scope to a Rimbaud-like passion for social responsibility. McFague goes so far as to depict this way of thinking as a form of "sacramentalism" in which "human beings as the *imago dei*" are said to reveal "the God-world relationship in a special way":

> Thus, in our models of God as mother of creation and as lover of the world, we can speak of God's incarnation in two ways: first, creation as a whole (God's body) is a sacrament or sign of the presence of God, and second, human beings, particularly those human beings especially open and responsive to God are sacraments or signs of God the lover. God becomes incarnated, "in the flesh," both in the body of the world as a whole and the bodies and spirits of certain creatures who have special capacity to respond to God as lover and hence to manifest that love.[35]

This is the language of the model. The God of the model "becomes incarnated" in the relationship between the responsive subject and spiritualized nature.

Before moving on to the next section, let us pause here and consider the extent to which McFague detaches herself from a traditional

---

33. McFague, *Models of God*, 192 n. 37.
34. McFague, *Models of God*, xi–xii.
35. McFague, *Models of God*, 135–36.

understanding of who God is. At one point McFague goes so far as to describe God as "the ultimate Subject whom we are to love with our whole heart, mind and soul simply because God *is* God."[36] But here she is appealing to a traditional model as part of her argumentation for extending the "subject-subjects" model to nature. Far from endorsing God as the ultimate Subject, McFague's theory of metaphor, as already seen, disowns the kind of transfer which "seems to rest on a confidence that things really *are* associated" and "that all things are connected among themselves because they are connected in God."[37]

McFague's kind of models disavow the "second-order" reference which Ricoeur discerns as "actually our fundamental, first-order reference [expressing] our ontological belonging to life, to beings, to the world, to Being."[38] As noted above, McFague states that the main criterion for "metaphorical theology" is pragmatic. As such, it would appear to claim the imprimatur of ordinary language which "obeys our interest for control, manipulation and pragmatic activities." In terms of truth, it reflects the language of what should be, as we conceive it, not the language of what is. It is on such terms that McFague proposes "Nature which is" as a term for God. She states: "The fullness of God cannot possibly be reflected only through human reality, and nature should be honored, as we are, by being a source of metaphors for God."[39]

Where does she accommodate such language for God? McFague's foray into the realm of metaphor pursues an admittedly subjectivist course. Her means of validating her models follows a path in which "remythologizing" joins hands with sub-rational engagement. Chapter 4 drew attention to a development, which Jung calls "the rebirth of the Platonic spirit," of locating metaphysical motifs in the subconscious mind.[40] McFague's proposal could well open the door for a God conceived in terms of Jungian archetypes, as for example the Lady of the Plants and Animals cited in the Introduction.[41]

---

36. McFague, *Super, Natural Christians*, 164. McFague's italics.
37. McFague, *Speaking in Parables*, 106.
38. Philibert, "Ricoeur as the Singer of Ruins," 133.
39. See McFague, *Super, Natural Christians*, 173–74.
40. Jung, *Aspects of the Feminine*, 119 and 122.
41. See Neumann, *The Great Mother*, 336.

NATURE WHICH ISN'T

This section considers McFague's suggestion that "Nature which is" could function as a source of language for God, as a variant on Thomas Aquinas' term "He who is" and Elizabeth Johnson's "She who is."[42] Here awareness of the lack of relation of the model to reality jostles against the attempt to look through the lens of the model. McFague acknowledges the philosophical difficulty of loving what is not accessible:

> But we are immediately drawn up short: we are trying . . . to see the world as it is so that we can love it rightly. But how, what, *is* it? How can we "see the world as it is"? There is no "natural" view of nature. We know that there is no innocent eye, that what we see is determined in large measure by where we stand.[43]

This is the dilemma of McFague's twofold approach. Access to the natural world, she says, is in large measure limited by the perspective of the model.

In the language of the model, the natural world is said to be connected with a God "who is on the side of life and its fulfillment"[44] while contact with nature promotes an attitude of love towards it. But some aspects of nature are not compatible with life and its fulfillment. I have entitled this section "Nature which isn't" to draw attention both to the distinction between model and reality and to the idealized assumption behind the term "Nature which is." McFague admits the incompatible aspects of nature but, in doing so, draws back from living in the model.

In *Super, Natural Christians*. McFague contrasts a model that has humane consequences with one that seeks to simply exercise control over nature. She refers to the former as the model of the "loving eye" and to the latter as the model of the "arrogant eye."[45] As already noted, McFague considers the notion that "God is on the side of life and its fulfillment" to be pragmatic rather than substantial. While her models are equivocal about access to the external world, the philosophical question of access is not the focus of interest for McFague. The main point is not whether access to the external world is possible but whether it is *beneficial*:

> We must remind ourselves that all seeing, all knowing is perspectival. The specific issue with which we are concerned—how

---

42. McFague, *Super, Natural Christians*, 173.
43. McFague, *Super, Natural Christians*, 32. McFague's italics.
44. McFague, *Models of God*, 192, n. 37.
45. See McFague, *Super, Natural Christians*, 32–36.

should we love nature?—will necessarily be based on perspectival knowing. The question is, which perspective, which kind of seeing, is better for nature?[46]

Here her twofold approach comes to the fore. On the one hand, the question of what is better for nature comes from "perspectival knowing." This is to stand back and make an ideological judgment. On the other hand, the activity of loving nature presupposes intimate encounter. On this latter point McFague introduces what she calls "a panentheistic God: that is . . . a view of the God-world relationship in which all things have their origins in God and nothing exists outside God, though this does not mean that God is reduced to these things."[47] "God," it should be noted, is the God of the model. One may compare this language for God with her disclaimers about theological language. The two types of "God-talk" interleave in a way that is not always easy to distinguish.

"How the metaphor [for God] refers we do not know," says McFague, "or, indeed, even if it does."[48] Nevertheless, she states: "We are letting the metaphor of the world as God's body try its chance. We are experimenting with a bit of nonsense to see if it can make a claim to truth."[49] Here is her twofold approach in a nutshell. On the one hand, she stands back from the model as in "experimenting with a bit of nonsense." On the other hand, the experiment can "try its chance" at operating beyond the nonsense level. The kind of truth at issue will be considered in chapter 7. The experiment allows McFague to describe the panentheistic God in detail: "God is the energy empowering the entire universe";[50] "God knows the world immediately just as we know our bodies immediately";[51] "God loves bodies";[52] "Evil is not a power over against God; in a sense, it is God's 'responsibility,' part of God's being, if you will. . . . God is involved in evil. But the other side of this is that God is also involved . . . in the suffering caused by evil."[53]

---

46. McFague, *Super, Natural Christians*, 33.
47. See McFague, *Models of God*, 72.
48. McFague, *Models of God*, 195–96 n. 13.
49. McFague, *Models of God*, 69.
50. McFague, *The Body of God*, 150.
51. McFague, *Models of God*, 73.
52. McFague, *Models of God*, 74.
53. McFague, *Models of God*, 75.

McFague goes on to outline human responsibility to "become partners with God in the care of the world."[54] But who is the God with whom we are to care for the world? In contrast with the arrogant, rationalistic sense of self giving rise to the subject-object model, she proposes "a more realistic [paradigm of the self and world], a more humane one, perhaps even a more Christian one."[55] Yet, despite the reference to Christianity, McFague has ruled out God as a source of values. She states that our notion of "love" is patterned on human types of love, e.g., of mother, lover, friend, which "*project a possibility*" that God's love can be seen through them. She rejects the possibility, which she calls "Barthian," that God defines love and that all human love only conforms to the divine pattern.[56] In terms of determining what is better for nature, McFague draws her values from the model of the "loving eye" influenced by what she calls a "sense of self in relation to the world," as seen above.[57] An external God is not, it seems, necessarily party to the world of the "loving eye."

In *Super, Natural Christians* McFague purports to present a cosmology based on ecological interdependence. She also considers the right to survive of cancer cells and the AIDS virus.[58] Interdependence *and* competition, while observable as factors in nature, become problematic in illustrating the character of God. The final paragraph of *Super, Natural Christians* reads:

> At sixty, I am once again six. I am filled with wonder at ordinary things—a child's smile, a dog's loping run, sticky new buds on a tree. But there is a difference between being sixty and six. The six-year-old does not flinch at the sight of a forest clear-cut or the eyes of a starving child. A Christian nature spirituality is not nature romanticism. Nor is it very optimistic about the future (the planet may well deteriorate). It is, however, determinedly realistic: it begins and ends with a hymn to the things themselves. A Christian nature spirituality praises God for the wonder of the ordinary and promises to work on behalf of the sick and outcast wonderful, ordinary creatures. A Christian nature spirituality is also determinedly hopeful because it believes that

---

54. McFague, *Models of God*, 76.
55. McFague, *Super, Natural Christians*, 92.
56. See McFague, *Models of God*, 192 n. 37. McFague's italics.
57. McFague, *Super, Natural Christians*, 92.
58. McFague, *Super, Natural Christians*, 152 and 57.

"Beam Me Up, Scotty"

the creator of these wonderful, ordinary creatures is working in, through and on behalf of us all.[59]

In this description, the sixty-year-old is aware that nature can be negative. How then does God (termed "Nature which is") work "in, through and on behalf of us all" (especially if the planet may well deteriorate)?

One might ask how a Christian nature spirituality can be determinedly hopeful while not being very optimistic about the future, similarly how a "hymn to the things themselves" can be determinedly realistic while the hymnist flinches at such things as the sight of the eyes of a starving child.[60] Nature as it is appears to be subject to challenge. A Christian nature spirituality "promises to work for the sick and outcast," to try and change things as they are rather than to sing hymns to them. Not only does the love of the "loving eye" come from a source independent of nature as it is. The love of the "loving eye" appears committed to a course that runs counter to nature as it is. On such terms, one might surmise that "Nature which is" becomes "Nature which is not yet." That this is not the biblical notion of "not yet" will be considered in the next section.

It should be recalled that nearly all detail about God is, for McFague, the language of models.[61] It is evident that *within* the model, the world (including humanity) is said to be dependent on the God of "panentheism."[62] But, in the absence of revelation, the God of the model depends on the human model-maker. On these terms the "is" of "Nature which is" is a very different notion to the "is" of the Thomist self-existing God.

ST. FRANCIS AND ST. CLARE

While her ecological model is said to give us "a way to think about ourselves as profoundly embodied, relational, responsive beings,"[63] McFague nevertheless looks beyond ecology in search of further inspiration for embodiment and interaction with the natural world. In this regard, she cites "the rich," "lived in" and symbolic medieval cosmology,[64]

59. McFague, *Super, Natural Christians*, 178.

60. Cf. McFague, *Super, Natural Christians*, 176 for her omission of the promise of a new earth.

61. See McFague, *Models of God*, 192, n. 37.

62. See McFague, *The Body of God*, 150.

63. McFague, *Super, Natural Christians*, 92.

64. See McFague, *Super, Natural Christians*, chapter 3.

and the "horizontal" approach that she discerns in the attitude to nature of Francis of Assisi.[65] But the assumptions behind medieval cosmology and a Franciscan attitude to nature are, I argue, at odds with McFague's assumptions. I will consider McFague's appeal to medieval cosmology in chapter 9. This section contrasts a search for human identity and spirituality through nature with the expectation that nature receives identity through redeemed humanity, the latter illustrated in a legend about St. Francis and St. Clare, recounted by G. K. Chesterton.

The Thomist depiction of "He who is" has a precursor in Augustine of Hippo's encounter with "the God who IS." I turn here to Augustine's account of how he rejects his earlier notion of a materialist God in the face of a direct experience of God: "Your light shone on me with its brilliance, and I thrilled with love and dread alike. I realized that I was far away from you. It was as though I were in a land where all is different from your own." Augustine reports hearing God's voice saying "I am the food of full-grown men. Grow and you shall feed on me. But you shall not change me into your own substance, as you do with the food of your body. Instead you shall be changed into me."[66] While this vision denies that God is connected with creation in a material way (except by implication in the Incarnation) it affirms the participation of humanity in the Godhead.

How then does the natural world fit in with this? Paul Fiddes states: "In the New Testament, according to Paul in Romans 8:19-22, the whole universe 'groans as if in the pangs of childbirth' (*NEB*), waiting for God to set it free, with its destiny deeply bound up with the redemption of God's human children."[67] In this regard Romans 8:19-23 is worth quoting in full:

> For the creation waits with eager longing for the revealing of the sons of God; for the creation was subjected to futility, not of its own will but by the will of him who subjected it in hope; because the creation itself will be set free from its bondage to decay and obtain the glorious liberty of the children of God. We know that the whole creation has been groaning in travail together until now; and not only the creation, but we ourselves, who have the first fruits of the Spirit, groan inwardly while we wait for adoption as sons, the redemption of our bodies (*RSV*).

---

65. McFague, *Super, Natural Christians*, 56–57, 66, 174.
66. Augustine, *Confessions* VII, 10.
67. Fiddes, *Participating in God*, 145.

Here the method of receiving identity runs in the opposite direction to the method described above, of a search for identity *through* nature. Through *human redemption*, says the apostle Paul, nature receives a new identity, free from the bondage of futility and decay: not only embodied humanity but also the renewed natural world will participate in the Godhead.

McFague alleges that traditional Christianity has left out the natural world. In *Super, Natural Christians*, she summarizes traditional Christianity as follows: "Christ came to earth to save humanity 2,000 years ago and will come again to usher the redeemed into heaven."[68] She goes so far as to draw attention to Genesis 1 in which nature is described as "good."[69] But she leaves out the tradition of what has happened to nature, in being subjected to futility, and omits what is promised to nature through human redemption.

There is a non-sequitur here. Though asserting that nature is "good," McFague also recognizes that nature is flawed, that there is such a thing as "fang and claw" and "survival of the fittest."[70] For McFague, something of the redemptive role appears to be undertaken by humans acting in a loving way towards nature.[71] She envisions a possibility that "the next step in evolution" may be "a cultural one of solidarity":

> The community model says that the well-being of the whole is the final goal . . . Utopias . . . that people imagine and sometimes try to create, give us clues to what such communities might be like. They are almost always ones in which the lion and the lamb . . . lie down together . . . The kingdom of God and the Eucharistic banquet are such clues for Christians.[72]

As I understand her, this redemptive method derives from a way of seeing things with a "loving eye" which in turn derives from a sense of identity through being in touch with nature.

McFague claims to find inspiration for her ecological model of the self and the world from Francis of Assisi. She writes:

> In letting things be what they are, we will learn how to care for them more appropriately. We will also begin to see how

---

68. McFague, *Super, Natural Christians*, 176.
69. McFague, *Super, Natural Christians*, 164–66.
70. McFague, *Super, Natural Christians*, 52.
71. See McFague, *The Body of God*, chapter 5.
72. See McFague, *Super, Natural Christians*, 157–58. Cf. McFague, *The Body of God*, 181.

interrelated and interdependent all of us are. Perhaps we will glimpse as well how these others are, now and then, images of the divine, even as we are. If we could develop such a sensibility, we might become, following Francis of Assisi, super, natural Christians. Developing this sensibility . . . involves the "loving eye," the eye that sees ourselves and others, including earth others, as profoundly related while at the same time able to respect real differences.[73]

In this regard, I draw attention to two instances of what G. K. Chesterton calls the true Franciscan spirit and to ask: which comes first for St. Francis, God or nature? And where does a sense of self fit in?

Chesterton states that "if there is one place in which the true Franciscan spirit can be found outside the true Franciscan story, it is in the tale of the Tumbler of Our Lady."[74] He goes on to say:

> But herein is the essential part of the parable. Our Lady's Tumbler did not stand on his head *in order* to see flowers and trees as a clearer or quainter vision. He did not do so; and it would never have occurred to him to do so. Our Lady's Tumbler stood on his head to please Our Lady. If St. Francis had done the same thing, as he was quite capable of doing, it would originally have been from the same motive . . . It would be *after* this that his enthusiasm would extend itself and give a sort of halo to the edges of all earthly things.[75]

McFague describes her "ecological model of self and world" as a way of seeing things. Chesterton says that the Franciscan spirit would never have thought of concocting a way of seeing things. The focus is somewhere else.

Chesterton also writes about "the beautiful friendship of St. Francis and St. Clare":

> I know no better symbol than that found by felicity of popular legend, which says that one night the people of Assisi thought

---

73. McFague, *Super, Natural Christians*, 66. See also 56. McFague quotes Bonaventure "Major Life of St. Francis," 8.6: "[St. Francis] called all creatures . . . by the name of brother or sister, because he knew that they all had in common with him the same beginning." She does not add that Bonaventure goes on to say: "However he reserved his most tender compassion for those creatures which . . . are used in Sacred Scripture as figures of [Christ]," nor does she refer to the story that follows about the curse, placed by St. Francis, on a sow that gobbled up a new-born lamb.

74. Chesterton, *St. Francis of Assisi*, 69.

75. Chesterton, *St. Francis of Assisi*, 71. Chesterton's italics.

the trees and holy house were on fire, and rushed up to extinguish the conflagration. But they found all quiet within, where St. Francis broke bread with St. Clare at one of their rare meetings, and talked of the love of God.[76]

In the legend the focus is on the love of God. Chesterton describes St. Francis and St. Clare as "the unconscious figures on the hill," not thinking about themselves or nature. Nature is depicted as entering into the human relationship with God. Chesterton describes nature as a "red halo" that embraced the two figures on the hill, a "flame feeding on nothing and setting the very air on fire."

Romans 8:19–23 tells us that nature is in bondage to decay. Nature will find its redeemed identity through the redemption of humanity. This story of St. Francis and St. Clare illustrates what that redemption might be like. I submit that the picture is very different from that suggested in McFague's "Christian nature spirituality."

---

76. Chesterton, *St. Francis of Assisi*, 110, 113.

6

The Other Side of Barth?

IN THE FIRST CHAPTER of *The Wizard of Oz,* Dorothy's farmhouse is whirled up into the air by a cyclone. The pressure of the wind on all sides lifts the house up and rocks it gently, as a baby is rocked in a cradle. At first Dorothy is frightened by her situation and deafened by the shriek of the wind. Eventually she crawls to her bed, climbs into it and falls asleep with her dog, Toto beside her.

In the above description, the safe place is high up in the air in the midst of a howling gale. Everywhere else is unsafe. We are not told the fate of the other farm buildings and stock but the small hole in the ground that functions as a cyclone cellar under the house says it all. It is dangerous to be above ground, unless you have found the only safe place in the eye of the storm. If one applies the picture of the cyclone to the Christian faith, it is one of outright hostility to anything apart from Dorothy's house. No quarter can be expected for earthly realities. In the picture supplied by the passage in Romans 8, however, current earthly reality, while in bondage to decay, looks forward to being set free. This picture is one of hope for the earth itself despite its current embattled situation.

I draw attention to the picture of the cradle effect in an otherwise destructive cyclone because I think it accords with a certain kind of theological method as it relates to world history in general and the biblical story in particular. I believe this kind of picture accords with Karl Barth's theological method. I have come to Barth through the eyes of feminist critics. I make no attempt to critique Barth's theology as a whole but rather

The Other Side of Barth?

attempt to assess his theological *method*, in particular as it impinges on the methods of his feminist critics. This book focuses on McFague's method which I judge to be influenced by Barth's method, probably unconsciously so. In order to explore Barth's method further, this chapter touches on the critique by another feminist writer, Catherine Keller.

McFague describes herself as an "erstwhile Barthian."[1] While both she and Barth attempt, in very different ways, to correct the effect of thinking stemming from the Enlightenment, neither, perhaps, is sufficiently critical of the *method* stemming from the Enlightenment philosophical heritage. McFague describes her approach as a view of truth "with heavy stress on what the implications of certain ways of seeing things (certain models) are for the quality of both human and non-human life."[2] She brings this kind of attitude to her "ecological model of self and world."[3] The notion of seeing things in a certain way is wholly compatible with a subject-object approach to external reality. The model of "the world as God's body" presents a different dynamic: the subject is said to treat the natural world as subject on equal terms, no longer seeing the world as an outsider but being in touch with spiritualized nature. But I query whether the difference in dynamic amounts to a departure from subject-object thinking. Instead I suggest that McFague's model amounts to an extension of subject-object thinking.

There is a third factor in this. As noted in Chapter 5, McFague presents a model of God in which human beings as the *imago Dei* are said to reveal the God-world relationship in a special way.[4] As I understand her, McFague extends this kind of thinking into a full-scale soteriology in relation to her cosmology. To my mind, her complex method is illumined by a comparison with Barth's soteriology in relation to his cosmology. I will outline this below. I turn now to the kind of God that Barth presents.

PHILOSOPHERS' GOD

In a series of essays collectively entitled *The Humanity of God*, Barth dissociates his theology from that of rationalist nineteenth century

---

1. McFague, *The Body of God*, 208.
2. McFague, *Models of God*, 192 n. 37.
3. McFague, *Super, Natural Christians*, 98.
4. McFague, *Models of God*, 135–36.

German Protestants. He describes their method of accommodating theology to philosophy:

> [T]he 19th-century theologians focused their attention on one particular point in relation to all the various world-views of their time: man's supposedly innate and essential capacity to "sense and taste the infinite" as Schleiermacher said, or the "religious *a priori*" as later affirmed by Troeltsch.[5]

Such theology seems to have shared the Kantian legacy of a soul-body divide in which the human concept or "religious idea," to use Tyrrell's terminology, was primary and the narrative content of the religion had a secondary function, which could be "demythologized."[6]

Barth recounts how he initially reacted against nineteenth century theology by going to the opposite extreme of emphasizing God's deity, "the image and concept of a 'wholly other'":

> We viewed this "wholly other" in isolation, abstracted and absolutised, and set it over against man, this miserable wretch—not to say boxed his ears with it—in such a fashion that it continually showed greater similarity to the deity of the God of the philosophers than to the deity of the God of Abraham, Isaac, and Jacob.[7]

Barth goes on to report a later theological starting-point: "It is when we look at Jesus Christ that we know decisively that God's deity does not exclude, but includes His *humanity*."[8]

Barth outlines his theological method: "From the fact that God is human . . . [it] follows first of all . . . [that "man"] is the being whom God willed to exalt as his covenant-partner":[9]

> We must affirm as second consequence the fact that through the humanity of God, a quite definite theme is given to *theological* culture in particular. . . . Since God in His deity is human, this culture must occupy itself . . . with the man-encountering God and the God-encountering man and with their dialogue and history, in which their communion takes place and comes

---

5. Barth, "Evangelical Theology in the Nineteenth Century," 20.

6. Cf. Barth, "Evangelical Theology in the Nineteenth Century," 29. Cf. also Tyrrell, *Christianity at the Cross-Roads*, 125. (See chapter 3.)

7. Barth, "The Humanity of God," 41.

8. Barth, "The Humanity of God," 46. Barth's italics.

9. Barth, "The Humanity of God," 50.

> to its fulfilment. For this reason theology can think and speak only as it looks at Jesus Christ and from the vantage point of what He is.[10]

Despite the claim to move away from an earlier philosophical God, Barth's theological starting point is still, to my mind, the concept or "religious idea," expressed in the term "Jesus Christ" or "the humanity of God." This concept is distinct from biblical history which is secondary to the concept.

The secondary function attributed to biblical history tends to detach it from the context of world history. Barth states: "Biblical history in the Old and New Testaments is not really history at all, but seen from above is a series of free divine acts and seen from below a series of fruitless attempts to undertake something in itself impossible."[11] The Nestorian-like division between the views from above and below contributes to Barth's abstract approach. Bultmann writes to Barth: "It has become increasingly plain to me that you have no inner relationship to history, such as you so strongly have to idealistic philosophy."[12]

The starting point of "Jesus Christ" is not conducive to a chronological approach to biblical history. In a letter to Bultmann, Barth writes:

> As I see it, one can and should read all theology in some sense backwards from [the one central figure in the NT]: down to anthropology, ethics and then methodology. . . . I have not become "orthodox" for this reason. I could list for you the points at which I have diverted a good deal from the paths of what can meaningfully be called "orthodoxy" and will continue to diverge on the stretches that are before me.[13]

In the *Church Dogmatics*, Barth gives further detail about the relation of Christ to the history of creation:

> What [the New Testament writers] have in view is the kingdom of God drawn near; the turning-point of the times, revealed in the name of Jesus Christ as the fulfilment of all the promises of the covenant of grace. To give to the Bearer of this name the honour due to Him, or rather to bear witness to the honour which He has, they venture the tremendous assertion that the

---

10. Barth, "The Humanity of God," 52–53. Barth's italics.
11. Barth, *Word of God and Word of Man*, 72.
12. Bultmann to Barth (Marburg, 31 December 1922). *Letters*, 4.
13. Barth to Bultmann (Basel, 24 December 1952). *Letters*, 107.

world was created through Him and in Him as through God, and in God, in God's eternal will and purpose.[14]

In this perspective, the one central figure of the New Testament representing "the turning-point of the times" appears to *take on*, in the sense of being retrospectively endowed with, a certain supra-historical persona.

Barth goes so far as to state: "The New Testament speaks plainly enough of the Jesus Christ who existed before the world was but . . . it does not speak of the eternal Son or Word as such, but of the Mediator, the One who in the eternal sight of God has already taken upon Himself our human nature."[15] One may contrast Barth's approach with the narrative direction of a statement by Augustine of Hippo: "when the fullness of time came she [Wisdom] was sent . . . in order that the Word might become flesh, that is become man."[16] Barth's divergence from orthodoxy takes on the nature of an a-historical soteriology in relation to biblical history.

Elsewhere Barth goes so far as to distinguish between "the historical Jesus" and "Jesus the Christ, the Son of the living God." In doing so, Barth makes a distinction between "history" and "real happening":

> However it may be with the historical Jesus, it is certain that Jesus the Christ, the Son of the living God, belongs neither to history nor to psychology; for what is historical and psychological is as such corruptible. The resurrection of Christ, or his second coming, which is the same thing, is not a historical event . . . our concern here is with an event which, though it is the only real happening *in* history is not a real happening *of* history.[17]

Barth has a philosophical approach to history. As such, the real happening *in* history has the ability to overarch the real happenings *of* history. McFague employs a similar distinction between the chronological and soteriological directions of history.

McFague states: "salvation is the *direction* of creation and creation is the *place* of salvation."[18] As will be seen in chapter 7, she applies the term "the common creation story" to popular evolutionism. In other words, evolutionary history in its linear trajectory supplies the "place" or theatre for salvation's overarching function. She writes:

14. Barth, *CD* III/1: 54.
15. Barth, *CD* III/1: 54,
16. Augustine, *The Trinity*, IV, 27.
17. Barth, *Word of God and Word of Man*, 90.
18. McFague, *The Body of God*, 180.

> Some natural theologies, theologies that begin with creation, try to make the claim that evolutionary history contains a teleological direction, an optimistic arrow, but our claim is quite different. It is a retrospective, not a prospective claim; it begins with salvation, with experiences of liberation and healing that one wagers are from God, and reads back into creation the hope that the whole creation is included within the divine liberating, healing powers. It is a statement of faith, not of fact; it takes as its standpoint a concrete place where salvation has been experienced—in the case of Christians, the paradigmatic ministry of Jesus and similar ministries of his disciples in different, particular places—and projects the shape of these ministries onto the whole. What is critical, then, in this point of view about the common creation story is not that this story tells us anything about God or salvation but, rather, that it gives us a new, contemporary picture with which to remythologize Christian faith.[19]

McFague's soteriology begins from human experiences of liberation and healing which are projected onto evolutionary history in an overarching fashion.

Barth's description of how Jesus came to be credited with being instrumental in the creation of the world might seem similarly dependent on human experience: the New Testament writers "venture the tremendous assertion" on the basis of their view of the kingdom of God drawn near. But Barth would have rejected the notion that human experience was the starting point of his theological method. Rather, he would have argued for a starting point of God's eternal will and purpose. To my mind, however, his retrospective method runs counter to access to his professed starting point.

Barth postulates a *divine* perspective (or divine enclosing human perspective) rather than a *human* "religious idea" for his conceptual vantage point.[20] But how does he gain access to this perspective? In the *Church Dogmatics*, he writes:

> Among the signs of the objective reality of revelation we have to understand certain definite events and relations and orders within the world. . . . Their nature as signs does not rest on a capacity resident in these particular creaturely realities as such, either to be or to become testimonies to revelation. Nor does it

---

19. McFague, *The Body of God*, 181.
20. See Barth, "The Humanity of God," 47.

rest on any *analogia entis*. It rests upon the divine foundation and institution.[21]

As already noted, Barth distinguishes between the historical Jesus (creaturely reality) and "Jesus the Christ, the Son of the living God" (the divine foundation and institution). As I understand him, Barth states that the New Testament writers "venture the tremendous assertion" which links the name of Jesus Christ (divine foundation and institution) with the Bearer of this name (creaturely reality). This is to say what the historical Jesus represents, not who he is.

Epistemologically, Barth purports to begin with the concept of the "divine foundation and institution" rather than with the narrative that supplies the content for it. For Barth, "the creaturely realities" do not point, or become testimonies, *to* revelation. Rather, they function as signs illustrating the prior concept. From the vantage point of the prior concept of "Jesus Christ," says Barth, theological culture must occupy itself with the biblical narrative. But, one may ask, where does the prior concept of Jesus Christ come from? If the revelation of God does not come through encounter with God mediated through the "creaturely realities" of word and sign how do we know about it? Does this epistemological conundrum constitute the other side of Barth?

THE CATHEDRAL

Chapter 5 compared McFague's theological method with the situation of the Wizard of Oz as he prepares for a balloon flight. I will continue to consider airborne experience in relation to experience on the ground as an illustration of her theological method in the next chapter. I discern something similar in Barth's method. But the tone is different. Barth's theology presents in a way that bears more affinity to Dorothy's house being borne aloft in a cyclone.

I have said that McFague's approach to her models is twofold. On the one hand she acknowledges the limitations of her subjective starting-point while on the other she wishes to overcome the subject-object divide by cultivating a "subject-subjects" model. There is also a third aspect to her method. Because she regards the "subject-subjects" model as beneficial, she wishes to superimpose it onto evolutionary history. I find a similarity of method in Barth although the content is quite different.

---

21. Barth, *CD* I/I: 224.

Barth emphasizes the starting-point of God's perspective. Secondary to this is the covenant-partnership of "man-encountering God" and the biblical narrative with which "man" must occupy himself. One might call this secondary aspect an ecclesiological model. Thirdly, Barth wants to read theology backwards "down to anthropology, ethics and then methodology."[22] In other words, his method superimposes soteriology (from the one central figure in the NT) onto everything else. But while McFague wishes to engage the natural world, Barth's ecclesiology tends to offer no quarter to what is outside it. This may account for its harsh relation to those on the ground as it were.

In writing about his ecclesiology, Barth refers to the notion of "correspondence." Seen from above, is "the mystery in which [God] meets us in the existence of Jesus Christ." Barth states that God wants "in His freedom actually not to be without man but *with* him and in the same freedom not against him but *for* him ... [in God's] free affirmation of man, His free concern for him, His free substitution for him—this is God's humanity."[23] And consequent to the concept of God's humanity is the covenant partnership and history, as noted earlier. For Barth, such consequences "result from the fact that we are asked about the *correspondence*—here the concept of analogy may come into its right—of our thinking and speaking with the humanity of God."[24] My question is: what kind of correspondence is at issue here?

Graham Ward cites "a famous attack on Barth" by Richard Roberts:

> Wherever the content of revelation and its time draws close to the reality common to humanity, ambiguity results, because the "reality" of revelation must both affirm and deny, recreate and annihilate at the same moment. This ambiguity is consistent with the double-edged quality of much of Barth's talk of man ... and is based upon the fundamental theological developments which led to the adoption of the "analogy of faith".[25]

---

22. Barth to Bultmann (Basel, 24 December 1952). *Letters*, 107.
23. Barth, "The Humanity of God," 48.
24. Barth, "The Humanity of God," 49–50.
25. See Ward, *Barth, Derrida and the Language of Theology*, 235. Ward cites Richard Roberts, "The Doctrine of Time in Karl Barth." See also the description of "the strategy by which Barth could trump modernity with the Reformation" by Hunsinger, *Disruptive Grace*, 293.

Ward observes that, for Roberts, 'this "ambiguity" is the great logical flaw whereby the *Church Dogmatics* rides above us like a Cathedral on a vast cloud'.

Ward argues further that this ambiguity is "a precursor for Derrida's *différance*." As I understand him, Ward suggests Barth's analogy of faith illustrates an unresolved tension of language between Barth's description of views "from above" and "from below." Such a textual strategy, says Ward, would place Barth's theological language in an allegorical relation to the tension that lies behind it. Ward detects a similarity here to Derrida's textual strategy:

> Discourse, for Derrida, is "allegorical metonymy". . . . "Metonymy" refers here to the unending chain of signifiers, each differing from each other, each displacing the meaning of the other. . . . Allegorical metonymy is, therefore, another description of the economy of *différance*. Barth's theology of the Word as a theological reading of *différance* is, then, *allegoria fidei* rather than *analogia fidei*.[26]

To my mind, however, Barth's *allegoria fidei* is more readily detected in the allegorical relation of the *content* of revelation to the *concept* of God enclosing humanity which is prior to it. Nevertheless, I would agree that Barth's view of the content of revelation in relation to common human experience can be aptly likened to that of a Cathedral riding above us on a vast cloud. In this sense, the view "from above" is superimposed on the view "from below." To employ the illustration from *The Wizard of Oz*, the cyclone which carries Dorothy's house superimposes itself on the reality on the ground. One might query whether Barth has quite given up his earlier presentation of an ear-boxing God.

At this point I return to a comparison of Barth's method with McFague's. Like Barth, McFague discerns two disconnected realities: the reality of faith and the reality of the "common creation story" or evolutionary history. As already seen, McFague identifies the ministry of Jesus and his disciples as "paradigmatic," that is, illustrative of the "wager" or assumed *concept* that "experiences of liberation and healing" are from God. She then "projects the shape of these ministries onto the whole," that is, onto evolutionary history.[27] Similarly, Barth uses the language of

---

26. See Ward, *Barth, Derrida and the Language of Theology*, 246. Ward cites Derrida, *Memoires for Paul de Man*.

27. McFague, *The Body of God*, 181.

projection in describing the relation between the Bible and life: "a new world projects itself into our old ordinary world."[28]

MYTH OR MINSTER?

This section is about demythologizing and what McFague calls remythologizing. Chapter 3 drew attention to Tyrrell's statement that "as man progresses he revolts against earlier and inadequate expressions of the religious idea."[29] McFague wishes to find new expressions of the religious idea that "God is on the side of life and its fulfillment," a new myth as it were.[30] I suggested above that Barth's theological starting point is the concept or "religious idea," expressed in the term "Jesus Christ" or "the humanity of God." Barth distinguishes the creation and nativity narratives from the genre of myth. Nevertheless I suggest that, in terms of method, these narratives could be said to function as expressions of Barth's "religious idea." Catherine Keller rejects the picture presented in Barth's reading of the creation narratives and presents an alternative reading from a feminist perspective.

The notion of demythologizing is canvassed in Barth's correspondence with Bultmann. The correspondence indicates the possibility of a contemporary form of mythological thinking in popular science. Bultmann writes to Barth:

> The situation today appears to me to be this: Man lives with the worldview which is projected by objectifying science; but he is increasingly aware . . . that he cannot understand his own existence in terms of this worldview. . . . You rightly say that my demythologizing has its source in the insight that the mythological view of the world and man is now outdated. But should it not be clear in the course of demythologizing that the decisive point is not the fact that it is outdated but the fact that the thinking of myth (contrary to its true intention) is objectifying? I do not replace mythical thinking with the thinking of objectifying science.[31]

---

28. See Barth, *The Word of God and the Word of Man*, 37.
29. See Lewis, "Fern-seed and Elephants," 122.
30. See McFague, *Models of God*, 192 n. 37.
31. Bultmann to Barth (Marburg, 11–15 November, 1952), *Letters*, 88, 95.

For Bultmann, the "thinking of myth" offers a dispensable projection of an underlying truth. He discerns a contemporary parallel to the earlier "mythological view of the world" in "objectifying science" (by which he seems to mean evolutionary history). He finds both earlier and later expressions inadequate for the current understanding of human existence.

In a further modification, Barth finds a parallel between evolutionary history and pagan mythology while distinguishing biblical creation from either:

> Natural science . . . may tell us the tale of millions of years in which the cosmic process has gone on . . . Continuation is quite a different thing from . . . sheer beginning, with which the concept of creation and the Creator has to do . . . At best a myth may be parallel to exact science; that is, a myth has to do with viewing what has always existed and will exist . . . in the . . . Babylonian myth of creation, for example, it is quite clear that we are concerned with a myth of growth and decay which fundamentally cannot be brought into connexion with Genesis 1 and 2.[32]

Barth differentiates here between "sheer beginning" and continuation. A myth, he says, has to do with viewing what has always existed and will exist. He indicates that the Babylonian myth of creation functions as a projection of the idea of growth and decay. But while the content is different, I am not convinced that Barth's approach to Genesis 1 and 2 differs from this in terms of *method*. One could argue that, for Barth, the narratives in Genesis function as an illustration of the "concept of creation" or "sheer beginning."

Barth goes on to state that the world "gives us no information about God as the Creator."[33] He indicates that access to the story of creation can be found in Christ: "By becoming man in Jesus Christ, the fact has also become plain and credible that God is the Creator of the world." We may note that Barth writes about the *concept* of creation. Similarly, the "fact" of Incarnation is heavily conceptual. I stated above that, for Barth, the content of revelation appears to bear an allegorical relation to the concept of God enclosing humanity. In other words, the content is projected from the concept. But Barth rejects the term "myth" for the Genesis narratives in favor of "saga."

---

32. Barth, *Dogmatics in Outline*, 51.
33. Barth, *Dogmatics in Outline*, 52.

Dustin Resch reports on Barth's distinctions in the *Church Dogmatics* between myth, saga and "historicist history":

> Barth's rather meagre treatment of the infancy narratives in the *CD* can be helpfully augmented by briefly examining his discussion of the creation narratives in *CD* III/I where he lays out his understanding of literary genre in an analogous context.... Barth believes that the content presented on the New Testament infancy narratives is closely related to the event attested in the Genesis creation narratives. Barth characterizes the creation narratives as saga (*Sage*). Saga is, for Barth, a literary form that uses "intuitive and poetic pictures" to depict a prehistorical reality of history (*praehistorischen Geschichtswirklichkeit*). While saga is used to express events that are genuinely historical in the sense that they took place in space and time, it does so by presenting it in its immediate relation to God.... Unlike myth, saga does not express a timeless state of God and the world, but depicts events that are genuinely historical. Unlike historicist history, saga is not confined to evaluating events according to their connection and analogy with other events in creation. While the creation events are entirely saga, owing to the fact that they present God's creation of the world to which there is no other analogy in creation, most of Scripture contains elements of saga interwoven in greater or lesser degrees with historical narrative. This mixture of saga and historical narrative is because all biblical events after creation presuppose both a connection with the history that went before it, as well as a relationship immediate to God. In the miracle stories of Scripture, in which God's immediacy to history is particularly evident, the use of saga becomes more pronounced.[34]

Barth's treatment of the infancy narratives will be considered in the next section. Resch finds a similar literary genre in Barth's approach to the creation stories which function as "intuitive and poetic pictures" portraying a pre-historical reality presented in its immediate relation to God.

If the creation stories can be classed as intuitive and poetic pictures can they also be classed as dispensable? In other words, are they open to demythologizing and "remythologizing"? Catherine Keller goes so far as to sketch an alternative beginning, identifying the *tehom* (deep) of Genesis 1:2 as a feminized locus for creation. She expresses opposition to a tradition in which "the Word of the Creator, as Son of the Father" unifies

---

34. Resch, *Barth's Interpretation of the Virgin Birth*, 72–73. Resch cites Barth, *CD* III/I: 78–90.

itself "over *against* the feminized chaos."[35] Keller outlines her pro-chaos reading of Genesis 1:2 as the reverse of Barth's cosmology:

> What if we begin instead to read the Word from the vantage point of its own fecund multiplicity, its flux into flesh, its overflow.... Inversely to Barth's logocentric doctrine of the creation, a tehomic theology derives the incarnation from the chaosmic width of creation. A chaosmic Christ would represent the flow of a word that was always already materialized, more and less and endlessly, a flow that unblocks the hope of an incarnation, in which all flesh takes part. But this new creation will not come forth *de novo ex nihilo*. It takes place within the shared, spatio-temporal body of all creatures.[36]

According to this description, Barth proposes a cosmology summed up in the Incarnation while Keller proposes an Incarnation summed up in the cosmology.

Keller's alternative reading would accord with Barth's understanding of the genre of myth expressing a timeless state of God and the world. In her reading a "chaosmic Christ" represents a process "always already materialized, more and less and endlessly." Keller contrasts a positive view of the *tehom* with Barth's negative view. While aligning Barth with the patristic tradition, she also asserts that Barth is not entirely orthodox: "Barth never quite affirms the classic creation from nothing. He does it one better: the fathers were too soft on the chaos. God would not create *from* such horror. Barth endows *das Nichtige* with the personality of a rebellious, death-dealing monster of chaos."[37] One may compare Barth direct:

> As this Word is spoken and repeated in the history of the covenant . . . it is thereby constantly decided that the hay^ethah of chaos is final—this world *was*. God will not allow the cosmos to be definitively bewitched and demonised or His creation totally destroyed, nor will He permit the actual realisation of the dark possibility of Gen. 1:2.[38]

---

35. Keller, *Face of the Deep*, 19.
36. See Keller, *Face of the Deep*, 18–19.
37. See Keller, *Face of the Deep*, 18–19. Keller's italics. She cites Barth, *CD* III.I:105.

38. Barth, *CD* III/I: 109. Cf. also Barth: "this whole realm that we term evil—death, sin, the Devil and hell—is *not* God's creation, but rather what was excluded by God's creation, that to which God has said 'No.' And if there is a reality of evil, it can only be the reality of this excluded and repudiated thing, the reality behind God's back, which He passed over, when He had made the world and made it good" (*Dogmatics in Outline*, 56–57).

In this presentation, "saga" appears to unify itself over against "myth." The dark possibility of Gen 1:2 is never realized.

Keller presents the inverse of Barth's doctrine of creation. The protagonists are the same as his as well as the scene of action; it is the outcome which is different. As an intuitive and poetic picture, the Word is either spoken over against the dark possibility of chaos or the possibility of chaos (no longer dark) "unblocks the hope of an incarnation." In some sense McFague would endorse Keller's presentation. As seen in Chapter 5, McFague writes of God's incarnation in terms of her model of "God as mother of creation."[39] In this model God could perhaps be understood as "already materialized."[40] In another sense, McFague wishes to superimpose "experiences of liberation and healing that one wagers are from God" onto evolutionary history, as seen above.[41] In method McFague follows Barth.

One further point can be noted here. Keller identifies Barth's doctrine of creation as "logocentric." Ward, on the other hand, detects in Barth's theology of the Word a theological reading of *différance*. If Ward is right, ambiguity is the keynote of Barth's method. This is not the kind of "logocentrism" that would be recognized by Steiner.

MASTER'S METAPHOR?

This book is about how language works, theological language in particular. McFague states that "much if not all religious language and a great deal of theological language" relies on metaphor: "that is, language that is literally appropriate to personal, social or political human relationships or to the natural world is applied metaphorically to God."[42] I agree with this but it depends what is meant by metaphor. McFague compares her metaphorical method with the green glasses of the Wizard of Oz.[43] In general she approaches the method from the Wizard's point of view:

39. See McFague, *Models of God*, 135–36.

40. McFague also favors an organic model "derived from the common creation story" in which "the multifarious character of the present universe in intricacy, complexity, and diversity at the macroscopic, microscopic and middling levels approaches the realm of infinite difference" (*The Body of God*, 55). Cf. her remarks on chaos theory in *The Body of God*, 229–30 n. 74.

41. McFague, *The Body of God*, 181.

42. McFague, *Models of God*, 23.

43. See McFague, *Metaphorical Theology*, 41–42.

unlike the inhabitants of Oz, one must be aware of the potential for deception. In this kind of attitude one sees what lies behind the metaphorical picture.

I have claimed a kind of similarity between Barth's theological method and McFague's. I also stress that there are significant differences. Barth's approach to the creation narratives may serve to pinpoint both similarity and difference. Resch reports that, for Barth, the creation narratives depict a pre-historical reality of history. Unlike the potential deception of McFague's metaphorical pictures, such "intuitive and poetic pictures" are said to be "genuinely historical." Like McFague's approach, Barth sees what lies behind the pictures, a pre-historical reality of history in its immediate relation to God. In other words, Barth's approach encourages a view over God's shoulder as it were. One sees the humanity of Jesus Christ before the world was, through the eternal sight of God.

At this point I will recall Lewis's distinction between a Master's and Pupil's metaphor outlined in chapter 2. McFague draws attention to Lewis's distinction in her description of the scientific "low-view" of models. She claims that the "low-view" of models is similar to "C. S. Lewis's description of a 'Master's' metaphor in which one knows what one wants to say and illustrates it for others, as contrasted with a 'Pupil's' metaphor in which the speaker is in the position of learner and has no means other than the metaphor to express the subject."[44] Lewis gives the example of a Master who has a mathematical access to the concept that space may be finite. The Master offers a picture of the Flatlander Sphere as a way of access to the concept for his non-mathematical students.

In chapter 2, I stated that the "low-view" of scientific models, as described by McFague, does not do justice to the Master's approach. As described by Lewis, the Master intends the metaphor to refer to what it purports to describe. Further, despite his alternative access to the facts, the Master will probably make use of his Pupil's metaphor. I suggest that Barth's approach to the creation narratives accords with that of Lewis's Master. As will be seen, Barth would be open to making use of the "intuitive and poetic pictures." Nevertheless, his method does seem to claim a prior and independent access to the "facts."

The method is perhaps at its clearest in Barth's treatment of the Virgin Birth. As seen above, Resch writes: "In the miracle stories of Scripture, in which God's immediacy to history is particularly evident, the use

---

44. McFague, *Metaphorical Theology*, 87–88.

of saga becomes more pronounced."⁴⁵ The notion of "God's immediacy" governs the way the "intuitive and poetic pictures" are to be received. In writing about the nativity of Christ, Barth distinguishes between "the thing" and "the sign." The "thing" is the "mystery of the Incarnation." The "sign" is the "miracle of Christmas":

> Why does the miracle of Christmas run parallel to the mystery of the Incarnation? If in the Incarnation we have to do with the thing, here we have to do with the sign. The two should not be confused. The thing which is involved in Christmas is true in and for itself. But it is indicated, it is unveiled in the miracle of Christmas."⁴⁶

Here the miracle is the sign of the mystery. We may compare Barth's remarks above that particular "creaturely realities" function as "signs" consequent on the prior divine "foundation and institution."⁴⁷

Barth goes on to emphasize that "the reality of the Incarnation" is in no sense dependent on the miracle: "The true Godhead and the true humanity of Jesus Christ in their unity do not depend on the fact that Christ was conceived by the Holy Spirit and born of the Virgin Mary." He indicates how the miracle should be received:

> [E]very time people want to fly from this miracle, a theology is at work, which has ceased to understand and honour . . . the mystery of the unity of God and man in Jesus Christ, the mystery of God's free grace. And on the other hand, where this mystery has been understood and men have avoided any attempt at natural theology, because they had no need of it, the miracle came to be thankfully and joyously recognised. It became, we might say, an inward necessity at this point.⁴⁸

The "miracle of Christmas" becomes an "inward necessity," secondary to the prior concept of the Incarnation.

If, for Barth, one must first be in the position of the Master (i.e. share God's perspective) *before* the miracle can be recognized, a hiatus between views "from above" and "from below" would seem likely. The sense that the language of faith operates like a great Cathedral riding above ordinary ways of speaking and thinking is borne out by A. N. Prior's depiction of

---

45. Resch, *Barth's Interpretation of the Virgin Birth*, 72–73.
46. Barth, *Dogmatics in Outline*, 96.
47. Barth, *CD* I/I: 224.
48. Barth, *Dogmatics in Outline*, 100.

"Barthian Protestant" in a fictitious dialogue about the possibility of the discussion of religion in secular terms. Barthian Protestant states:

> "I have always felt that it must be possible to give an adequate explanation of religious faith on the hypothesis that it is an illusion . . . It is also possible to explain the fact of faith, and the corresponding sociological fact of Israel and the Church, on the assumption that it is *not* an illusion—that God is real, and faith is his gift, and 'sacred history' the story of his strategy . . . I have held that . . . there is nothing to choose between the two [hypotheses], and that one just jumps the way one has to. Faith . . . is an inward miracle of God's mercy . . . I do not begin . . . with doctrines that look rational but prove not to be so, but present you with 'nonsense' right from the jump . . . *Of course*, the laws of thought and the laws of grammar, forbid us to confess our faith . . . But God, with whom all things are possible, comes to our rescue, and takes up our words and our thoughts and *makes* them carry his meaning . . ."[49]

If the sociological fact of Israel and the Church defies the laws of thought and grammar, the relationship between religious history and secular history is remote indeed.

I find in this depiction some similar ingredients to my illustration from *The Wizard of Oz*. The belief of the inhabitants of Oz is an illusion. By contrast, "the fact of faith" for Barthian Protestant only looks like an illusion since God is able to make sense out of this apparent illusion. But, as seen in chapter 5, the supposed wizard attempts to make sense out of his own illusion in his farewell speech to the citizens of Oz. We may note something here which will be explored in the next chapter. McFague describes her models of God as "a bit of nonsense." But she also asks whether her model of the world as God's body "makes sense'" in terms of an "incarnational understanding of Christianity and an organic interpretation of postmodern science."[50]

Barth comes close to admitting the similarities and also the differences between his method and McFague's in his essay, "The Humanity of God." Barth outlines three alternative epistemological positions: the

---

49. I have quoted key points from two consecutive speeches by "Barthian Protestant" here. See Prior, "Can Religion be Discussed?" 7–9. Prior comments: "This is not a wild guess at what Barth might [say]. The idea that nonsense may be given sense by a sheer act of omnipotence is repeated again and again in his *Prolegomena to Church Dogmatics*."

50. See McFague, *The Body of God*, 150.

position of theological existentialism, his own position which he describes as "close to" the existentialist position, and a possible development of the existentialist position which sounds to me similar to that held by McFague and Keller:

> It is not yet clear whether and in what sense a genuine, concrete dialogue, history, and communion between God and man is envisioned [in the theological existentialism of Rudolf Bultmann and his followers, close to which we find ourselves here] or whether it is concerned merely with a repristination of the theology of the believing individual who reflects on himself in his solitude (this time on his reality and unreality) and explicates himself. The fact that to date neither the people of Israel nor the Christian community appears to have constitutive meaning for his theology causes one concern. And what can be the meaning of the "overcoming of the Subject-Object-Scheme," recently proclaimed with such special enthusiasm, so long as it is not made clear and guaranteed that this enterprise will not once more lead to the anthropocentric myth and call into question anew the *intercourse* between God and man and thus the *object* of theology. Certainly existentialism may have reminded us once again . . . that one cannot speak of God without speaking of man. It is to be hoped that it will not lead us back into the old error that one can speak of man without first, and very concretely, having spoken of the living God.[51]

Barth's fear that, in an attempt to overcome "the Subject-Object-Scheme," existentialism might develop into anthropocentric mythology seems to have been realized in McFague's and Keller's approaches. Barth distances himself from such a development but he does not distance himself from existentialism *per se*. For Barth, the individual who reflects upon himself and explicates himself is said to give way to speaking about the living God but, insofar as Barth's position is "close to" the existentialist position, the human *concept* of God is primary. A genuine, concrete dialogue, history, and communion between God and man may be envisioned in Barth's theology but in what sense? Does the dialogue speak through the voice of the existentialist thinker? Should the biblical narrative not be allowed to speak with its own voice?

McFague distinguishes between Barth's and Bultmann's position. Bultmann, she says, limits the good news [of salvation] "to the *pro nobis*; one does not talk about the New Testament as *Historie* (objective, factual

---

51. Barth, "The Humanity of God," 54.

history) but as *Geschichte* (the meaning of the events for the persons who encounter them)."[52] If Barth conceives "saga" in its immediate relation to God, Bultmann conceives the New Testament in its immediate relation to us. Does not the kind of anthropocentric mythology espoused by McFague tend to be conceived in its immediate relation *pro nobis*?

---

52. McFague, *Speaking in Parables*, 31.

7

Making Sense?

IN THE LAND OF OZ, most of the journeys happen on foot but Dorothy and her friends sometimes travel by air in the arms of the Winged Monkeys. On the first occasion the Monkeys deliver the travelers into the power of the Wicked Witch of the West. The second time the tables are reversed. Dorothy and her companions are carried back to the Emerald City after having destroyed the Witch. On the second journey, the four companions initially set out on foot. There is no road between the Witch's castle and the Emerald City and, by mistake, they travel away from the Emerald City. Then Dorothy summons the Winged Monkeys to her aid, gaining a bird's eye view on the return journey of the territory to the west. In the first flight the Monkeys are agents of evil, in the second of good. Their behavior is governed by whoever wears the Golden Cap.[1]

McFague states that her theological method employs what she calls a retrospective arrow. The method begins with the ministry of Jesus and his followers. It then travels backwards to the dawn of evolutionary history, projecting the experience of salvation onto that history.[2] In some sense this method may be compared with Dorothy's journey from the Witch's castle. She experiences the "salvation" of destroying the Witch by tipping a bucket of water over her. She then embarks on a journey which takes her away from her goal. But the rescue by the Winged Monkeys could, on

---

1. See Baum, *The Wizard of Oz*, chapters 12–14.
2. McFague, *The Body of God*, 181.

McFague's terms, be said to project Dorothy's experience of salvation onto the pathless distance between the land to the west and the city.

McFague presents her cosmology as "a way of speaking of God's relation to all matter, all creation, that 'makes sense' in terms of an incarnational understanding of Christianity and an organic interpretation of postmodern science":

> It helps us to be *whole* people within our faith and within our contemporary world. Moreover, the model does not reduce God to the world nor relegate God to another world; on the contrary, it radicalizes both divine immanence (God is the breath of each and every creature) and divine transcendence (God is the energy empowering the entire universe). Finally, it underscores our bodiliness, our concrete physical existence and experience that we share with all other creatures: it is the model on the side of the well-being of the planet, for it raises the issue of the ethical regard toward *all* bodies as all are interrelated and interdependent.[3]

For McFague, it is the model or overview which purports to "make sense" of the world and to be of ethical benefit.

Dorothy's journey does not, on its own terms, attempt to "make sense" of reality on the ground in the same way. If anything is to be done about evil it is done directly. Dorothy douses the Witch with water and unexpectedly destroys her. Dorothy's action releases the Winkies from the power of the Witch. The Winkies invite the Tin Woodman to rule over them and by the end of the book he does so.[4] A mere journey in the arms of the Winged Monkeys would not have the desired effect. But McFague's method operates differently: her method of promoting the well-being of the planet belongs to a way of thinking, not to an external event. Secondly, it must be recalled that McFague refers here to the God of her model, not the living God. I will return to what is meant by "an incarnational understanding of Christianity and an organic interpretation of postmodern science" later. Thirdly, McFague's caveat about the external reference of her model-metaphors comes to the fore. On the one hand, McFague disclaims the possibility of reliable reference: "we must remind ourselves that all seeing, all knowing is perspectival."[5] On the other hand, she wants to project her perspective onto evolutionary

---

3. McFague, *The Body of God*, 150. McFague's italics.
4. See Baum, *The Wizard of Oz*, chapters 12–13; 23.
5. McFague, *Super, Natural Christians*, 33.

reality, which would suggest that evolution could claim its own ontological status independent of human perspective. Fourthly, McFague claims that her method "underscores our bodiliness" and connects us with the rest of creation. But does the method really achieve this? Is it not more about concepts than direct engagement?

Writing in the nineteen nineties, McFague describes what she terms "resistance" from Protestants "to a 'nature' spirituality, a spirituality that finds renewal and hope coming from what the eye sees and not just what the ear hears."[6] She states that for a time she shared this resistance: "As a Protestant and erstwhile Barthian, I was myself for many years such a resister. Only 'the Word' that reached my ears conveyed the presence of God, never the sights before my eyes." In describing herself as an *erstwhile* Barthian, McFague wishes to dissociate herself from Barth. She writes: "Barth saw creation as enclosed within election and totally defined by it."[7] But does not McFague also define the natural world in terms of her model? She writes:

> To say that sin has an ecological dimension means that we must view beings, organisms, in relation to their environment. The environment of all beings, according to our model of the universe as God's body, is the "divine *milieu*": we live and move and have our being, along with other beings, in God. Therefore, sin or living a lie will be living disproportionately, falsely, inappropriately within this space, refusing to accept the limitations and responsibilities of our place. Moreover, this space, place, has been further defined and qualified for Christians by the cosmic Christ, the embodied life paradigmatically expressed in the liberating, healing, inclusive ministry of Jesus of Nazareth.[8]

If Barth sees creation to be defined by election, McFague sees the "universe as God's body" defined by "the cosmic Christ," in accord with her "ecological" notion of good and evil.

I suggest that McFague continues to demonstrate some similarity to Barth's method, even in distancing herself from it. In Barth's case, the central figure of Jesus Christ is seen, through the lens of the eternal sight of God, as already human before the dawn of creation.[9] The method relies heavily on perspective. To use the illustration from *The Wizard of Oz*,

---

6. See McFague, *The Body of God*, 208.
7. McFague, *The Body of God*, 221 n. 6.
8. McFague, *The Body of God*, 115.
9. Barth, *CD* III/1: 54. See chapter 6.

the journey is governed by the perspective of the wearer of the Golden Cap. When the Witch wears the Cap, the Witch governs the journey. While it would be too much to say that McFague regards Barth's theology as evil, she evidently considers that his perspective is connected with the kind of "living a lie" that she wishes to correct. What kind of truth factor she invokes at this point is a further question.

Chapter 6 drew attention to what appears an uncompromising attitude from Barth to reality on the ground. Despite her claims to the contrary, I am not convinced that McFague avoids this problem. Her way of seeing through the lens of her model would seem to similarly impose her model on external reality. How, one may ask, does this affect our experience of "bodiliness"?

RELATIVISM

McFague wishes her "metaphorical theology" to make sense. In other words she aims for coherence within a relativistic framework. Chapter 3 drew attention to her frame of reference. She states that "there is indeed no way behind our constructions to test them with the reality they presume to represent."[10] She contends that constructions are productive of reality: while external reality exists, the only way of reaching it is to create versions of it. On these terms she upholds the possibility of producing better constructions on the understanding that the notion of "better" is relative to a particular perspective and particular time.

If one sees this description of linguistic reference in terms of ethics, the perspective is that of the wearer of the Golden Cap. The Witch creates her own reality by enslaving Dorothy and the Winkies. Dorothy creates an alternative reality by liberating the Witch's slaves. Beyond these versions are the realities of good and evil. But, according to McFague, there is no way behind the different versions to test them for correspondence to such realities. At the most, she says, one might be better relative to the other. But, in the absence of an external benchmark, how could this be demonstrated? McFague's theory of language contrasts with the kind of "truth-values arrived at across time and consensus" referred to by Steiner.[11] While I have taken the illustration of the Golden Cap from *The Wizard of Oz*, one must continue to ask whether McFague's assumptions

---

10. McFague, *Models of God*, 26.
11. Steiner, *Real Presences*, 119. See chapter 3.

are in accord with the assumptions of the story. I will take up this point in the next chapter.

As already seen, the relativistic nature of McFague's thinking does not preclude the ethical imperative:

> [W]e must remind ourselves that all seeing, all knowing is perspectival. The specific issue with which we are concerned—how should we love nature?—will necessarily be based on perspectival knowing. The question is, which perspective, which kind of seeing, is better for nature?[12]

But where is God in the ethical imperative? As noted above, McFague states that God is the energy empowering the entire universe. But this is part of a "way of speaking" about "God's relation to all matter." In other words, this kind of transcendence is part of the model. As seen in chapter 5, McFague draws her values from the model of the "loving eye" influenced by what she calls "our deepest, most basic sense of self in relation to the world."[13] She states that our notion of "love" is patterned on a projected possibility that God's love can be seen through the screen of human loves.[14] She rejects the understanding that "God defines love and that all human love only conforms to the divine pattern."[15] For McFague, there is no ethical reference point beyond ideology. Put simply, we are at the mercy of the wearer of the Golden Cap.

McFague spells out the kind of thinking that motivates her relativistic paradigm: "Two of the greatest influences on my thinking . . . have been process philosophy and feminist epistemology."[16] I will briefly consider both. The connection with process philosophy is touched on below. Margaret Whitford, editor for feminist psychoanalyst, Luce Irigaray, draws attention to an inherent conflict in feminist epistemology: women are currently caught between deconstruction of the subject and an unresolved search for a sense of worth and meaning. Whitford sums up the epistemological predicament for postmodern feminists:

> On the one hand, they share with postmodernist thought the radical critique of the modernist Enlightenment inheritance; on

---

12. McFague, *Super, Natural Christians*, 33.
13. McFague, *Super, Natural Christians*, 92. See chapter 5.
14. McFague, *Models of God*, 192 n. 37.
15. McFague attributes this understanding which she rejects to Barth (*Models of God*, 192 n. 37).
16. McFague, *Super, Natural Christians*, 2.

the other hand, the emancipatory thrust of feminism is rooted in the Enlightenment.[17]

In this context, says Whitford, Irigaray wishes to retain the emancipatory thrust, warning "against displacing the male/female binary before the female side has acceded to identity and subjectivity."

The current critique of the modernist Enlightenment not only undermines the emancipatory thrust which is rooted in the Enlightenment. It also undermines what Steiner terms "a semantics of correspondence." Writer on sociology and feminist theology, Elaine Graham states:

> Derrida's profound scepticism toward views of meaning as fixed and absolute enables all discourse to be exposed as provisional, and appeals to 'truth' and 'consensus' as illusory. Binary oppositions, especially those which characterize masculine and feminine as fixed, self-authenticating 'metaphysical presences', are undermined as unstable, slippery concepts which deny any notion of language as revealing a reliable external 'reality'.[18]

The deconstructionist context is at odds with the emancipist thrust, a tension evident in Irigaray's thinking.

Graham indicates that Irigaray hopes to find an alternative source of identity for women outside "patriarchal" authentication. But her search for female identity carries its own contradiction. Graham writes: "By placing the female body outside patriarchal culture, the more effectively to challenge androcentric norms, Irigaray risks rendering women's bodies immaterial and rhetorical, rather than empirical and rooted in social relations."[19] The tendency is toward projected abstraction rather than what McFague calls "bodiliness." Irigaray's response to a deconstruction of meaning is to attempt to retain the male/female binary without the "metaphysical presences" which authenticate it. On such terms her search moves away from signification and embodiment.

Postmodern thinking carries the dilemmas of self-reference and self-authentication. The difficulty with such thinking is that everything is projected from the subject rather than focused on what is outside the subject, hence the disembodying effect. One can never arrive at "bodiliness" on such terms. To deconstruct the subject would be a further step on a pathless journey. McFague's project does not take that step but the

---

17. Whitford, *The Irigaray Reader*, 12–13.
18. Graham, *Making The Difference*, 184.
19. Graham, *Making The Difference*, 137–38.

attempt to find meaning in models may in the long run have a similar effect. As seen in chapter 5, the attempt to test one model against another can only be conducted *within* the current model. The effect in relation to science will be seen below.

TWO STORIES

In her project to make sense of "an incarnational understanding of Christianity and an organic interpretation of postmodern science" McFague states that her "personal/ organic model" is "compatible with interpretations of both Christian faith and contemporary science, although not demanded by either."[20] I question whether it is endorsed by either. This section considers what she means by an organic interpretation of postmodern science and how she relates this interpretation to Christianity. The next section engages more specifically with her notion of "an incarnational understanding of Christianity."

McFague argues for a "personal/organic model" associated with a kind of thinking found in process theology. "Process thought moves toward a social view of agency (every entity or actual occasion is an agent, including God)," she says.[21] Earlier she writes: "We have lost the sense of belonging in our world and to the God who creates, nurtures, and redeems this world and all its creatures, and we have lost the sense that we are a part of a living, changing, dynamic cosmos that has its being in and through God."[22] It is ironic that she situates the remedy for this state of deprivation in a model-metaphor which does not claim access to reality. We have already seen her disengagement from the "metaphor of transference" which, by her admission, "seems to rest on a confidence . . . that all things are connected among themselves because they are connected in God."[23]

A further disengagement is evident in McFague's appeal to science. She uses the term "science" but what she means is something more like a popular philosophy of the nature and origin of the universe.[24] She admits that "an organic interpretation of postmodern science" is a reading

20. McFague, *The Body of God*, 150.
21. McFague, *The Body of God*, 140. Cf. also 31.
22. McFague, *The Body of God*, 34.
23. McFague, *Speaking in Parables*, 106.
24. See McFague, *The Body of God*, 40–41.

or picture of reality.[25] She argues for "a working cosmology" in terms of evolutionary history or, as she prefers to call it, "the common creation story." She favors "the common creation story" as opposed to the "Genesis myth" which, she says, "does not strike most people as a working model or construct within which the ordinary events and details of their lives can be understood."[26]

McFague outlines a rationale for the "personal/organic model" in *The Body of God*, the third in her series on language for God. The fourth book, *Super, Natural Christians*, explores the model from the perspective of living *within* it, as it were from the inside. At this point the "personal/organic model" becomes the "subject-subjects model." I have already noted this development in chapter 5. As I indicated, this kind of model operates independently of external reality, at the expense of scientific credentials. At one point McFague observes, "in science models can be and are tested by investigating the properties one expects to be present and if the expectations prove to be correct, one concludes that the model *is* a description, albeit imperfect and partial, of reality."[27] But the "personal/organic model" is not, by this standard, a scientific model. She describes the "common creation story" as "a narrative . . . that, while accepted in broad outlines by the majority of contemporary practicing scientists, relies on many assumptions, includes many unknowns, and can be interpreted in a variety of ways . . . ."[28] Clearly McFague feels at liberty to interpret the narrative in her own way.

McFague rejects natural theology as a means to "make sense" between evolution and creation, choosing instead to follow what she calls "a theology of nature":

> Natural theology tries to harmonize (or find points of contact between) belief and knowledge of the world; a theology of nature attempts to reconceive belief in terms of contemporary views of the natural world. A theology of nature does not solicit the help of science to provide a basis for or to confirm faith, but uses the contemporary picture of reality from the sciences of its day as a resource to reconstruct and express the faith.[29]

---

25. See McFague, *The Body of God*, 91–97.
26. McFague, *The Body of God*, 112.
27. See McFague, *Metaphorical Theology*, 99. McFague's italics.
28. McFague, *The Body of God*, 40.
29. McFague, *The Body of God*, 65–66.

Such an approach not only reconstructs the faith, it also re-construes history.

I have already suggested that McFague's method may owe something to Barth. Chapter 6 noted Barth's stance towards the Genesis creation narratives. Barth classifies these narratives as "saga," that is, a literary form that uses "intuitive and poetic pictures" to depict "a prehistorical reality of history."[30] While not denying the genuine historicity of the narratives, Barth nevertheless conceives this genre in its immediate relation to God. McFague would appear to treat the "contemporary picture of reality" suggested by evolutionary history in a somewhat similar way. The picture is intuitive in offering "a working model or construct within which the ordinary events and details of [life] can be understood." The method does not to deny the "historicity" of the narrative, but presents it in its immediate relation, not to God but to us.

McFague's "theology of nature" engages with evolutionary history as "story," describing it as "a historical narrative with a beginning, middle and presumed end":[31]

> The common creation story is both common and uncommon. It is common because it is the story of everything that is, of how the universe began fifteen billion years ago and how it evolved into some hundred billion galaxies of which our Milky Way is one. Hence everything that exists . . . has a common beginning and a common history: at some level and in a remote and intimate way, everything is related to everything else . . . . The common creation story is uncommon because it is the wildest, most outrageous, most awesome tale conceivable: from an initial explosion, an infinitely hot, infinitely dense matter/energy event billions of years ago, the entire universe has evolved into its present complexity, diversity, size and age.[32]

In this context, McFague's use of the term "historical" is linked with the literary quality of the narrative. Despite the presumed end, its historicity resides in its lack of completion: "In our new cosmic story, time is irreversible, genuine novelty results through the interplay of chance and law, and the future is open. This is an unfinished universe, a dynamic universe, still in process."[33] By contrast, adds McFague, other cosmologies

---

30. Resch, *Barth's Interpretation of the Virgin Birth*, 72–73.
31. McFague, *The Body of God*, 105.
32. McFague, *The Body of God*, 27.
33. McFague, *The Body of God*, 104–5.

"including mythic ones such as Genesis and even earlier scientific ones, have not been historical, for in them creation was finished."

Notwithstanding this story-like character, there is a suggested link with science and hence with actual world history. While allowing that scientists debate "the big bang theory itself"[34] and that details about the evolution of the earth and its life-forms are "highly contested," McFague maintains that "the *direction* of the evolutionary process toward diversity and the *nature* of . . . 'interdependence'" is compatible with "the most hard-nosed evolutionary theory."[35] But, as noted above, McFague's "theology of nature" engages with "the contemporary picture of reality" rather than with evolutionary theory direct. McFague's appeal to hard science is not sustained.

I turn now to C. S. Lewis who also highlights the story-like character of evolutionary history: "Let no one say we are an unimaginative age: neither the Greeks nor the Norsemen ever invented a better story."[36] But Lewis makes a clear distinction between the story and the "biological theorem." What he terms "the Myth of popular Evolutionism" predates scientific theory: "If popular Evolutionism were (as it imagines itself to be) not a Myth but the intellectually legitimate result of the scientific theorem on the public mind, it would arise *after* that theorem had become widely known."[37] But, says Lewis, this is by no means the case. He finds evidence of the story in "Keats's *Hyperion*, nearly forty years before the *Origin of Species*" and also in a letter about the *Nibelung's Ring* from Wagner, dated 1854.[38] Secondly, the Myth is not a hypothesis in a scientific sense. In "the science, evolution is a theory about *changes*: in the Myth it is a fact about *improvements*."[39] (Lewis cites J. B. S. Haldane: "We are therefore inclined to regard progress as the rule in evolution. Actually it is the exception, and for every case of it there are ten of degeneration.") Thirdly, and unlike the Myth, the biological theorem *per se* "makes no cosmic statements, no metaphysical statements, no eschatological statements."[40] By contrast, McFague's project follows the line of the popular myth.

34. McFague, *The Body of God*, 40.
35. McFague, *The Body of God*, 45. McFague's italics.
36. Lewis, "Funeral of a Great Myth," 117.
37. Lewis, "Funeral of a Great Myth," 111. Lewis's italics.
38. Lewis, "Funeral of a Great Myth," 112.
39. Lewis, "Funeral of a Great Myth," 114. Lewis cites Haldane, "Darwinism Today."
40. Lewis, "Funeral of a Great Myth," 114.

In pursuing a "theology of nature," McFague claims to follow the biblical pattern. She states that theologies "always have paid and always should pay serious attention to the picture of reality operative in their culture."[41] She finds this cultural kind of cosmological perspective "in both the Jewish and early Christian traditions."[42] In place of the biblical picture of reality, McFague wishes to substitute a postmodern picture with its own implications for the relation between God and the world, alongside a reconstructed ethical component. Here she distinguishes between conscious and unconscious reconstruction. "For centuries," she says, "people have lived for the most part unknowingly within the constructs of Christian reflection."[43] By contrast, McFague advocates "a planetary perspective" with conscious emphasis on "the *consequences* of proposed constructions for those who live within them":

> Broadly speaking, the encompassing agenda would be to deconstruct and reconstruct the central symbols of the Jewish and Christian traditions so as to be on the side of life and its fulfillment, keeping the liberation of the oppressed (including the earth and all its creatures) in central focus.[44]

This kind of "planetary agenda" derives not from a postmodern cosmological picture *per se* but from a truncated and remodeled Christianity superimposed on the cultural picture. One might ask whether McFague's perspective not so much remythologizes the Christian faith in terms of the "common creation story" as remythologizes the "common creation story" in terms of elements from the Christian faith.

In one sense McFague disclaims the "improvements" that Lewis discerns in the popular myth of evolution As noted in chapter 6, McFague's method disowns the "optimistic arrow" in the direction of evolutionary history *per se*.[45] But, in another sense, she reengages the "optimistic arrow" through the optimistic construction that her method superimposes onto the evolutionary story. She wishes to borrow from what she terms the constructs of Christian reflection in a conscious way. Deconstructed

---

41. McFague, *The Body of God*, 28–29. But cf. Augustine's description of various ancient theories about the nature of world history (see *City of God XII*, 10–14). See also below for the incompatibility of the Incarnation with a Platonic cosmology.

42. McFague, *The Body of God*, 65.

43. McFague, *The Body of God*, 69.

44. McFague, *The Body of God*, 67–68. McFague's italics.

45. See McFague, *The Body of God*, 181.

and reconstructed, such reflection can then serve as a means to the "liberation of the oppressed (including the earth and all its creatures)."

In a further sense, however, the popular evolutionary story already engages with liberation. "[The Myth] arose in the Revolutionary period," says Lewis. "But for the political ideals of that period it would never have been accepted. That explains why the Myth concentrates on Haldane's one case of biological 'progress' and ignores [the] ten cases of 'degeneration.'"[46] By the Revolutionary period, Lewis means the era of Keats and Wagner, the Romantic period in other words. It is the Romantic era (following the French Revolution) which is the source of the quest for "liberation," including what Whitford calls the "emancipist thrust" of feminism.

Lewis indicates that, if believed, the popular evolutionary story has the effect of an enchantment from which the world needs to be awakened.[47] Put in terms of *The Wizard of Oz*, those who believe the myth are, for Lewis, in a similar state to that of the inhabitants of Oz. While McFague does not commit herself to naïve belief in the story, she wishes to make conscious use of it. Here she places herself in line with the policy of the Wizard. In one sense she agrees that the spell must be broken: she advocates a state of awareness of proposed constructions and their consequences. But in another sense she wishes to perpetuate the enchantment while adding newly constructed symbols of the Jewish and Christian faith. This is a far cry from making sense on scientific terms.

I have entitled this section "Two stories." The alternative story is the one commencing in Genesis. "The Genesis myth," says McFague, "does not strike most people as a working model or construct within which the ordinary events and details of their lives can be understood."[48] But evolutionary history also has its problems as a working model, hence the desire to superimpose symbols of the Jewish and Christian traditions. Such symbols or "experiences of liberation" have the effect of initiating an ethic which runs counter to the notions of "the fang and the claw" and "survival of the fittest."[49] I turn now to McFague's other stated aim of making sense in the context of "an incarnational understanding of Christianity."

---

46. Lewis, "Funeral of a Great Myth," 122.
47. Lewis, "Funeral of a Great Myth," 123.
48. McFague, *The Body of God*, 112.
49. See McFague, *Super, Natural Christians*, 52 cf. 152, 157–58.

THE POSSIBILITY OF THE INCARNATION

In *Metaphorical Theology*, the first of her series on language for God, McFague appears to disown the Incarnation. She writes: "The basis of the sacramental universe within Christianity . . . is the incarnation: the sense of divine immanence in the Hebrew tradition is brought to its apotheosis in the Johannine assertion that 'the Word became flesh and dwelt among us.'"[50] But, she remarks: "many of us no longer believe in a symbolic, sacramental universe."[51] Nevertheless, she reengages the motif of incarnation in terms of a panentheist God in her third book, *The Body of God*:

> Panentheism is, I would suggest, a strong motif in both Hebrew and Christian traditions that take seriously the mediation of God to the world. These traditions deny, on the one hand, a picture of God as an external super-person (or Unmoved Mover) distant from and alien to the world and, on the other hand, a view of God as immediately available to the mind of human beings or as identified with natural processes. Rather, the panentheistic tradition is found in all those passages in the Hebrew Scriptures that mediate the divine presence through human words and acts as well as natural phenomena and in the New Testament in its central declaration that "the Word was made flesh" in Jesus of Nazareth. In all these instances, mediation and incarnation are central and, therefore, are open to, or ought to be open to, the embodiment of God, especially in its panentheistic form of the world (universe) as God's body and God as its spirit.[52]

Here I believe she is reconstructing a central symbol of the Christian tradition rather than deploying the orders of reality in which the Incarnation would make sense.

What frame of reference is at issue here? McFague notes Wolfhart Pannenberg's objection to Barth's in principle dissociation of the doctrine of creation from scientific descriptions of the world: "If theologians want to conceive of God as the creator of the real world, they cannot possibly bypass the scientific description of that world."[53] One might rephrase this to read: if theologians want to engage a scientific description of the world, they cannot possibly bypass the creator (and redeemer) of the real world.

50. McFague, *Metaphorical Theology*, 10
51. See McFague, *Metaphorical Theology*, 11–13.
52. McFague, *The Body of God*, 150.
53. See McFague, *The Body of God*, 221 n. 5. McFague cites "The Doctrine of Creation and Modern Science."

Does McFague's method solve the problem by removing God as creator, as well as scientific description, from the real world? Evolutionary history engages with world history as a series of events in chronological order. The Incarnation would traditionally be understood as the entry of the creator into world history in a chronological sense. But the retrospective method espoused by Barth and McFague runs counter to this.

Chapter 6 noted Bultmann's comment to Barth: "It has become increasingly plain to me that you have no inner relationship to history, such as you so strongly have to idealistic philosophy."[54] Similarly, McFague's project of re-imagining the Christian tradition in terms of evolutionary history cannot, to my mind, proceed without making the historical component a matter of concepts rather than of living engagement. The effect on the Christian story is similarly conceptual: she wishes to deconstruct and reconstruct the central symbols of the Jewish and Christian traditions. Her project to make cosmological sense in terms of science and theology does not, in fact, engage with either on cosmological terms. Her appeal to hard science notwithstanding, McFague deploys a myth projected from the contemporary sciences. She also engages a myth projected by the Jewish and Christian traditions. McFague would seem to reengage the "thinking of myth" which Bultmann wants to discard while combining elements from creation and evolution, contrary to Barth's insistence on a distinction between the two.[55]

Let us pause here and consider the interface between theology and cosmology. In this regard, let us compare Barth and Lewis on the Apostles' Creed. Barth begins with dogmatics. He states: "Precisely from this dogmatic standpoint it must be clear that the whole of theology is . . . not a mere historicism, that the history is valid, the history which penetrates into the present day, *hic et nunc*."[56] On Barth's terms, this is to engage with soteriology (the history which penetrates into the present day) rather than historicity (a mere historicism). The link with actual world history is at best tenuous. Barth states that the name of Pontius Pilate "in connexion with the Passion of Christ makes it unmistakably clear that this Passion of Jesus Christ . . . took place . . . in the centre of the world-history in which our human life is played out."[57] For Barth, however, the prior

---

54. Bultmann to Barth (Marburg 31 December 1922) *Letters*, 4.

55. See Bultmann to Barth (Marburg, 11–15, November, 1952), *Letters*, 88, 95 and Barth, *Dogmatics in Outline*, 51.

56. Barth, *Dogmatics in Outline*, 12.

57. Barth, *Dogmatics in Outline*, 109.

creedal statement that God is creator of heaven and earth is not part of world history in the same way: "If we are to take [creation] seriously, it must at once be clear that we are not confronted by a realm which in any sense may be accessible to human view or even to human thought."[58] For Barth, the events outlined in the Creed do not interact with world history so much as intersect world history at the point of the crucifixion.

Resch quotes Barth on his theological evaluation of Scriptural history and saga:

> The decision about its nature as revelation, the confirmation of its reality as the Word of God, is reached by the fact that in its "historical" parts and also particularly and precisely in its "non-historical" (or sagas)—although always in connection with the former—it attests the history of the great acts of God as genuine history, and that this witness is received and accepted through the power of the Holy Spirit.[59]

Barth appears to connect or reconnect "non-historical" saga with "genuine history." What he means by "genuine" may be difficult to determine. To my mind this is reminiscent of his distinction, noted in chapter 6, between a real happening *in* history as opposed to a real happening *of* history.[60] As in much of what Barth has to say about biblical history, I gain the impression that the events tend to *become* "genuine history" (through the attestation of the Holy Spirit).

Barth admits that his approach to biblical history is a departure from orthodoxy.[61] But the content of his theology seems largely orthodox. Chapter 6 noted his assertion that the doctrine of creation is distinct from pagan mythology.[62] Lewis agrees: "Some hazy adumbrations of a doctrine of the Fall can be found in Paganism; but it is quite astonishing how rarely outside Christianity we find—I am not sure that we ever find—a real doctrine of Creation."[63] But Lewis has a more traditional approach to the historical relevance of the creeds. Lewis goes so far as to

---

58. Barth, *Dogmatics in Outline*, 51.

59. See Resch, *Barth's Interpretation of the Virgin Birth*, 73. Resch cites Barth, *CD* III/I, 82.

60. Barth, *Word of God and Word of Man*, 90

61. Barth to Bultmann (Basel, 24 December 1952) *Letters*, 107.

62. Barth, *Dogmatics in Outline*, 51.

63. Lewis, "Some Thoughts," 93.

maintain that the creedal statements offer a template for understanding the direction of world history.[64]

A note about the use of the term "historicism" may serve to highlight the difference between Barth and Lewis. Barth uses the term "historicism" to mean events which can be evaluated according to their connection and analogy with other historical events. By contrast, Lewis uses the term "historicism" to mean a false belief that ultimate meaning can be discovered in the historical process without the aid of divine revelation. "On certain great events (those embodied in the creeds)," writes Lewis, "we have what I believe to be divine comment which makes plain so much of their significance as we need, and we can bear, to know. On other events . . . we have no such comment."[65] Lewis writes that evolutionism "when it ceases to be simply a theorem in biology and becomes a principle for interpreting the total historical process is a form of Historicism."[66] In Lewis's opinion, one should guard against the kind of coherent world-view that comes from embroidering on the modest claims of Christianity and the sciences.

Chapter 6 cited an observation about Barth's theological method in which the "reality" of revelation must both affirm and deny, recreate and annihilate at the same moment the "reality common to humanity."[67] Such a conception is hardly conducive to a full-blooded interaction between God and humanity, much less an Incarnation. If, in Barth's thinking, the realm of creation is not accessible to human view or even to human thought, one might then ask whether the intuitive and poetic pictures offered by the biblical genre of "saga" do not have a kind of intermediary function between otherwise incompatible realities. Barth's remarks about the miracle of Christmas functioning as a *sign* of the mystery of the Incarnation may serve to indicate Barth's method of reconciling the two.

Where does McFague sit with this? "A theology of nature," says McFague, "does not solicit the help of science to provide a basis for or to confirm faith, but uses the contemporary picture of reality from the sciences of its day as a resource to reconstruct and express the faith."[68] Her project to make sense of "an incarnational understanding of Christianity

---

64. See Lewis, "Historicism."

65. Lewis, "Historicism," 145.

66. Lewis, "Historicism," 132. Lewis also says that when "a village woman says that her wicked father-in-law's paralytic stroke is a "judgment on him" she is a Historicist."

67. See Graham Ward, *Barth, Derrida and the Language of Theology*, 235.

68. McFague, *The Body of God*, 65–66.

and an organic interpretation of postmodern science" is realized in a personal/organic *model*. This kind of model, McFague reminds us, is not a description but rather a paradigm or way of seeing things.[69] One might ask whether the personal/organic model does not have a kind of intermediary function for McFague between otherwise incompatible realities, in parallel with Barth's notion of "sign."

Let us return at this point to Pannenberg's objection to Barth's in principle dissociation of the doctrine of creation from scientific descriptions of the world. The realms of faith and fact constitute incompatible realities only if the doctrine of creation is detached from world history. But how could the Incarnation occur on such terms? McFague states that the Incarnation lacks the credibility in our time that it would have had in first century Mediterranean times and the Middle Ages.[70] In fact, the notion of incompatible realities is an ancient one: Lewis notes "the Platonic view that the Divine and the human cannot meet except through a *tertium quid*."[71] The Incarnation as an event in world history explodes the categories of philosophy in its idealistic tendencies, whether ancient or modern.

McFague goes so far as to endorse Hebrew and Christian traditions which "take seriously the mediation of God to the world."[72] But she does not attempt to factor the Incarnation as such into her cosmology. What she wishes to retain from the biblical tradition is not the Incarnation, but what she calls "mediation" (with a small 'i' for "incarnation"). She states: "In its traditional form the claim [that the Word became flesh and lived among us] is not only offensive to the integrity and value of other religions, but incredible, indeed absurd in light of postmodern cosmology."[73] She goes on to say:

> It is not the exclusive claim that matters, for one would assume that the source, power, and goal of the universe . . . would be embodied in many forms. . . . Rather, it is both the concrete, physical availability of God's presence ("became flesh") and the likeness to ourselves, a human being ("lived among us") that matter.

---

69. See McFague, *The Body of God*, 157.
70. McFague, *The Body of God*, 136–37.
71. Lewis, *The Discarded* Image, 79.
72. McFague, *The Body of God*, 150.
73. See McFague, *The Body of God*, 159–60.

But in eschewing the exclusive claim of Christianity, the model eschews particularity. It does not become flesh in that sense.

Bultmann disclaims engagement both with biblical "mythology" and the "worldview of objectifying science." For Barth, biblical "saga" would seem to intersect world history in the crucifixion under Pontius Pilate. McFague's evolutionary cosmology could perhaps be said to intersect hard science. But the link is tenuous. Her contemporary picture coming from the sciences of the day unashamedly espouses popular evolutionism. As such, it resembles the "worldview of objectifying science" in Bultmann's sense. McFague superimposes a selected sample of biblical symbols onto her cosmology, retaining the color but not the substance of the Incarnation in the process. Her project relies on projected pictures rather than on substance. I submit that her attempt to "make sense" between disparate disciplines bears a closer affinity to making popularized sensibility between the two.

THE WIZARD AND SCIENCE

It is my contention that McFague's appeal to metaphor is an exercise in illusion and that her claim to "make sense" is no exception to this. She finds common ground between Christianity and postmodern science, not in terms of external reality by means of natural theology, but in terms of a contemporary "working model or construct within which the ordinary events [of life] can be understood."[74] In other words, her reconciliation is conducted on existentialist terms. The appeal to science has the appearance of engaging with external reality but this is deceptive since her model-metaphors disclaim this intention. The appeal to Christianity enables the ethical application but this occurs in the absence of external epistemological validation.

As I judge, McFague's attempt to overcome the subject-object divide is in essence an attempt to overcome the dichotomy between existentialism and positivism. She herself appears to have a foot in both camps. At the same time she expresses her distance from Barth and Bultmann and also from positivism. She finds a remedy for both ways of thinking in her understanding of metaphor. She writes:

> It may be an oversimplification to put the distinction between Barth and Bultmann in terms of objective versus subjective: yet it

74. McFague, *The Body of God*, 112.

is, I believe, not only accurate but essential, for this is the shoal on which they founder. . . . If one takes metaphor to be the crucial constitutive of language, the subjective-objective split is false.[75]

It is common knowledge since Thomas Kuhn and his work on the theory-laden context within which science operates that science is a metaphorical enterprise at heart, that it is constructive and interpretive, and that therefore it is closer to philosophy and even theology than anyone thought fifty years ago during the heyday of positivistic science.[76]

Metaphor is said to bridge the subjective-objective split. But on what terms?

McFague distinguishes between the "subjective cul-de-sac of Bultmann (all that can be said of God must be said in terms of my own transformed life)" and the "objective presumption of Barth (his peculiar epistemology which recognizes the Kantian limits in all instances but one, the biblical revelation)."[77] But Barth's claim that "the whole of theology" validates "the history which penetrates into the present day" does not operate in the order of objective scientific reality: this is the burden of Pannenberg's objection about him. In other words, Barth's apprehension of the biblical revelation does not fill the postmodern epistemological vacuum nor does it to overcome the subject-object divide. Barth admits a similarity in his thinking to Bultmann's existentialism, as seen in chapter 6.[78] To my mind the *faith* aspect of his method functions somewhat similarly to McFague's notion of a model. McFague's engagement with a "theology of nature" would introduce science to this arena, as "a metaphorical enterprise at heart."

Let us turn now to Turbayne's Wizard. Here is a variant on the theme of the subject-object divide. As already noted, Turbayne critiques positivism but does not critique positivist parameters.[79] Turbayne pays tribute to the primacy of "the facts." This does not prevent him from engaging with metaphor, which he judges to deviate from "the facts," but it does supply the terms on which the deviation is proposed. Ricoeur states that Turbayne's "examples of model-metaphors are borrowed not from restricted areas of physics but from the order of meta-scientific world

---

75. McFague, *Speaking in Parables*, 31–32.
76. McFague, *The Body of God*, 93.
77. McFague, *Speaking in Parables*, 33–34.
78. Barth, "The Humanity of God," 54.
79. See Ricoeur, *The Rule of Metaphor*, 253–54.

views, where the border between model and scientific myth tends to be erased."[80] Turbayne places himself on the fault-line between "fact" and "not fact," unlike Ricoeur's more nuanced frame of reference. We may compare this borrowing from the neighborhood of scientific myth with Bultmann's remark about the projections of "objectifying science." The content is similar but the context is different. Bultmann's theology resides in a subjective cul-de-sac, says McFague. Such thinking does not share Turbayne's concern with facts.

Turbayne promotes the use of metaphor within a positivist framework. But he also acknowledges that access to "literal truth" depends on the linguistic agency of metaphor. He writes:

> The attempt to re-allocate the facts by restoring them to where they "actually belong" is vain. It is like trying to observe the rule "Let us get rid of the metaphors and replace them by the literal truth." But can this be done? . . . I have said that one condition of the use of metaphor is awareness. More accurately speaking, this means *more* awareness, for we can never become wholly aware. We cannot say what reality is, only what it seems like to us, imprisoned in Plato's cave, because we cannot get outside to look."[81]

At this point Turbayne undermines his own premise. How can metaphor constitute a misallocation of "the facts" if there are no such things? How can one become more *aware* of the misallocation on such terms? As I judge, McFague follows Turbayne in her respect for facts, witness her appeal to hardnosed evolutionary theory. She also claims that we have no access to external reality but only multiple interpretations.

An appeal to metaphor as a means to reconcile subject and object does not, on these terms, make sense but it may appear to do so. I have stated that Turbayne places himself on the fault-line between "fact" and "not fact." I judge that McFague does the same thing. In effect, Turbayne and McFague operate in two orders of reality. The appeal to "the facts" belongs to positivist parameters. The appeal to "metaphor" belongs to subjectivist parameters. But the order of meta-scientific world views may seem to encompass both. McFague's engagement with popular evolutionism sits comfortably at the point where the border between scientific model and scientific myth tends to be erased.

80. Ricoeur, *The Rule of Metaphor*, 253.
81. Turbayne, *The Myth of Metaphor*, 64 (Turbayne's italics).

Making Sense? 143

In such a framework "metaphor" acquires a new role. We may recall the final option assigned to Turbayne's Wizard with regard to a linguistic metaphor for the events of nature:

> The third course is to be fully aware of the presence of the disguise; aware that there are no proper sorts into which the facts must be allocated, but only better pictures or better metaphors . . . and then to treat the language metaphor as a myth . . . [so that] when the "initiated" say "it is not true," one is able to answer by acting *as if* it were true.[82]

In this way of thinking, attention moves from truth in the sense of "the facts" to a "better" way of acting. In other words, "better" takes on the meaning of "better value." There is a separation at this point between truth and value.

In *The Body of God* McFague discusses the rival merits of two scientific readings of the universe:

> Within the scientific community itself there is considerable debate concerning the picture of reality emerging from postmodern science, a debate characterized by two camps: the unifiers versus the diversifiers, reductionism versus holism, or the machine versus the organic model.[83]

"The point to emphasize," says McFague, "is that both positions are ideologies, both are readings."[84] We have a choice between the two.

That said, she adds "a third and attractive option." She spells this out: "we can accept reductionism as a successful method of research as well as the physical base of all levels of nonliving and living entities and, at the same time, opt for the holistic, organic view as the picture of reality or metaphysics with which theology should be in conversation."[85] There is a subtle shift of categories at this point. In the third option, the machine model moves into the realm of "a successful method of research," the realm of fact in other words. The organic model moves into the realm of metaphysics with which theology should be in conversation. McFague then dissociates her third option from external verification. The choice,

---

82. Turbayne, *The Myth of Metaphor*, 216–17. Turbayne cites Stewart, *The Myths of Plato*. He states here: "the distinction between *bona fide* science, so-called, and scientific mythology is so tenuous that it cannot be sharply drawn."

83. See McFague, *The Body of God*, 91–92.

84. McFague, *The Body of God*, 92.

85. McFague, *The Body of God*, 93.

she says, is between pictures of reality, not between reality and a picture of reality. She states that "factors other than correspondence with reality must enter." Here she makes the remark that science "is a metaphorical enterprise at heart."

One might ask what becomes of the method of successful research on such terms. In answer, McFague proceeds to redefine "objectivity," going so far as to question a claim to scientific objectivity stemming from "some forms of traditional, Western (male) epistemology." She suggests that a feminist "view from the body" would counteract the bias of research and offer "a stronger objectivity" by broadening the base of participation:

> [The] two key notions [of this approach] are embodiment and praxis (versus disembodiment and theory): knowledge or truth is not concerned with neutral (read masked) abstractions corresponding to eternal verities but with situated, embodied sites of insight and need, oriented toward increasing inclusivity and betterment.[86]

The territory is no longer "fact" but "inclusivity and betterment."

McFague does not explain the use of the term "masked" in this context and does not acknowledge a debt here to Turbayne. As I understand her, she suggests that ideology cannot be measured for correspondence to external truth but that "a stronger objectivity" can be obtained through a pooling of ideological approaches.[87] In other words, the Golden Cap must be shared. I will look more closely at the effect of this kind of thinking on ethics in chapter 10. McFague associates "betterment" with a feminist emphasis on a "view from the body."[88] We have noted above the tendency towards projected abstraction in a postmodern feminist search for embodiment.

McFague's appeal to "a stronger objectivity" moves away from focus on the external world but, as noted, she retains a respect for "the facts." I suspect that the model of successful research functions for McFague in the way that "crucified under Pontius Pilate" operates for Barth. There is a point of intersection between different orders of reality which has a verifying effect but does not fundamentally alter the theological parameters. Her examples of model-metaphors, borrowed from the order of meta-scientific world views, facilitate the movement away from external

---

86. See McFague, *The Body of God*, 95–96.
87. See McFague, *The Body of God*, 96.
88. See McFague, *The Body of God*, 95.

correspondence. The subject-object divide is overcome at the expense of the object.

This kind of thinking relies on an arbitrary juggling of different frames of reference. Turbayne states that we are imprisoned in Plato's cave because we cannot get outside to look. He retains the notion of an outside: this is fundamental to the Wizard's cautionary proviso that, in departing from the realm of "fact," one must remain conscious of "pretense." Similarly, McFague states that "we must remind ourselves once again that we are dealing with models, not descriptions, and also that all models have limitations, including, of course, the one we have put forward."[89] The reminder would seem all the more necessary if the claim to "a stronger objectivity" is applied to the ethically redemptive component which McFague wishes to graft onto popular evolutionism.

What is lost in such thinking is *access* to what is outside. One may ask what effect this will have on the future of the sciences. One can agree that all models have limitations. Nature, says Lewis, "gives most of her evidence in answer to the questions we ask her."[90] But, in the absence of access to reality and external standards, how could such questions be asked or assessed? There is a further question here: do the alleged prisoners in Plato's cave have the ability to recognize the limitations of their models? Put differently, what frame of reference would permit the Wizard to operate *outside* the frame of the inhabitants of Oz?

As I judge, McFague's project only serves to expose a deep contradiction of the post-Cartesian legacy. Chapter 4 drew attention to a disjunction between the modern notion of objectivity and the modern tendency towards a subjectivist epistemology. Here one may discern the seeds of a subject-object divide. McFague's relativistic approach would make the notion of objectivity increasingly nominal. At the same time she detaches the term "objectivity" from its Cartesian orientation and redeploys it ideologically.

In writing about the popular evolutionary myth, Lewis sums up an epistemological predicament:

> The Myth cannot even get going without accepting a good deal from the real sciences. And the sciences cannot be accepted for a moment unless rational inferences are valid: for every science claims to be a series of inferences from observed facts.... But at

---

89. McFague, *The Body of God*, 157.
90. Lewis, *The Discarded Image*, 223.

the same time the Myth asks me to believe that reason is simply the unforeseen and unintended by-product of a mindless process at one stage of its endless and aimless becoming. The content of the Myth thus knocks from under me the only ground on which I could possibly believe the Myth to be true.[91]

The sciences rely on the validity of observed facts as well as of inference. The Wizard has another agenda.

I began this chapter by likening McFague's soteriological method to the bird's eye view obtained from traveling, in the arms of the Winged Monkeys, from beyond the castle of the Witch of the West back to the Emerald City. I suggested this analogy in order to illustrate the retrospective nature of her method. The ontological abstinence entailed is clearer in terms of the Emerald City itself. It must be remembered that the City is green only due to the green glasses of its inhabitants. As in McFague's method, greenness is projected onto the City.

Turbayne goes so far as to conclude that access to "the facts" is governed by illusory propensity of metaphor. On such terms the Wizard cannot take off his own glasses. On the other hand, Turbayne's method (and McFague's as well) relies on awareness of the City as it is. There is a contradiction here but, as with Lewis's remarks about the evolutionary myth, the consequences are not taken. What is of interest is the attractive and apparently beneficial prospect of imposing the green color on the otherwise inaccessible City.

McFague's project would seem to occupy a shadowy space in which the projections of "mythology" and "objectifying science" (as discerned and rejected by Bultmann) overlap with the realm of the "as if" (promoted by Turbayne), a space which would put the counter-realm of solid facts in jeopardy.[92] McFague states that "many of us no longer believe in a symbolic, sacramental universe."[93] Her relativistic notion of truth is, she says, not concerned with "eternal verities." Does such disengagement amount to a linguistic hiatus in which, as Lewis states, "all our thinking is nonsensical"?[94] I will return to this question in chapter 10. The next two chapters explore an alternative approach.

---

91. Lewis, 'The Funeral of a Great Myth', 118.

92. Ricoeur associates Turbayne's notion of "pretense" in metaphor with "bad faith" although, he says, Turbayne "does not use those terms" (*The Rule of Metaphor*, 252).

93. See McFague, *Speaking in Parables*, 106.

94. Lewis, "Bluspels and Flalansferes," 50.

8

"A Reality Comes to Language"

IN *THE WIZARD OF OZ* Dorothy travels from the Land of Oz to the farm in Kansas by means of the Silver Shoes. She takes three steps, whirling through the air at a great rate. Then suddenly she stops. She lands on the grass and rolls over several times before she knows where she is. Eventually she sits up and looks about. She is home at the farm.[1]

Chapter 2 made use of this illustration to draw attention to Ricoeur's theory of the operation of metaphor. Ricoeur describes a threefold method of metaphorical reference: at the level of the expression itself, at the level of the journey from vehicle to tenor and at the level of external reference. He describes the arrival at external reference in terms of *discovery*. In "poetic experience," says Ricoeur, "something other than the poet speaks even as he speaks, and . . . beyond the control of the poet, a reality comes to language."[2]

Ricoeur writes about "the air of *rightness* that certain more fortunate instances of language and art seem to exude":

> Does not the fittingness, the appropriateness of certain verbal and non-verbal predicates indicate that language not only has organized reality in a different way, but also made manifest a way of being of things, which is brought to language thanks to semantic innovation? It would seem that the enigma of

---

1. See Baum, *The Wizard of Oz*, chapter 23.
2. Ricoeur, *The Rule of Metaphor*, 253–54.

> metaphorical discourse is that it 'invents' in both senses of the word: what it creates, it discovers; and what it finds, it invents.[3]

The "enigma of metaphorical discourse" brings two things together. There is an interface between poetic invention and the reality, beyond the control of the poet, which comes to the poetic language. Ricoeur continues:

> What must be understood, therefore, is the interconnection of three themes. In the metaphorical discourse of poetry referential power is linked to the eclipse of ordinary reference; the creation of heuristic fiction is the road to redescription; and reality brought to language unites manifestation and creation.

In this way, language which owes much to the poet's invention joins forces with the reality it seeks to describe. In terms of *The Wizard of Oz*, the journey ends in contact with the ground in a way that makes itself felt.

Lewis also uses the term "rightness" in describing how the imaginative power of metaphor provides access to external reality. Lewis argues for "a kind of truth or rightness in the imagination itself" since "all our truth, or all but a few fragments, is won by metaphor."[4] He goes on to say:

> And thence, I confess, it does follow that if our thinking is ever true, then the metaphors by which we think must have been good metaphors. It does follow that if those original equations, between good and light, or evil and dark, between breath and soul and all the others, were from the beginning arbitrary and fanciful—if there is not, in fact, a kind of psycho-physical parallelism (or more) in the universe—then all our thinking is nonsensical.

While Lewis goes further than Ricoeur in highlighting the function of metaphor in conceptual language, both are at one, I believe, in the notion that "something other than the poet speaks even as he speaks," to use Ricoeur's way of putting it.

Ricoeur uses the terminology "heuristic fiction" to describe the *modus operandi* of metaphorical reference. McFague also uses the terms "fiction" and "heuristic" in describing her kind of theology. As already seen, her theology is said to be "mostly fiction."[5] McFague writes: "To say that metaphorical theology is experimental is to emphasize its as-if

---

3. Ricoeur, *The Rule of Metaphor*, 239.
4. Lewis, "Bluspels and Flalansferes," 49–50.
5. McFague, *Models of God*, xi.

quality, its heuristic quality of finding out for itself."[6] She goes on to say that this kind of theology "must be willing to play with possibilities and as a consequence, not take itself too seriously." One gains the impression that "fiction" does not mean the same thing for McFague that it does for Ricoeur. Metaphorical discourse "invents" in two senses, says Ricoeur: "what it creates, it discovers; and what it finds, it invents." By contrast, McFague seems to use the term "heuristic" in one sense only. Her kind of metaphor experiments but does not, as I judge, claim to find.

Chapter 4 noted McFague's desire for theology to engage with life through various literary genres. McFague writes: "theological discourse, which has for the most part been discursive and conceptual, may well be in need of radical correction."[7] She goes on to say, "If the parable (and its close cousins, story and confession) are seen as primary forms for theology, then the content of theology might well be different than it has been in the past." But what is the basis for her literary approach? McFague goes so far as to state: "Without assuming an idealistic perspective (the world out there is only what subjects say it is), a moderate Kantianism (and we are all, one way or another, Kantians) insists that in a sense ... all theology, philosophy, physics, and art is autobiography."[8] I submit that her existentialist leaning colors her treatment of story and confession: the spectacles she wears tend to give it an inward focus.

What I present below is my attempt to engage with the literary intention and flavor behind McFague's statement that "in a sense, all theology, philosophy, physics, and art is autobiography" and to consider where she stands in relation to Ricoeur and Lewis among others. I begin with science (in the genre of nature writing) before moving to art (in the form of "parable") and theology (in the form of "vocational autobiography"). I then reflect on her notion of "myth"" and what she might mean by the need to "remythologize" Christianity.

SECOND NAÏVETÉ AND NATURE WRITING

McFague makes a distinction between the secondary language of conceptual theology and the primary language of religion which makes use

---

6. McFague, *Models of God*, 37.
7. McFague, *Speaking in Parables*, 82.
8. McFague, *Speaking in Parables*, 147–48.

of imagery derived from basic biological realities.[9] She sums up Ricoeur's position on the role played by metaphor in this respect: "metaphor constitutes the first stage of interpretation and hence is intrinsically connected, on the one hand, to its depths in symbol and, on the other hand, to emerging conceptualization."[10] McFague states that, for Ricoeur, symbols "are rooted in reality at a cosmic, prelinguistic level, while metaphors are the linguistic innovation of symbols, interpreting and reinterpreting them," adding that symbols and metaphors "are in a symbiotic relationship, for symbols give roots in the cosmos and lived world to metaphor, while metaphors bring symbols to language, clarify symbols, and display the endless associations and connections of symbols."[11] From this we may draw the conclusion that, for Ricoeur, symbols constitute the link with the reality which metaphor brings to language.

We might assume that Ricoeur's engagement with reality at a cosmic, pre-linguistic level would form the basis for what McFague discerns as conceptual theology's need for radical correction. But McFague's summation of Ricoeur's position is couched on a different premise. She writes:

> We must first note ... that in [Ricoeur's] overall perspective the purpose of theological language is finally a religious, existential one. Theological language must gain distance and be different from religious language *because* it is only in this way that modern people, deprived of a naive harmony with the sacred cosmos via symbols, can experience that connection—as a "second naiveté" through the indirect mediation of interpretation.[12]

Here McFague seems to detach religious metaphor from its depths in symbol and here, I submit, she misrepresents Ricoeur. Her claim that "modern people" must stand back from this primary religious language would seem at odds with what Ricoeur means by "heuristic fiction."

McFague states that "modern people" are deprived of a naïve harmony with the "sacred cosmos." But, as she admits elsewhere, this is not Ricoeur's position. Chapter 4 cited her remark that "modern consciousness" is not in sympathy with the notion "that ... the universe is in some sense sacramental, that God is somehow the true and original father, that all things are connected among themselves because they are connected

---

9. See McFague, *Metaphorical Theology*, 118.
10. McFague, *Metaphorical Theology*, 120.
11. McFague, *Metaphorical Theology*, 202–3 n.12.
12. McFague, *Metaphorical Theology*, 119. McFague's italics.

"A Reality Comes to Language"   151

in God."[13] But "modern consciousness" in this respect is out of sympathy with Ricoeur's position. McFague goes on to indicate that Ricoeur aligns his position with a sacramental universe: "it is the index of the situation of man at the heart of the being in which he moves, exists and wills, that the symbol speaks to us." In McFague's depiction of "modern consciousness" we are a long way from Lewis's notion that "good" metaphors provide the material for thought and that without them all our thinking is nonsensical. We are a long way from Ricoeur's first stage of interpretation which is prior to conceptualization. For McFague it seems to be the other way round.

In the course of her remarks about him McFague admits her distance from Ricoeur. She finds him "less than satisfactory in specifying one of the crucial functions of models—their ordering, systematic potential for comprehensive interpretation."[14] She illustrates what she means with an example of her own:

> To take an example Ricoeur does not use, if we ask what it means to call God "father," we cannot answer this question by staying at the level of metaphors and models but must move to a level of broader and more comprehensive categories including not only "father" but also other metaphors as well as concepts which both limit and complement it.[15]

Here McFague demonstrates her own method. She takes a metaphor derived from the biological reality of human fatherhood, steps back from it and then explores and limits it at the level of "comprehensive interpretation."

In her claim that the "indirect mediation of interpretation" is a means to connect "modern people" with the "sacred cosmos," McFague uses the phrase "a second naïveté." She implies that this is what Ricoeur means by it. We may recognize the phrase as Ricoeur's since it occurs in his critique of Turbayne: "The problem afflicting Turbayne is that of

---

13. See McFague, *Speaking in Parables*, 106–7.

14. McFague, *Metaphorical Theology*, 119–20.

15. McFague, *Metaphorical Theology*, 121. McFague disclaims "a thorough presentation of the intricacies of Ricoeur's various arguments" about the two forms of language—conceptual and symbolic (*Metaphorical Theology*, 213 n. 25). She appears to underestimate what Ricoeur calls the "dynamism of meaning" supplied by metaphorical discourse in enabling philosophical discourse to "think more" which constitutes "the 'soul' of interpretation." See Ricoeur, *The Rule of Metaphor*, 303. Cf. also Lewis, "The Language of Religion," 164–79.

demythologized myth: does it still have its power as speech? Is there something like metaphor-faith beyond demythologization? A second *naïveté* beyond iconoclasm?"[16] Ricoeur alludes here to the ontological reference of metaphor. He goes on to say "it seems difficult to maintain the ontological abstinence of the 'as if' without believing in the descriptive and representative value of the model." It is the descriptive and representative value of the model (beyond the "as if") which I judge to be the point at which Ricoeur and McFague part company.

I used the illustration of Dorothy's journey to the farm in Kansas in Chapter 2 to indicate the reference of metaphor (her arrival at the farm) in spite of the loss of literal reference (the Silver Shoes falling off in the desert). Contrary to McFague's depiction, this second naïveté is not an attempt by modern people to return to harmony with the cosmos through conscious interpretation but the combination of poetic intuition and something beyond the control of the poet whereby "a reality comes to language." McFague seems to deny the *efficacy* of metaphorical reference for modern people. By her account, modern people do not take the road of redescription to journey's end, the sudden bump of arrival and rolling over several times. Rather, modern people remain suspended so to speak in the mid-air of their interpretive paradigm.

I turn now to the genre of nature writing. In *The Body of God* McFague writes about the kind of relationship we should have with other animals, consequent upon making ourselves aware of the implications of "the common creation story."[17] She states: "What such study often does is return us to a state of wonder, curiosity, and affection that we as children had for other animals." She adds that this childlike wonder and ability to play together "in a mixed community" is lost in adulthood. Nevertheless she urges that "we can make at least a partial return to this mixed community by way of a 'second naïvete,' a way that involves educating ourselves on our genuine, deep, and concrete forms of interrelatedness with other life-forms."[18] At this point McFague adds a footnote: "The phrase 'second naïvete' is Paul Ricoeur's and refers to the possibility of returning to the most basic roots of our being by a conscious, informed route when the intuitive acceptance found in our own youth and the youth of

---

16. Ricoeur, *The Rule of Metaphor*, 254. See chapter 2.
17. McFague, *The Body of God*, 118–21.
18. McFague, *The Body of God*, 121.

the human community is no longer possible for us."[19] While McFague attributes the phrase to Ricoeur she does not annotate this appeal to him. McFague does not repeat here that the purpose of "a second naïveté" is to regain a link with the cosmos through the agency of interpretation. Rather, she states that its purpose is a return to "the most basic roots of our being."

I submit that it is not Ricoeur whom McFague follows here, but Rimbaud. Chapter 5 drew attention to a similarity between McFague and Rimbaud in proposing a sub-rational sense of self as a means of access to the world, which also facilitates social responsibility towards the world. As noted, McFague wishes to promote an "ecological model of self and world":[20]

> Our assumption is that how we see the world, whether with an arrogant or a loving eye, depends upon our deepest, most basic sense of self in relation to the world. Our thesis is that a sense of self coming from touch rather than from sight gives us a way to think about ourselves as profoundly embodied, relational, responsive beings, as created to love others, not to control them.[21]

In this method, the conscious assumption about "how we see the world" interacts with the less than conscious "basic sense of self in relation to the world" to supply "a way to think about ourselves." This dynamic constitutes McFague's ecological model. One may compare what McFague says of "the possibility of returning to the most basic roots of our being" with what Ricoeur says of poetic experience: "it is the index of the situation of man at the heart of the being in which he moves, exists and wills, that the symbol speaks to us." While the term "being" is common to both, McFague connects it with the inner self while Ricoeur looks outwards for it.

McFague distinguishes "childhood experiences of a love for nature" (first naïveté) from "the education of that love through the mediation of nature writing" (second naïveté).[22] She states:

> Nature writers do not write about nature in general but about a particular locale, a place they care about, a place that has influenced them, that they want to know intimately and share with others. They recognize and celebrate the wildness or otherness

---

19. McFague, *The Body of God*, 247 n. 28
20. McFague, *Super, Natural Christians*, 98.
21. McFague, *Super, Natural Christians*, 92.
22. McFague, *Super, Natural Christians*, 119.

of this place in two ways: through accuracy and imagination, through a naturalist's scientific attention to detail and a poet's aesthetic attention to particulars. Finally, the experience which is both theirs and shared with the reader, the experience of the wild other(s) in this place, is a second naïveté experience. It is not the direct, innocent encounter of the child, but a mediated account, a well-informed, imaginative interpretation by an adult.[23]

The phrase "a second naïveté" is Ricoeur's but McFague uses it in a different sense. She acknowledges the intimacy of access in nature writing. The suggestion that adults are somehow less in touch with such reality is wholly her own.

In describing nature writing McFague admits her relativized ontology: "We have insisted that there is no such thing as an innocent eye, that we always see from particular contexts, that all sight is embodied (the eye of the body versus the presumably pure eye of the mind)."[24] Her focus is on experience of nature, not nature direct. It must be recalled that McFague's project is to "remythologize" the relationship between God and the world.[25] What she says about nature writing cannot be read separately from this interpretive paradigm.

In understanding McFague's project, I believe that one must always distinguish between the ontological reference of the model and the experience of living *within* the model. While attention to the natural world is a factor in McFague's project, she situates it within "a way of thinking about ourselves." This delimits the ontological reference of the model. In her attempt to live *within* the model McFague appeals to the kind of experience which is mediated through nature writing. But, as I judge, this places a frame around the genre which would not be shared by nature writers themselves. It is with this paradigm in mind that I would read what McFague has to say in response to the approach of early twentieth century American naturalist John Muir who, she claims, "neither sentimentalized nor objectified nature." McFague concludes:

> The loving eye, then, is the eye of the second naïveté, educated so as to help us embrace intimacy while recognizing difference. This is the eye trained in detachment in order that its attachment

---

23. McFague, *Super, Natural Christians*, 131.
24. McFague, *Super, Natural Christians*, 114–15.
25. See McFague, *Models of God*, chapter 2.

will be objective, based on the reality of the other and not on its own wishes or fantasies.²⁶

The model itself could embrace this way of thinking. But this is distinct from engaging with the other, including God as other, *outside* the model.

I have queried whether McFague's frame of reference is compatible with the scientific method. I go further and ask what effect such thinking has on the imagination. McFague acknowledges that imagination is a product of the "right" brain.²⁷ But the kind of imagination that comes from delving into "the most basic sense of self," said to be in touch with the natural world, is perhaps more akin to subconscious wishes and fantasies than the disciplined kind needed for detailed nature writing or poetry. One might ask about the possible effect on a literary approach to theology. I turn now to her engagement with parable and religious autobiography.

PARABLE

Chapter 7 drew attention to McFague's hope to "make sense" in terms of "an incarnational understanding of Christianity and an organic interpretation of postmodern science."²⁸ In this context she describes her notion of a panentheist God. She goes so far as to say, "the panentheistic tradition is found in all those passages in the Hebrew Scriptures that mediate the divine presence through human words and acts as well as natural phenomena and in the New Testament in its central declaration the 'the Word was made flesh' in Jesus of Nazareth."²⁹ Elsewhere she writes: "Many theologians today feel that an incarnational theology, a theology from above such as the Johannine 'Word became flesh' perspective, is not possible in a time when the credibility of God of is undermined."³⁰ As a response to modern skepticism, she proposes that Jesus can be interpreted as "a parable of God."

---

26. McFague, *Super, Natural Christians*, 116. McFague cites Richard Austin, *Baptized into Wilderness*.

27. McFague, *Metaphorical Theology*, 195 n. 3. McFague cites Lucy Bregman, "Religious Imagination: Polytheistic Psychology Confronts Calvin" for "an intriguing list that includes the 'left' and 'right' brains, equating literalism with the left and symbolism with the right."

28. McFague, *The Body of God*, 150.

29. See McFague, *The Body of God*, 150.

30. McFague, *Metaphorical Theology*, 49.

What then does McFague mean by "parable"? She describes Ricoeur's approach:

> Ricoeur [suggests] that parables work on a pattern or orientation, disorientation and reorientation: a parable begins in the ordinary world with its conventional standards and expectations, but in the course of the story a radically different perspective is introduced that disorients the listener, and finally, through the interaction of two competing viewpoints, tension is created that results in a redescription of life in the world.[31]

McFague cites Ricoeur directly in connection with the notion of Jesus as "a parable of God":

> As soon as the preaching of Jesus as the "Crucified" is interwoven with the narratives of his "deeds" and his "sayings," a *specific possibility* of interpretation is opened up, by what I call here the establishment of a "space" of intersignification: by a *specific possibility*, I mean the suggestion to read the proclamation of Jesus as "the parable of God" *into* the proclamation by Jesus of God "in parables." To entirely disregard this possibility would require that we disconnect the parables from the Gospel.[32]

One may note that Ricoeur calls Jesus *the* parable of God, not *a* parable of God.

I maintain that presenting Jesus as *a* parable of God moves him into the interpretive paradigm. McFague states: "A metaphorical statement is, as we recall, always a judgment of similarity (and difference) between two thoughts: Jesus 'is and is not' God . . . we cannot make the illegitimate move of identifying Jesus with God."[33] She is at pains to emphasize the possibility that "other religions can make the claim that they also contain metaphorical expressions of divine reality."[34] She goes so far as to distance us from Jesus: "we 'are and are not' his followers." At this point the interpretive frame comes to the fore: "Just as a parable puts distance between Jesus and God, so it puts distance between Jesus and his

---

31. McFague, *Metaphorical Theology*, 46–47. McFague refers to Ricoeur, "Biblical Hermeneutics," 122–28.

32. See McFague, *Metaphorical Theology*, 205 n. 46. McFague cites Ricoeur, "Biblical Hermeneutics," 105. (Italics in the text as cited).

33. See McFague, *Metaphorical Theology*, 51.

34. See McFague, *Metaphorical Theology*, 51–52. Here McFague admits: "A parabolic christology relativizes Jesus' particularity while universalizing the God of whom Jesus is a metaphor."

"A Reality Comes to Language" 157

followers: we reflect his ways but in our own ways, and there are other ways besides his. Christians judge his way to be a good, perhaps the best, way but it is not exclusive."[35]

In terms of an understanding of "parable," I detect a difference between Ricoeur's procedure and McFague's, which I categorize as literary engagement and disengagement respectively. In considering McFague's procedure, let us recall Barth's distinction between "thing" and "sign" in relation to the story of the Virgin Birth. For Barth, the concept of the Incarnation (thing) precedes the narrative (sign).[36] Similarly, McFague's judgment of similarity and difference (Jesus "is and is not" to be identified with God) takes precedence over the biblical narrative. The term "parable" is then equivalent to Barth's usage of "sign" in relation to "thing." In McFague's case, the "thing" is unequivocally the prior "religious idea." To my mind, Ricoeur's procedure has a different flavor. The crucified Jesus as "the parable of God" is the radically different perspective which further disorients those who listen to his proclamation of God "in parables." In this latter procedure, there is no protection for the listener or reader. It is this engagement or vulnerability which supplies the space for a redescription of life in the world.

We reflect Jesus's ways, says McFague, but in our own ways. At one point she writes: "we do not interpret the parable, but the parable interprets us."[37] She also says, "As a true and novel metaphor, Jesus as parable reorders and upsets our familiar, conventional understandings of God by means of the unfamiliar, unconventional pattern he introduces."[38] But she places this reordering in a context:

> What the parables stand for is opposition to *all* forms of idolatry and absolutism, *even* the new orientation to reality brought about through the parables' redescription of reality. The permanent function of parables is to enhance consciousness of the radical relativity of human models of reality, even when these models are "divinely inspired," that is, based on the new way of the kingdom.[39]

---

35. McFague, *Metaphorical Theology*, 54.
36. Barth, *Dogmatics in Outline*, 96.
37. McFague, *Speaking in Parables*, 71.
38. McFague, *Metaphorical Theology*, 50.
39. McFague, *Metaphorical Theology*, 47. McFague's italics.

McFague goes so far as to cite Ricoeur in this regard. She claims that Ricoeur "says that the reorientation in a parable is of an open-ended and relative sort, which does not allow us to remake our world according to a new set of rules and standards."[40] But does Ricoeur say this?

Admittedly, Ricoeur draws attention to the ability of religious language to relativize human models of reality. But it does so by placing them in a new light which *is* the new way of the kingdom. He calls "the symbol 'Kingdom of God' the 'limit referent' which presides over ... the limit-experiences which religious language claims to redescribe."[41] At the same time he distinguishes his position from that of Barth's supernaturalism of the Wholly Other:

> *[T]he eruption of the unheard in* our discourse and *in* our experience constitutes precisely one dimension *of* our discourse and *of* our experience.... If this were not so, the claim of the Scriptures that Christian self-understanding in fact is the understanding of authentic human existence would fail entirely. It is precisely as extreme that religious language is appropriated. And it is this appropriateness of limit-expressions to limit-experiences which is signified by our affirmation that religious language, like all poetic language, in the strongest sense of the word, redescribes human experience.[42]

Ricoeur emphasizes the *interaction* of two competing viewpoints. The kind of conceptual distance espoused by McFague would preclude the eruption of the unheard in the limit-expressions of limit-experiences, to use Ricoeur's terminology.

McFague states: "No *one* parable tells us of 'the kingdom of God,' and even all together they do not add up to a definition of the kingdom, to a doctrine or concept of the kingdom."[43] In the footnote she amplifies her remark in terms of an observation by Ricoeur:

> Ricoeur makes this point in a very telling fashion in the following statement: "It is not enough to say that the Parables say nothing directly concerning the Kingdom of God. We must say in more positive terms, that taken *altogether, they say more than any rational theology*. At the very moment that they call

---

40. See McFague, *Metaphorical Theology*, 47. She cites Ricoeur, "Biblical Hermeneutics," 126 (*Metaphorical Theology* 205 n. 44).

41. Ricoeur, "Biblical Hermeneutics," 122.

42. Ricoeur, "Biblical Hermeneutics," 127. Ricoeur's italics.

43. McFague, *Metaphorical Theology*, 43. McFague's italics.

"A Reality Comes to Language"

for theological clarification, they start shattering the theological simplifications which we attempt to put in their place."[44]

One might ask how the parables can shatter theological simplifications if, on McFague's terms, it is only through the distancing of conceptual language that modern people can experience connection with the cosmos. If one must always begin with the theological concept, can one gain access to the means that would critique and shatter it?

In *Speaking in Parables*, McFague offers the example of the parable of the Wedding Feast for which she uses the version in Matthew 22.[45] She states: "The first thing to do with a parable is to read it, several times, work out the relations of those involved, highlight the subtleties of the story—in other words, let the story penetrate *us*, rather than look for possible interpretations of it."[46] But despite this advice, McFague does not quote the parable in full but only quotes Matthew 22:1-10, leaving out the next four verses. She goes on to say that the parable is not "a story with a 'moral' or with 'one point.'"[47] Yet she discerns the point of the story in a distinction between the "logics of merit and grace": the "first invitations are offered to the worthy: the second invitations are proffered with no regard to worth." She concludes: "What we see, then, in the parable of the Wedding Feast is not a new reality but the same reality in a new perspective."[48] A key problem with this interpretation is the omission of verses 11-14. The guest who has no wedding garment belongs to the second group who are invited "with no regard to worth." Yet this guest is ejected from the feast. "Bind him hand and foot," says the king, "and cast him into the outer darkness; there men will weep and gnash their teeth." The parable ends with its own interpretation: "For many are called, but few are chosen."[49] Where, as a new perspective toward the same reality, is the logic of grace as opposed to the logic of merit here? Does not the parable shatter McFague's theological clarification?

---

44. McFague cites Ricoeur, "Listening to the Parables of Jesus" (*Metaphorical Theology*, 204 n. 33). The italics are in the quotation.
45. See McFague, *Speaking in Parables*, 68-72.
46. McFague, *Speaking in Parables*, 68-69. McFague's italics.
47. See McFague, *Speaking in Parables*, 69-70.
48. See McFague, *Speaking in Parables*, 70.
49. See Matt 22:13-14 (*RSV*).

VOCATIONAL AUTOBIOGRAPHY

"Metaphorical thinking," says McFague, "is the way human beings, selves (not mere minds) *move* in all areas of discovery, whether these be scientific, religious, poetic, social, political, or personal."[50] She emphasizes the existential nature of human thought, including "the highly 'existential' genres in which the Scriptures are written—the passion story, hymns, letters, sermons, poetry and so on."[51] But I find that she leaves out what Ricoeur calls "the eruption of the unheard in our discourse and in our experience."[52] In *Speaking in Parables*, she devotes a chapter to confession in the form of autobiography.[53] The chapter is entitled "Autobiography: The Unity of Life and Thought" and includes among others the lives and writings of the Apostle Paul, Augustine of Hippo and Pierre Theilhard de Chardin. In this context she asserts that "we are all, in one way or another, Kantians" and that "a moderate Kantianism . . . insists that in a sense, all theology, philosophy, physics, and art is autobiography."[54]

McFague distinguishes a moderate Kantianism from "an idealistic perspective (the world out there is only what subjects say it is)," but also adds: "In a real sense, what the world *is* is what we say it is and we say it is what *we* are." She continues:

> It is hard to deny where modernity has landed us—after Galileo toppled us from the centre of the universe, human beings are, curiously, back there again, albeit in a somewhat different guise. In a sense we are "stuck" with our centrality: we cannot, finally, get outside of ourselves, we cannot jump out of our skins.[55]

From the inescapability of the self, McFague moves to the desirability of focus on it: "what many voices increasingly are saying—from the

---

50. McFague, *Speaking in Parables*, 58. McFague's italics.

51. See McFague, *Speaking in Parables*, 61–62.

52. In writing about Scripture as a "poetic text," McFague cites Ricoeur on poetic language ("Biblical Hermeutics," 89): "in the very measure that the first-order reference is abolished, another power of speaking the world is liberated, although at another level of reality. This level . . . is an eclipsing of the objective, manipulable world, an illumining of the life-world, which seems to me the fundamental ontological import of poetic language." But even at this poetic level I think McFague misses "the ontological import." She goes on to class Scripture as an ontological *stance*. (See *Metaphorical Theology*, 59 and 206 n. 62.)

53. See McFague, *Speaking in Parables*, chapter 7.

54. McFague, *Speaking in Parables*, 147–48.

55. See McFague, *Speaking in Parables*, 147–48. McFague's italics.

existentialist tradition to the women's movement—is, "Why should we want to [escape]?" She adds that "what we all seek is not happiness or achievement but to be ourselves—to realize the destiny that is me: to create, to recognize, to realize one's own daimon."[56]

McFague finds the "truth" of an autobiography in a harmony between outward events and inward growth which can be recognized by the reader:

> In order for the reader to be able to say, "Yes, here's the person," the accomplishment must have integrity both as an art object (it must be unified and patterned in an aesthetically satisfying way) and as a moral reality (the imagery must be evocative in such a way that the reader is brought to "feel" that the autobiographer's interpretation is true; it is, in other words, his or her master form).[57]

By "master form," McFague means "a dominant vision of that self." She states: "Each incident in a good autobiography should be seen as part of a process, an unfolding; disparate incidents should be bound together from a particular point of view and given thereby 'sense,' 'meaning.'"[58] This meaning can be a theological meaning. "As in Paul's or Augustine's case," says McFague, "one *does theology* and one *theologizes life*."[59]

McFague states that "autobiography is intended to be a metaphor of the self... realized only in and through the details of an actual, historical life."[60] The story invites self-discovery both by the author and the reader:

> This is, I believe, at the heart of the perennial fascination with the story of Jesus (not the theology of his person and work but the story in the synoptic gospels): there is, often even among agnostics, the suspicion that if I knew this story better, I would somehow come to know myself better.[61]

But if the story is intended to provide a "dominant vision of the self," one might ask why McFague omits the theology of Jesus's person and work.

McFague states that Paul's letters are an intermediary form between parable and confession, wrought out if Paul's own experience and

---

56. McFague, *Speaking in Parables*, 148.
57. McFague, *Speaking in Parables*, 156.
58. See McFague, *Speaking in Parables*, 152–53.
59. McFague, *Speaking in Parables*, 157. McFague's italics.
60. McFague, *Speaking in Parables*, 151.
61. McFague, *Speaking in Parables*, 150.

utilizing the experience theologically.⁶² She casts the apostle Paul as a kind of existentialist biographer. "Metaphors spill from him," she says, ". . . hammered out through the agony and passion of his own life and through his commitment to the lives of his charges. Many of them come out of a world-view already at hand . . . but Paul renews them by setting them in the context of God's radical love, the unfamiliar that provides a new context for the familiar so that it is seen anew."⁶³ Although centered on his own life, it is his vocational understanding of the self, according to McFague, which enables the apostle to avoid self-absorption:

> It seems as if Paul's theological concern derives principally from his vocational drive: that is, he attempts to think as precisely as possible about relations between God and human beings in order to bring his brothers and sisters to a genuine and permanent commitment. The method and the concern parallel the parables very closely because what Paul's theologizing consists of is metaphor after metaphor attempting to evoke indirectly the graciousness of God for the purpose of winning commitment to him.⁶⁴

From this description, Paul begins with theology (the graciousness of God) which then becomes an existential challenge to others. The challenge is expressed through "metaphor after metaphor." The aim is to "win commitment."

I noted above that McFague draws attention to "the perennial fascination with the story of Jesus," even among agnostics. McFague attributes the fascination to the moral effect of the story, "the suspicion that if I knew this story better, I would somehow come to know myself better." But is it the story one would need to know better or God in Christ through the story? I recall at this point Barth's remark about the theological existentialism of Bultmann and his followers: "Certainly existentialism may have reminded us once again . . . that one cannot speak of God without speaking of man. It is to be hoped that it will not lead us back into the old error that one can speak of man without first, and very concretely, having spoken of the living God."⁶⁵ I do not find that McFague first, and very concretely, speaks of the living God. In her understanding, the metaphors

---

62. See McFague, *Speaking in Parables*, 158–59.
63. See McFague, *Speaking in Parables*, 161–62.
64. McFague, *Speaking in Parables*, 160–61.
65. Barth, "The Humanity of God," 54.

of the apostle's life seem to be an expression of his existential vocation rather than spilling forth from encounter with Christ.

As already seen, McFague casts doubt on the divinity of Christ. That point aside, what is the relationship between "religious autobiography" and the personal encounter which they write *about*? Lewis raises a similar question with regard to Bultmann: "What is gained by trying to evade or dissipate this shattering immediacy of personal contact by talk about 'that significance which the early church found that it was impelled to attribute to the Master?' This hits us in the face. Not what they were impelled to do but what impelled them."[66] In describing Paul's letters as religious autobiography, McFague wishes the reader to be able to say, "Yes, here's the person." But which person? Jesus or Paul?

MYTH

I have taken the liberty in this book of using incidents from *The Wizard of Oz* to contrast what Ricoeur calls "metaphorical truth" with a way of thinking about metaphor which tends towards illusion. This is not to be confused with the story itself. Lewis goes so far as to say that authors of children's books are less likely than other writers to use language in a meaningless way.[67] *The Wizard of Oz* assumes that the Witch of the West is really evil in terms of an external standard. Would "evil" have any meaning on any other terms? At one point McFague seems to admit this kind of thinking:

> It is one of the unfortunate assumptions that metaphor and myth belong to the childhood of the human race, or at best are mere embellishments of truth we can have, now that we are logically and technically advanced, in some more direct way, whether philosophically, scientifically, or existentially. But if new meaning is always metaphorical, then *there is no way now or ever to have strange truth directly*. We are always children, primitives, when it comes to new insight into such matters as love, life, death, God, hope and faith. The point is, of course, that apart from metaphor, that is, apart from primal language, we would not "see" such matters at all . . .[68]

66. Lewis, "Fern-seed and Elephants," 197.
67. Lewis, "Bluspels and Flalansferes," 49.
68. McFague, *Speaking in Parables*, 40–41.

But if we would not see such matters at all apart from primal language, what does this say about modern people, deprived of a naïve harmony with the cosmos via symbols?

McFague states that "modern people" can only experience connection with the cosmos "through the indirect mediation of interpretation."[69] She claims to speak for Ricoeur at this point. But does she? McFague wishes to regain access to metaphor and myth but on what terms? She writes: "We must not forget the crack in the foundation beneath all our imaginings and the conceptual schemes we build upon them. That crack is exemplified by the 'is not' of metaphor which denies any identity in its assertions."[70] The alleged crack in the foundation beneath all our imaginings and the conceptual schemes we build on them would seem the point of McFague's departure from Lewis and Ricoeur.

What exactly does McFague mean by "myth"? It must be recalled that her project of "remythologizing" is a response to a tradition of "demythologizing."[71] In *Speaking in Parables*, McFague offers a three-way contrast between the theological methods of Barth and Bultmann and the linguistic method of biblical metaphor.[72] She describes Barth and Bultmann as "the giants of contemporary theology" and says they pose the question: "How can our words be appropriate to today's people so that God's action can take place through them?"[73] She goes on to say that this is a task always undertaken by theology. One must query, however, whether theology has always focused so radically on "today's people"? McFague's remark is, however, relevant to her own method. It is the radical focus on "modern people" which would seem to color her notion of metaphor and myth.

In comparing Bultmann with Barth, McFague states that Bultmann critiques "the mythological categories of the New Testament in contrast to perennial 'existential' categories of human self-understanding":

> Bultmann translates the myths not into metaphysics (which is still quasi-objective) but into existentialist categories. Thus we find his solution to the Kantian limit—there is no way to talk about things "out there"—in terms of limiting the good news

---

69. McFague, *Metaphorical Theology*, 119.
70. McFague, *Models of God*, xii.
71. See McFague, *Models of God*, 32.
72. See McFague, *Speaking in Parables*, 30–35.
73. McFague, *Speaking in Parables*, 30.

to the *pro nobis*; one does not talk about the New Testament as *Historie* (objective, factual history) but as *Geschichte* (the meaning of the events for the persons who encounter them).[74]

Contrary to Bultmann, McFague demonstrates an interest in "myth." But I cannot help suspecting that existentialist categories have a predominating function in her approach to the mythological.

McFague's remarks about J. R. R. Tolkien's *The Lord of the Rings* are revealing in this respect. I compare what she says with Lewis's observations in his review of *The Lord of the Rings*. Lewis writes:

> Probably no book yet written in the world is quite such a radical instance of what its author has elsewhere called 'sub-creation'. The direct debt (there are of course subtler kinds of debt) which every author must owe to the actual universe is here deliberately reduced to the minimum. Not content to create his own story, he creates, with an almost insolent prodigality, the whole field in which it is to move, with its own theology, myths, geography, history, palaeography, languages and orders of beings—a world 'full of strange creatures beyond count'.[75]

A story in which the direct debt to the actual universe is reduced to the minimum does not at first sight appear to accord with Ricoeur's notion of a reality coming to language. Lewis anticipates this kind of objection: "The value of myth," he says, "is that it takes all the things we know and restores to them the rich significance which has been hidden by the 'veil of familiarity.'"[76]

McFague grants all this. She states that the world of *The Lord of the Rings* is a "Secondary World" complete in itself, that its "focus is not on human transformation but on the struggle of good and evil forces in the world, a struggle of mythic proportions [which] can be resolved mythically."[77] She says that "what the mythic pattern, the heightened renditions of good and evil . . . allow for is what Tolkien elsewhere has called 'recovery,' seeing things as we were meant to see them."[78]

So far Lewis and McFague are in agreement. But they differ about the effectiveness of the myth in its engagement with life. Lewis poses the

---

74. McFague, *Speaking in Parables*, 31.
75. Lewis, "Tolkien's *The Lord of the Rings*," 112–13.
76. Lewis, "Tolkien's *The Lord of the Rings*," 120.
77. McFague, *Speaking in Parables*, 133.
78. McFague, *Speaking in Parables*, 134.

question: "why, if you have a serious comment to make on the real life of men, must you do it by talking about a phantasmagoric never-never land of your own?"[79] Lewis supplies his answer to this: "Because, I take it, one of the main things the author wants to say is that the real life of men is of that mythic and heroic quality." As he explains earlier, "the most obvious appeal of the book is perhaps also its deepest."[80] He cites an episode in the history of Middle Earth: "there was sorrow then too, and gathering dark, but great valour, and great deeds that were not wholly vain. *Not wholly vain*," repeats Lewis and adds, "it is the cool middle point between illusion and disillusion."

But McFague does not find this quality appealing. She pays tribute to the "mythic" or "parabolic" aspect of the novel: "The unfamiliar, the sight of things in their singularity, is accomplished by the deformation of the familiar in the direction of the larger than life: this is the mythic way to stretch reality, to open the cracks into it."[81] But having so to speak opened the cracks to the unfamiliar, McFague seems to wish to close them again. She continues: "But it is not an entirely satisfactory way for human beings, for . . . the action . . . is largely external, and little reformation through moral choice and persuasive grace takes place."

McFague's observation about "cracks" may take us back to her remark cited above: "We must not forget the crack in the foundation beneath all our imaginings and the conceptual schemes we build upon them. That crack is exemplified by the 'is not' of metaphor which denies any identity in its assertions."[82] This is to endorse what McFague calls the Kantian limits with no way (and perhaps no wish) to talk about things "out there." In her remarks about *The Lord of the Rings* McFague draws back from opening "the cracks to the unfamiliar," beyond subjective limits. As narrative, she finds the myth unsatisfactory. She would prefer the action to be redirected towards reformation through moral choice and persuasive grace. One may see a similar response on her part to the parable of the Wedding Feast in terms of moral choice and persuasive grace above. The focus of *The Lord of the Rings* "is not on human transformation," says McFague,

---

79. Lewis, "Tolkien's *The Lord of the Rings*," 120.

80. Lewis refers to *The Lord of the Rings*, vol 1, chapter 2 ("Tolkien's *The Lord of the Rings*," 116).

81. See McFague, *Speaking in Parables*, 134–35.

82. McFague, *Models of God*, xi–xii.

"but on the struggle of good and evil forces in the world."[83] But without that focus how do we know what is meant by good and evil?

By contrast, Lewis expresses the appeal of the unfamiliar in his observations on characters in *The Lord of the Rings* which are "almost alien (one would think) to the author's habitual imagination, figures . . . so brimming with life (not human life) that they make our sort of anguish and our sort of exaltation seem unimportant."[84] Lewis continues: "Such is Tom Bombadil, such the unforgettable Ents. This is surely the utmost reach of invention when an author produces what seems to be not even his own, much less anyone else's. Is mythopoeia, after all, not the most, but the least, subjective of activities?"

If mythopoeia is the least subjective of activities, what becomes of McFague's statement that "a moderate Kantianism . . . insists that in a sense, all theology, philosophy, physics, and art is autobiography"? Here perhaps the divergence between McFague and Lewis (along with Tolkien and Ricoeur) is most evident. For an author who produces what seems not even his own, much less anyone else's, must demonstrate the "reality [which] comes to language" *par excellence*.

I will conclude with a comparison between McFague's usage of the "common creation story" and what Lewis says about writing science fiction. This is as close as I will come to discussing what it might mean to say that all physics is autobiography. In defending his science fiction against a scientific critic, Lewis states that he included "just enough astronomy to create in 'the common reader' a 'willing suspension of disbelief.'"[85] In *Out of a Silent Planet*, Lewis had made use of the popular tradition that Mars has canals. Later he disclaims the expectation that this fictional device needed to be scientifically accurate. His critic, he says, "has caught me carving a toy elephant and criticises it as if my aim had been to teach zoology. But what I was after was not the elephant as known to science but our old friend Jumbo." For Lewis, however, Jumbo has his own ontological reference. McFague, on the other hand, makes use of a popular picture of evolutionary history which she calls "the common creation story." The value of the story for McFague is that it is "the view of reality current in our time."[86] Like Lewis, McFague offers at best a loose association with

---

83. McFague, *Speaking in Parables*, 133.
84. Lewis, "Tolkien's *The Lord of the Rings*," 116.
85. Lewis, "A Reply to Haldane," 99.
86. McFague, *The Body of God*, 28.

scientific accuracy. But, in disclaiming Lewis's poetic kind of ontological reference, does McFague not present a version of evolutionary history very much *pro nobis*?

9

Three Kinds of Sacramentalism

WHEN DOROTHY AND HER friends travel southwards from the Emerald City, they come across a land like a large china plate in which everything is made of china including the people. The people are much smaller than Dorothy. The travelers have to be very careful as they walk through this strange land because everything is very easily broken. If the china figures are broken they must go to the mender's shop.[1]

The picture of a land composed of china may serve to illustrate a traditional kind of sacramentalism. In the story the people look and behave like real people although they are more fragile. The reader is not told who the mender is but in real life a real person would have made the figures and would mend them if they broke. The relation between the land of china figures and our world could be designated as both analogous to our world and dependent on it. McFague describes this kind of sacramentalism:

> For a traditional sacramental sensibility, the bread and wine of the Eucharist are symbols of divine nurture; they do not merely "point to" spiritual food, but really and truly *are* spiritual food. The things of this world participate in and signify what transcends our world. The sacramental sensibility depends upon a belief that everything is connected, that the beings of this world are analogously related to God (Being-Itself), and hence can be sacramentally related to God. The analogy of being by

1. See Baum, *The Wizard's Illusion*, chapter 20.

> which all that *is* is because of its radical dependence on God ties everything together in a silent ontological web which reverberates with similarity within dissimilarity out to its farthest reaches. Even a corpse, says Augustine, is like God to the extent that it still has some degree of order left in its decaying flesh and emerging skeleton. In such a universe, everything holds together, everything fits, everything is related.[2]

As already seen, McFague does not subscribe to this kind of sacramentalism. She writes: "The medieval sacramental sensibility is not ours, either in theory or practice. Our time is characterized by disunity, by skepticism that anything is related to anything else, and by secularity."[3]

But McFague is not satisfied with merely discarding traditional sacramentalism. On the one hand she wishes to take seriously "the characteristics of the contemporary sensibility." On the other hand she also wishes to broaden the understanding of "what counts as 'true'" which, "in our positivistic, scientifically oriented society is what corresponds with 'reality,' with the 'facts.'"[4] Literalism, says McFague, is more absolute now than in earlier times:

> It is not only that many people have lost the practice of religious contemplation and prayer, which alone is sufficient to keep literalism at bay, or that positivistic scientism has injected a narrow view of truth into our culture. While both are true, it is also the case that we do not think in symbols the way our forbears did. That is to say, we do not see the things of this world as standing for something else; they are simply what they are. A symbolic sensibility, on the contrary, sees multilayered realities, with the literal level suggestive of meaning beyond itself. While it may have been more justified for people in earlier times to be biblical literalists since they were less conscious of relativity, as symbolic thinkers, they were *not* literalists.[5]

In this regard, I detect three meanings in McFague's usage of the word "literal." Firstly, she makes reference to a positivist demarcation between literal facts and matters sensed within the subject. McFague calls this a "narrow view of truth." The second meaning of "literal" applies to epistemology in general. In this sense "literal" refers to a broad belief

---

2. McFague, *Metaphorical Theology*, 5–6. McFague's italics.
3. McFague, *Metaphorical Theology*, 6.
4. McFague, *Metaphorical Theology*, 4.
5. See McFague, *Metaphorical Theology*, 5. McFague's italics.

Three Kinds of Sacramentalism

in external reference, held by "people of earlier times" in contrast with relativism. The third distinction is an older one, that between "literal" and "symbolic." "A symbolic sensibility," says McFague, "sees multilayered realities, with the literal level suggestive of meaning beyond itself."

McFague uses the word "literal" in the first sense in likening contemporary literalism to realistic art which offers a copy of what it represents. She states that, in a literalistic understanding, "'true' religious language is also a copy of what it represents; in other words, a literal or realistic representation of God's nature." To illustrate the point she adds, "If the Bible says that God is 'father' then God is literally, really, 'father'; the word 'father' and the associations of that word truly refer to God's nature."[6] McFague critiques this kind of literalistic approach to religious language. She expresses a wish to reinstate some kind of sacramental flavor, along the lines suggested by Old Testament scholar, Phyllis Trible, that poetry is "like a finger pointing to the moon."[7] "Either to equate human words with divine reality or to see no relationship between them is inappropriate," concludes McFague. But what kind of relationship between human words and divine reality does she have in mind?

There is much to be said, I believe, for an alternative to contemporary literalism (in the first sense of the word). In recognizing the symbolic sensibility of pre-Enlightenment ages, McFague rightly detects the possibility of poetic truth in religious language. But she does not endorse this kind of truth. As already seen in this book, McFague detaches modern sensibility from the classical type of metaphor in which a word is transferred "from what it usually means to some other object."[8] She offers "God the Father" as an example of this type of metaphor. She writes: "the Christian symbolic universe does *not* hold together for most of us.... We do not, like Bunyan's Pilgrim, see ourselves as ... taking upon ourselves the biblical or other traditional symbols or stories and making them our own through transference."[9] In other words, McFague would distance contemporary Christian sensibility not only from equating human words with divine reality in a literal way but also with finding a relationship between them.

---

6. McFague, *Metaphorical Theology*, 5.

7. McFague, *Metaphorical Theology*, 7. McFague cites Phyllis Trible, *God and the Rhetoric of Sexuality*, 16.

8. See McFague, *Speaking in Parables*, 106–7.

9. McFague, *Speaking in Parables*, 107.

McFague seems to confuse the poetic reference of classical metaphor with the allegorical reference of the figures in *Pilgrim's Progress*. I will look at allegory in some depth in the next chapter. I believe that McFague's existentialist leaning has the tendency to take any attempt at "remythologizing" in an allegorical direction. By this I mean that her existentialist impetus finds expression in pictures or models which refer back to the conceptual categories which project them. If she retains the flavor of classical metaphor it takes shape *within* the model. In the last chapter I discerned this tendency in McFague's stated wish to return to the primary language of the Christian tradition and also in the way that she enlists nature writing for her project.[10] I find a similar tendency in her stated wish to reinstate a "new sacramentalism" within her subject-subjects model. All told, I would question whether a symbolic sensibility is possible in a relativist epistemology.

This chapter takes something of a grand tour through the vagaries of Western thinking. In this I follow McFague. From the parameters of medieval cosmology I move to a search for a similar sense of integration in contemporary sensibility. I then go on to consider the consequences of McFague's mooted "horizontal sacramentalism." While I critique the direction of McFague's kind of sacramentalism I agree that a simple return to medieval cosmology is not an appropriate way forward. The chapter concludes with an alternative to the one suggested by McFague.

DRESDEN CHINA COUNTRY

Chapter 4 noted the kind of linguistic sacramentalism which was associated with a popularized medieval cosmology. The cosmology, says Lewis, had begun to develop in late antiquity:

> In the last age of antiquity many writers . . . were, perhaps half-consciously, gathering together and harmonising views of very different origin: building a syncretistic model, not only out of Platonic, Aristotelian and Stoical, but out of Pagan and Christian elements. This Model the Middle Ages adopted and perfected.[11]

Denys Hay describes this hierarchical system:

---

10. See McFague, *Metaphorical Theology*, 118–20 and McFague, *Super, Natural Christians*, chapter 6.

11. Lewis, *The Discarded Image*, 12.

> The whole created universe was regarded as a vast ladder of ascending entities running unbroken from the edge of Hell to the infinite and ultimate unity of God. In this divinely appointed order each individual object or concept was both part of some greater whole and itself a microcosm of inferior creation. In either aspect it was integrally involved in the 'Great Chain of Being'.[12]

The model entailed elaborate correspondences. Hay continues:

> It was possible to argue from one part of the cosmic hierarchy to another; to define the relations of father to family or of pope to emperor, from the superiority of the heart to the limbs or the sun to the moon. And once such a correspondence had been established it had all the compulsion of eternal and inescapable truth.

Eternal truth was, in this sense, a matter of speculation. But there is more at stake here.

As noted in chapter 4, E. L. Mascall states that, according to the medieval view, the external world is to be perceived in a trans-sensory sense, offering access to a transcendent "intelligible object of which it is the manifestation."[13] McFague also draws attention to this way of thinking:

> The culture of the Middle Ages was extroverted, not introverted; people looked outward to find signs of God in nature, rather than inward to find the divine within themselves. . . . In this subject-subjects model, nature as a whole as well as particular, individual creatures certainly do not have intrinsic value: they are not subjects in their own right. Medieval people did not pay attention to nature in order to care for it better, nor did they have a romantic desire to bond with it. On the contrary, nature for them had a higher calling—in fact, the highest calling. Like the Bible, it was a book, the book of nature, which humans were to learn to read rightly in order to find their way to God. But the natural world was certainly not an object either; it was not a commodity that people could use and destroy at will. Rather, it was a way God had chosen to lead humans into the divine presence. Thus, its subjectivity, its *persona*, its particular individuality in whole and in its parts, was symbolic: *it signified God for humans.*[14]

12. Denys Hay, *The Medieval Centuries*, 56.

13. Mascall, *Words and Images*, 36–38. Mascall quotes from Kant, *Critique of Pure Reason*.

14. McFague, *Super, Natural Christians*, 53–54. McFague's italics.

Despite its hierarchical nature, McFague offers the medieval picture of the universe as a case-study for her subject-subjects model.

I have given this section the heading "Dresden china country" in order to bring some pictorial sense to the symbolic character of the medieval cosmos. But the picture does not do justice to its complexity. McFague offers a useful outline of its vertical and horizontal development:

> Medieval sacramentalism owes its roots to the dual Greek heritage, the two traditions of Plato and Aristotle, the one focused on the otherworld and the other on this world. While Plato saw nature as patterned on what lay beyond it, the eternal forms, Aristotle began the process of horizontal connections among earth's lifeforms: we were related to the plants through the nutritive soul, to the animals through the sensitive soul, and to other humans through the rational soul. . . . Although Augustine's Neoplatonism certainly stressed the vertical, introverted direction, Thomas Aquinas's allegiance to Aristotle qualified it with horizontal, extroverted motifs: natural law, secondary causation, grace as perfecting rather than replacing nature.[15]

"The Thomistic universe," continues McFague, "is a panorama filled to the brim with different reflections of divine being, each imaging that glory *in its own way* . . . each creature has its being, its existence, in a manner appropriate *to it alone*." But despite the medieval focus on the natural world, she goes on to say that "the emphasis from the beginning appears to be on the vertical, not the horizontal, on nature as a way to God and not on the value of individual, different things and creatures."[16]

In search of a horizontal emphasis, McFague finds an alternative case study in Martin Buber's model of I-Thou relationship which "includes developing a relationship not only with God and other human beings but also with nature." She cites Buber's insistence that "we can and should have an I-Thou relationship with a tree." Here she quotes Buber direct:

> The tree is no impression, no play of my imagination, no value depending on my mood; but it is bodied over against me and has to do with me, as I with it—only in a different way. . . . The tree will have a consciousness, then, similar to my own? Of that I have no experience. . . . I encounter no soul or dryad of the tree, but the tree itself.[17]

---

15. McFague, *Super, Natural Christians*, 57.
16. See McFague, *Super, Natural Christians*, 57–58. McFague's italics.
17. McFague, *Super, Natural Christians*, 100. McFague cites Buber, *I and Thou*, 8.

Three Kinds of Sacramentalism

McFague adds that, in her impression of Buber, "the intense moments of connection, of real relationship, between Thous are fleeting and rare; most of the time we live in the I-It world . . . of individuality, difference, and use."[18] She distinguishes between the I-It relationship which Buber sees as necessary for everyday experience and the I-Thou relationship which "is quite separate from knowing the other in its embodied, concrete, particular otherness." The real relationship, says McFague, is based on a mystical connection, "the relationship that through each thing unites us to God."[19]

The mystical connection is the point at which McFague parts company with Buber. She states: "For all his helpfulness in extending spirituality to the natural world as well as his insistence that our relation with nature be one of subject to subject, Buber comes very close to a nature-supernature dualism. What we know about others—their individuality, their embodied differences, their concrete reality—does not contribute to their real being as intimations of the Divine."[20] She admits that Buber "does not intend this dualism" and goes on to quote him: "The aim of relation is relation's own being . . . through contact with every *Thou*, we are stirred with a breath of the *Thou*, that is, of eternal life." McFague situates what she terms Buber's "subject-subjects model" within the milieu of twentieth century existentialism, at base a model of "one individual with God: I and Thou." While attracted to a style of thinking associated with Buber, McFague states that in some ways she prefers the medieval view because it resembles an ecological model in suggesting "a cosmology, not just a psychology, a way of being in the world rather than a way for an individual to find God."[21]

A comparison of Buber's style of thinking with that of medieval cosmology raises further issues. Mascall reports a critique by Martin Buber's followers of the "I-it" attitude of Western Catholic theism "on the ground that it postulates as the realm of our experience a world of passive and inactive objects in which the possibility of any direct responsible confrontation of human persons with a personal God is to all intents and purposes absent."[22] Mascall's defense of the scholastic tradition offers a

---

18. See McFague, *Super, Natural Christians*, 101.
19. See McFague, *Super,* Natural *Christians*, 101.
20. See McFague, *Super, Natural Christians*, 101–2. McFague cites Buber, *I and Thou*, 62–63.
21. McFague, *Super, Natural Christians*, 102–3.
22. Mascall, *Existence and Analogy*, 182.

useful insight into the matters at stake. One may contrast his conclusions with McFague's.

Mascall suggests that the critique by Buber's followers applies to modernist, rather than to scholastic, philosophy:

> Such a criticism would, I think, be perfectly valid of a Cartesian universe, in which the direct object of human experience is simply a realm of intra-mental ideas and in which any possibility of knowing other existents than ourselves arises simply from the accuracy with which our ideas copy them. . . . But it does not hold, I would maintain, against a view . . . which I believe to be that of the scholastic tradition in its full vigour, according to which existence is an activity and indeed the most fundamental of all activities, and which claims that in our experience of the objects of perception we are entering into a living relationship with fellow creatures whose very existence declares the incessant creative energizing act of God.[23]

Mascall goes on to consider the effect of "I-Thou" language in relation to the world:

> I do not think it is altogether adequate to describe this as simply an 'I-Thou' as contrasted with an 'I-it' relation; such a form of words would tend to suggest either that we are confronted only with beings that are alive and personal, or else that we ought to react to every being in our environment as if it were alive and personal, whether in fact it is so or not.[24]

We may note that McFague's "subject-subjects model" appears to move towards responding to everything in the environment as if it were alive and personal. McFague asserts: "The so-called primitive urge to anthropomorphize nature is a correct one."[25] I will consider her procedure in this respect more fully below.

Mascall defends Western Catholicism as a means to overcome "ruthless exploitation which has been so calamitous a feature of the modern world":

> It is not, I think, necessary either to deny or personify lifeless matter in order to get what we need; it is sufficient to realize that even the lifeless 'it' is the subject of an activity which enables it

---

23. Mascall, *Existence and Analogy*, 182–83.
24. Mascall, *Existence and Analogy*, 183.
25. McFague, *Super, Natural Christians*, 53.

to be the object of, and to contribute to, our own experience. In existing it is not just passive, but is performing, on its own level of being, an activity—the activity of existing—which, on a vastly higher level and in the analogical mode proper to rational beings composed of soul and body, we too perform. If the radically analogical character of the act of existing is fully understood, we shall be able, without falling into the fallacy of personifying the lower creation, to recognize sub-human creatures, whether animate or inanimate, as partners with us in the activity of existing and as combining with us in the hierarchical order of the universe to praise and glorify God.[26]

In this way of thinking, even lifeless matter is in some sense regarded as "subject" although in a sense very different from that envisaged in "subjectification of the world" as described by McFague. On the other hand, McFague's concept of the world as God's body appears to be a short step towards what Mascall calls "falling into the fallacy of personifying the lower creation."

I will return to a possible continuation of dialogue between followers of Buber and Mascall in the last section. At this stage we may note that Mascall and Buber are at one about what McFague calls the vertical direction of the natural world. It is this vertical direction which allows for experience of the objects of perception in an ontological sense. By contrast, McFague's theory offers an experience which is even less ontological than that of a Cartesian universe. In a Cartesian way of thinking, reports Mascall, "the possibility of knowing other existents than ourselves arises simply from the accuracy with which our ideas copy them." But, according to McFague, "we create the reality in which we live; we do not copy it."[27]

In chapter 7 I suggested that the attempt in McFague's project to overcome the subject-object divide reduces to occupying an overlap between existentialism and positivism. But McFague also critiques "positivistic" literalism as well as what she discerns as Buber's existentialist limitation. She indicates a desire to move beyond these ways of thinking. The next two sections consider her attempt to do so.

---

26. Mascall, *Existence and Analogy*, 183.
27. See McFague, *Models of God*, 26.

AN INTEGRATED SENSIBILITY?

"What we *know*," says McFague, "are the metaphors or projections of the self, the worlds it creates."[28] She goes on to state: "Without assuming an idealistic perspective (the world out there is only what subjects say it is), a moderate Kantianism (and we are all, one way or another, Kantians) insists that in a sense . . . all theology, philosophy, physics and art is autobiography." On this assumption, it is perhaps not surprising that we may be in danger of falling into the fallacy of personifying the lower creation. One may contrast this existentialist frame of reference with the positivist claim that what counts as "true" for us is what corresponds with "reality," with the "facts."

Let us return to the dichotomy in the Cartesian (or Kantian) legacy. Descartes, says McFague, is "the father of the modern notion of objectivity."[29] This is consonant with the positivist notion of factual truth. At the same time, the legacy is subjectivist since knowledge is anchored in individualistic and self-reliant thought.[30] This latter aspect leads to what McFague calls the Kantian limits or lack of access to things "out there." McFague writes: "For Descartes, knowledge was not to be found through a return to the gods, but by a turn inward, to the individual's internal thoughts: 'I think therefore I am.'"[31] The Cartesian (or Kantian) legacy leaves something out. The gods (or God) no longer validate epistemology. At the same time this legacy offers a kind of objectivity. The positivist claim of access to the facts rests on the "I-it" relation which Mascall attributes to "a Cartesian universe." But something is lost in the process.

McFague indicates that the Cartesian legacy has caused a loss of relationship with the natural world:

> Our world now is literalized. What once was rich in meaning, a subject responsive to many deep and sublime interpretations, becomes nothing more than an object to be analyzed, dissected, and commodified. Everything interesting, meaningful and living moves into our minds: "I think, therefore I am"—with these fatal words, nature loses its subjecthood.[32]

---

28. McFague, *Speaking in Parables*, 147–48. McFague's italics.
29. McFague, *Super, Natural Christians*, 74.
30. See McFague, *Super, Natural Christians*, 188 n. 10.
31. McFague, *Super, Natural Christians*, 74
32. McFague, *Super, Natural Christians*, 59.

Three Kinds of Sacramentalism

She traces the history of this development.

> Whereas people in the Middle Ages had lived in a world as subjects among many subjects, animal and plant ones (as well as angelic and demonic ones, with *the* Subject, God, presiding over everything), human beings were now alone. . . . Our ecological crisis at the close of the twentieth century is but the last stage in this long deepening of human solitude.

We may compare what McFague writes here with what Mascall says of a Cartesian universe. Mascall redirects the critique of the Catholic tradition to a modernist frame of reference. He indicates that it is this more recent kind of thinking which "postulates as the realm of our experience a world of passive and inactive objects in which the possibility of any direct responsible confrontation of human persons with a personal God is to all intents and purposes absent."[33]

According to Steiner, it would be an overstatement to remove God entirely from Cartesian thinking. But the sense that God operates as the point of integration with all that lives would seem reduced. McFague charts the effect in the history of Christianity:

> The interior, vertical route that starts with Augustine continues into the Reformation, especially in Martin Luther as well as into the twentieth century, epitomized in Existentialism. Nature falls into the background, serving as a backdrop or stage for God's important work: redemption. Nor did things fare much better in post-medieval Roman Catholicism. Counter-Reformation Catholicism was anti-nature, seeing divine action as limited to the supernatural, with nature as a mere foil to grace.[34]

Post-medieval Christianity retains the vertical route on less than ontological terms. There is an epistemological consequence in this. As seen in chapter 7, the *interior* vertical route does not provide a theatre for the act of redemption as an event in world history.

McFague outlines the modernist dilemma:

> The old easy commerce between the interior and the exterior, between the human and natural worlds, with both sharing similar qualities of imagination, subjectivity and purpose and meaning

---

33. See Mascall, *Existence and Analogy*, 182–83.

34. McFague, *Super, Natural Christians*, 58. McFague cites James A. Carpenter, *Nature and Grace*, 33 and Gabriel Daly, "Foundations in Systematics for Ecological Theology," 40.

(though in different ways), has long since broken down; and we are left alone, locked into our own minds.[35]

She wishes to restore "the old easy commerce" between different orders of reality on new terms. Her focus is on the human knower in relation to the world. "The main difficulty with post-Cartesian epistemologies," she says, "is that they do not figure in the figurer; they split mind and body, reason and imagination, subject and object, nature and history and end with something less than *human* knowing."[36]

To an extent McFague endorses the subjectivity as well as the communal nature of religious tradition. She endorses the "I-Thou" emphasis of Buber's thinking. She goes further in promoting the "I" as well as the "Thou," finding nineteenth century poet, Gerard Manley Hopkins a useful counter-example to the dichotomizing nature of post-Cartesian epistemologies. For Hopkins, she says, the world always has "the taste of me."[37] Elsewhere McFague goes so far as to praise Hopkins for continuing "the multi-dimensionality of the medieval world [in which] things are not just themselves—they signify more." Hopkins, she goes on to say, was an anomaly in his time: "few people beyond the seventeenth century had his integrated sensibility, the ability to see the natural and the supernatural worlds *together*."[38] Nevertheless she critiques Hopkins for the same reason that she critiques the medieval approach: "Things and people are diverse, unique, and particular only *as* they praise God and *in order to* praise God."[39]

McFague wishes to re-establish "the old easy commerce between the interior and exterior" on horizontal rather than vertical terms. She goes so far as to advocate a horizontal kind of sacramentalism.[40] But what she does not address is the loss of an external epistemology. The kind of verifying effect offered by positivist parameters is insufficient to restore interaction between different orders of reality. I suggested in chapter 7 that the model of successful research functions for McFague as a point of intersection from a positivist respect for "the facts" to the ethical frame which operates in the order of meta-scientific world views.

---

35. McFague, *Super, Natural Christians*, 59–60.
36. McFague, *Speaking in Parables*, 59. McFague's italics.
37. McFague, *Speaking in Parables*, 148.
38. McFague, *Super, Natural Christians*, 58–59.
39. McFague, *Super, Natural Christians*, 58. McFague's italics.
40. See McFague, *Super, Natural Christians*, 172–74.

But intersection is not integration. The other side of the dilemma is the solitude of subjectivism. One may ask whether it is possible to have an integrated approach to external reality without the vertical element. Does one not otherwise begin and end with autobiography?

"The main difficulty with post-Cartesian epistemologies," says McFague, "is that they end with something less than *human* knowing."[41] But what is the result if what we know constitutes a projection of the self? As seen above, McFague states a wish to overcome "positivistic" literalism through some kind of poetic sensibility. I would agree with McFague's endorsement of poetic sensibility as a means to relation in an "I-Thou" fashion with the natural world. But it depends what is meant by poetic sensibility. The common factor between metaphorical language and an "I-Thou" relation with the natural world is the vertical direction which McFague wishes to deny.

Christianity, says McFague, must add a "new sacramentalism" to seeing nature as subject.[42] She cites metaphor as the means to re-establish an integrated form of knowing. She states: "Metaphor is the language of 'a body that thinks'; it is, therefore, neither an embellishment of language nor a primitive form to be superseded by conceptual language, but *the* method of human thought."[43] But she also equates metaphors with projections of the self and distances "modern consciousness" from the classical type of metaphor arising from the Christian symbolic universe.[44] Human beings are now alone, she says. Will the route of the projected metaphor offer a remedy? Or is her attempt to attain an integrated sensibility achievable, contrary to her intention, only at the expense of access to "things out there"?

HORIZONTAL SACRAMENTALISM

Chapter 5 introduced McFague's notion of "sacramentalism" in which "human beings as the *imago dei*" are said to reveal "the God-world relationship in a special way." Here it is again:

> The model of God the creator as mother suggests an ontological (or cosmological) sacramentalism: the world is born from the

---

41. McFague, *Speaking in Parables*, 59. McFague's italics.
42. See McFague, *Super, Natural Christians*, 172.
43. McFague, *Speaking in Parables*, 60. McFague's italics.
44. See McFague, *Speaking in Parables*, 106, 147.

> being of God and hence will be like God. The model of God the savior as lover suggests a personal (or anthropological) sacramentalism: the world is in a responsive relationship to God as his beloved and hence will, in different ways, manifest that relationship.... Thus, in our models of God as mother of creation and as lover of the world, we can speak of God's incarnation in two ways: first, creation as a whole (God's body) is a sacrament or sign of the presence of God, and second, human beings, particularly those human beings especially open and responsive to God are sacraments or signs of God the lover. God becomes incarnated, "in the flesh," both in the body of the world as a whole and the bodies and spirits of certain creatures who have special capacity to respond to God as lover and hence to manifest that love.[45]

This kind of sacramentalism arises from a way of thinking about ourselves. It is, McFague indicates, the outworking of the model "the world as God's body."

The notion of "sacramentalism" appears in McFague's second book of her series on religious language. It is developed further in the fourth book of the series in which McFague goes so far as to propose a "sacred world order." If McFague had not already distanced her models from reference to reality it might appear that her form of sacramentalism alludes to the living God. How could all phenomena have the potential to reflect deity if they cannot point to divine reality? How could humanity (as the *imago dei*) be revelatory of the God-world relationship in a special way? The answer, I believe, is in the word "suggests." The model projects a possibility. Within the projected possibility there is a suggested "sacramentalism." The projected version of the world can be understood to have the potential to reflect the projected version of the deity. The old idea of vehicle and tenor operates *within the model,* but not outside it. The old idea of metaphorical reference is not abandoned; rather it is reissued within a subjectivist framework.

But the suggested sacramentalism is said to function in a horizontal way. The focus is not "on seeing God, but on seeing the tree (this particular tree) which, its own way, as itself, is *also* in God."[46] McFague writes: "The things of earth do not point away from the earth to God; rather, they are themselves the 'body' of God—one of the major metaphors that

---

45. McFague, *Models of God*, 135–36.
46. McFague, *Super, Natural Christians*, 172. McFague's italics.

Christians might now use from nature to speak of God."[47] The focus moves away from resemblance to God (despite her earlier suggestion that the world born from the being of God will be like God and that human beings, as the *imago dei*, are understood to reveal the God-world relationship in a special way). McFague claims the imprimatur of Francis of Assisi in focusing on the things of earth "rather than on their divine message."[48] "The Christian eye does not need training to see God," she says, "but to see other things, especially earth others—and *then* to see them in God."[49] As we have seen, this approach runs counter to Chesterton's assessment of "the true Franciscan spirit." St. Francis, says Chesterton, would begin with the supernatural. "It would be *after* this that his enthusiasm would extend itself and give a sort of halo to the edges of all earthly things."[50]

I stated above that the old idea of metaphorical reference is reissued in a subjectivist framework. But in describing her horizontal kind of "sacramentalism," McFague goes so far as to state that "natural forms . . . are not transparent to the divine" and that "'Nature' is not a metaphor for God." (We may note in passing that metaphor and transparency are linked together in this disclaimer.) McFague situates her disclaimer in her emphasis on particulars:

> The natural world is not a single entity but a marvelously rich, multidimensional, diverse, and intricate collection of lifeforms and things. It is precisely this character of the natural world that presents itself to us as a new and exciting way to speak of God. (Actually, it is not new at all, but appears so to post-Enlightenment Christians, especially Protestants, who narrowed the world to themselves and God.)[51]

McFague's wish to embrace a traditional approach on horizontal terms comes to a head in terms of "Catholic" and "Protestant" elements of a "sacred world order," as will be considered below.

What McFague calls remythologizing is the product of an experimental thought process. "As we begin this experiment," she says, "we must once again recall that a metaphor or model is not a description. We

---

47. McFague, *Super, Natural Christians*, 174.
48. See McFague, *Super, Natural Christians*, 172–74.
49. McFague, *Super, Natural Christians*, 172. McFague's italics.
50. See Chesterton, *St Francis of Assisi*, 69–71. Chesterton's italics. See chapter 5.
51. McFague, *Super, Natural Christians*, 173.

are trying to think in an as-if fashion about the God-world relationship, because we have no other way of thinking about it."[52] One may see the progression from a consciously hypothetical way of thinking to "living in the model" in what she has to say about resurrection of the body. She commences in an experimental fashion:

> What if, we are asking, the "resurrection of the body" were not seen as the resurrection of particular bodies that ascend, beginning with Jesus of Nazareth, into another world, but as God's promise to be with us always in God's body, our world? What if God's promise of permanent presence to all space and time were imagined as a worldly reality, a palpable, bodily presence?[53]

From projecting a possibility she then moves to the kind of awareness that comes from looking through the lens of the model:

> What this experiment with the world as God's body comes to, finally, is an awareness, both chilling and breathtaking, that we as worldly, bodily beings are in God's presence. It is the basis for a revived sacramentalism, that is, a perception of the divine as visible, as present, palpably present in our world.... We meet the world as a Thou, as the body of God where God is present to us always in all times and in all places. In the metaphor of the world as the body of God, the resurrection becomes a worldly, present, inclusive reality, for this body is offered to all: "This is my body."[54]

McFague uses the language of "Thou" for encounter with "the world as God's body" which echoes Buber's "I-Thou" relationship. In writing about Buber, McFague distances herself from a mystical element in this relationship. Her language here might give a different impression.

We have seen that McFague moves away from the vertical element in traditional "sacramentalism." The "chilling and breathtaking" direction of McFague's experiment is not mysticism *per se*. What is at stake here will take some unraveling. McFague proposes a "revived sacramentalism" in place of "the interior, vertical route" or aural tradition, of Protestantism in particular. She advocates a return to what she calls a visual tradition in which it is not "just a book, the scriptures, that is special as the medium

---

52. McFague, *Models of God*, 70.
53. McFague, *Models of God*, 69–70.
54. McFague, *Models of God*, 77.

Three Kinds of Sacramentalism

of divine presence, but the world is also God's dwelling place." In this respect she reports a discussion with feminist writer, Rosemary Ruether:

> The aural tradition criticized here is obviously only one version of a Logos theology, and one peculiar to Protestantism. I am grateful to Rosemary Radford Ruether for a comment on this point in a letter dated May 16, 1986, in which she writes of "the strong current in neo-Platonism which cultivates a 'cosmic piety' of the visible world as an embodied God, found in Hermetic theology and even in Plotinus and in Plato's *Timaeus*. This tradition flows into a Christian sacramentality which sees the whole cosmos as sacramental, i.e., the bodying forth of the divine Logos. This is a very different understanding of Logos from the 'heard word' that is absent. It is Logos as Ground of Being bodying forth in not only human being, but all visible things. This older cosmos theology needs to be given more credit for a view very similar to yours."[55]

Ruether detects a similarity between McFague's view and what she calls "this older cosmos theology," the various strands of which entailed different theological expressions. What they had in common was a strong sense of ontological affirmation. By contrast, McFague's notion of ontological affirmation is confined to her models as we have seen. In what sense is McFague then at liberty to invoke "the divine Logos"?

In McFague's experiment of "the world as God's body," she wishes to avoid both what she calls the vertical element and pantheism but the position may be difficult to sustain. The closest McFague comes to positing a "divine Logos" would seem her depiction of a panentheist God. She states that her panentheist way of thinking "does not totally identify God with the world any more than we totally identify ourselves with our bodies"[56] and that the view that God is not exhausted by all finite beings is "compatible with our model of God as the spirit that is the source, the life, the breath of reality."[57] Feminist writer Grace M. Jantzen comments: "At least some forms of panentheism, while stressing that the world is inseparable from God, nevertheless also hold that 'God's inclusion of the world does not exhaust the reality of God.'"[58] Jantzen goes on to remark:

---

55. See McFague, *Models of God*, 200 n. 9.
56. McFague, *Models of God*, 71
57. McFague, *The Body of God*, 149.
58. See Jantzen, *Becoming Divine*, 271, n. 5.

Insofar as this means that God could exist without the world, or that there is a 'part' or 'aspect' of God somehow beyond or other than the world, this collapses after all into dualism, and is not analogous with the relationship between a person and her body as I sketch it. If, on the other hand, it merely means that God is not reducible to physicalism, then it does not differ from panentheism. I suspect that 'panentheists' often shuffle rather uneasily between these two positions.

The possibility of an uneasy shuffle between two positions could be even greater for McFague, given her acknowledged distinction between the God of the model and the possibility of a God beyond all models.[59]

Within the model, McFague goes so far as to address the world as Thou. Elsewhere she qualifies what she means by treating the world as subject: "There is nothing mysterious or creepy about this: we are not suggesting that trees and mountains are conscious, purposive subjects, but only that their raison d'être is not to be objects for us."[60] Nevertheless, her proposed "subjectification of the world" appears to move in a pantheistic direction: "It is the recognition," she says, "similar to the notion of the *anima mundi* in medieval times and the early Renaissance, that other things have life and vitality."[61] In this regard, McFague quotes soul-ecologist, Thomas Moore: "A striking building stands before us as an individual every bit as soulful as we are."[62] McFague does not explain how a building could be every bit as soulful as we are without being conscious and purposive. We may recall Mascall's remark about falling into the fallacy of personifying the lower creation.

Despite the lack of external reference in her thinking, McFague states a wish to overcome the individualistic tendency of existentialism in favor of "a cosmology, not just a psychology, a way of being in the world rather than a way for an individual to find God."[63] I gain the impression that she seeks a form of cultural existentialism if such is possible given the individualistic tendency of existentialist thinking. She wishes to construct a "sacred world order," having the flavor of and yet distinct from

---

59. See McFague, *Models of God*, 195–56 n. 13.

60. McFague, *Super, Natural Christians*, 111.

61. McFague, *Super, Natural Christians*, 112.

62. McFague, *Super, Natural Christians*, 112. McFague cites Moore, *Care of the Soul*, 268.

63. McFague, *Super, Natural Christians*, 102–3.

the medieval order.⁶⁴ Similarly, Jantzen proposes "a feminist religious symbolic." Jantzen's proposal may serve to illustrate the terms on which such constructions are built:

> Because of the identification in the western symbolic of the female with the material, for women to project a divine horizon . . . it is necessary that this female divine cannot be pure spirit, a disembodied God, but thought of in female terms."⁶⁵

An emphasis on the material, however, is not to be confused with external reference. Jantzen distances herself from process theology because of its "ontological realism" which she finds "somewhat less promising territory for the new ground of a feminist philosophy of religion intent on developing a feminist symbolic of the divine."⁶⁶ Nevertheless, she asserts that "if the claims of process thought are treated not as metaphysical truths but as dimensions of a religious symbolic, so that the divine indicates what we consider most worthy and to be valued, then many of their ideas blend well with a feminist approach."⁶⁷ An ethical movement which is not anchored in ontological realism would seem in accord with what we have already seen in McFague.

In describing her proposed "sacred world order," McFague uses the terms "symbol" and "Catholic" to indicate similarity to the medieval order and "metaphor" and "Protestant" to indicate distance from it:

> Our thesis is that the Catholic sensibility is greatly to be desired; that its insistence on a sacred world order is right and needed but that such an order must be one that satisfies the steely-eyed Protestant head-shaking at how bad things really are and how different things are. . . . The Catholic sensibility is symbolic, seeing connections, similarities, and unity among all parts of the whole; the Protestant sensibility is metaphorical, seeing differences, divergences and deterioration but *also* surprising and profound relations.⁶⁸

---

64. McFague, *Super, Natural Christians*, 51–52.
65. Jantzen, *Becoming Divine*, 269.
66. Jantzen, *Becoming Divine*, 257.
67. Jantzen, *Becoming Divine*, 258.
68. McFague, *Super, Natural Christians*, 52. McFague adds the disclaimer: "Needless to say, either of these mind-sets can exist in actual Catholics and Protestants; and both can exist in the same person or culture—and I believe they should."

But "sacred" in this projected sense is not "sacramental," traditionally understood. One may compare this with what Lewis has to say about classic "sacramentalism" in which transcendent reality has a symbolic echo in our material world. Lewis distinguishes pagan from Judaeo-Christian symbolism:

> [W]hen you hear in the thunder the voice of a god you are stopping short, for the voice of a god is not really the voice from beyond the world, from the uncreated. By taking the god's voice away—or envisaging the god as an angel, or servant of the Other—you go further. The thunder becomes not less divine but more. By emptying nature of . . . divinities—you may fill her with Deity, for she is now the bearer of messages.[69]

McFague's "sacred world order" stops short at the level of the model or thought experiment. She rejects the vertical or message-bearing route in an external sense. Even her panentheist tendencies are less ontological than the voice of a god heard in thunder.

We have seen that McFague proposes a symbolic universe on subjectivist terms. At the same time she associates "metaphor" with "steely-eyed Protestant head-shaking at how bad things really are and how different things are." (This contrasts with her treatment of "metaphor" as the means of integration in overcoming the Cartesian dichotomy.) The dual functions of connection (Catholic) and disconnection (Protestant) are reminiscent of the difference between "living in the model" and actual lived experience. The head-shaking component, while not Barthian in content, carries what I would consider a Barthian orientation which is perhaps what McFague means in labeling it "Protestant." Chapter 6 noted a Barthian disjunction between the content of revelation and earthly reality. To my mind, the Barthian method lends itself to a type of Platonic division between heaven and earth. It is foreign to the biblical interactive God evidenced in the intervention, by Yahweh, at Babel. I will return to a comparison of Catholic and Protestant sensibilities in the next section.

It must be recalled that McFague's project rejects the "classic sacramental perspective" on feminist grounds.[70] McFague states that it is the task of metaphorical theology to "break the hegemony over the Western

---

69. Lewis, *Reflections on the Psalms*, 71.
70. McFague, *Metaphorical Theology*, 10–11.

religious consciousness" of the metaphor "God the father."[71] She cites a feminist perception "of the profound structural implications of this model as a form of ecclesiastical, social, political, economic and personal oppression." But to relativize this metaphor is to relativize external epistemology. I suspect that the consequences in ecclesiastical, social, political, economic and personal terms are yet to be charted.

This is not to say that the way in which the metaphor "God the father" has been understood and the kind of sacramental universe which has been influential in the Western consciousness are beyond challenge. This is not the place to engage with the metaphor "God the father" as it affects women. Here I will attempt to sketch a possible alternative to the medieval sacramental universe. Rather than dismantling a traditional sacramental model and reissuing something similar in a subjectivist framework the way forward may lie in divesting the medieval cosmos of its non-biblical elements.

COMING ALIVE

Lewis describes the medieval view of the cosmos as a syncretistic model. But it was not a model in McFague's sense. McFague reports that "the culture of the Middle Ages was extroverted, not introverted; people looked outward to find signs of God in nature, rather than inward to find the divine within themselves."[72] She goes so far as to cite physicist Hanbury Brown in this respect:

> When religious beliefs lose touch with reality they are likely to turn *inwards* and present a picture of the world which is no more than a mirror of ourselves, and such a picture . . . is potentially dangerous. If our system of religious beliefs is to form a coherent world-view, as it did in the Medieval Model, it must look *outwards* to what contemporary science is telling us about the world around us.[73]

But in our postmodern skepticism, can we find a way of looking outwards? As already seen in this book the kind of metaphor espoused by McFague is what she calls the metaphor of juxtaposition, in keeping with

---

71. McFague, *Metaphorical Theology*, 29.

72. McFague, *Super, Natural Christians*, 53–54.

73. McFague, *The Body of God*, 221 n. 5. McFague cites Brown, *The Wisdom of Science*, 172. Italics are in the text.

"our alienation and disbelief."[74] This kind of metaphor poses no challenge to post-Cartesian dichotomies.

"Metaphorical theology" claims to overcome alienation to the natural world. At the same time it draws back from an external God as the source of connection. In such thinking external epistemology is discarded in favor of a subjectivist epistemology with the result that alienation to the natural world is overcome *within* the model. This kind of model is what Barth would call anthropocentric myth. It is, says McFague, a projection of a possibility. The model of the "world as God's body" does not reflect the world as it is but as it might be. It relates to external reality not in imitating it but in being productive of it.[75]

Let us pause to consider a likely trajectory of a search for an integrated sensibility in a subjectivist frame of reference. The extent to which we are all Kantians is the extent to which we rely on our categories of understanding for access to the external world. Steiner maintains that this route to knowledge has until recently been underpinned by spokes of meaning which ultimately lead to God. Jung, on the other hand, discerns an alternative source of meaning in the Platonic motifs or archetypes of the subconscious mind. The attempt to hold the interior worlds of Kantian categories and Jungian archetypes *together* would result in an inversion of traditional sacramentalism, access to the natural world stemming from (and qualified by) the conscious categories of understanding *above* the mythological archetypes of the subconscious mind.

What then is the alternative? I return here to McFague's distinction between "Catholic" and "Protestant" sensibilities. "'Protestant' stands for the disjunctive, divided, skeptical, postmodern mind-set that sees difference and difficulties wherever it turns," says McFague.[76] But is "Protestant" a useful term in this context? The postmodern mind-set owes much, I believe, to what McFague calls the Kantian limits which cast doubt on access to "things out there," in particular if Kantian thinking is detached from the sense of linguistic "presence" which is ultimately, according to Steiner, anchored in God. But, in this latter respect, Protestantism, at least at its inception, did not discard the sacramental universe. Its development had an earlier impetus. As seen above, McFague reports that "the interior, vertical route that starts with Augustine continues into the

---

74. McFague, *Speaking in Parables*, 107–8.
75. See McFague, *Models of God* 192 n. 37 and McFague, *Speaking in Parables*, 58.
76. McFague, *Super, Natural Christians*, 52.

Three Kinds of Sacramentalism 191

Reformation and especially in Martin Luther as well as into the twentieth century, epitomized in Existentialism."[77] The vertical route continues even if, as McFague asserts, "nature falls into the background" in key forms of Protestant thinking.

Let us now return to the "linguistic sacramentalism" which characterized but also predated the medieval era.[78] In this context, Graham Ward draws attention to Ernst Hoffmann's research into ancient Greek understandings of "logo-centrism."[79] Ward reports differing approaches to "logo-centrism" in pre-Socratic philosophers, Heraclitus and Parmenides. For Heraclitus "the word of the multitude is lifeless and only through the Logos can it become animated." For Parmenides, on the other hand, "Logos *is*, words do not have true being, only relative existence to it." This, comments Ward, "is the difference between the word as sacrament and the word as symbol." It could be said that Catholic sensibility has more affinity with symbolic connectedness while Protestant emphasis on an aural tradition and personal relationship with God has more affinity with the sacramental aspect of language. It is noteworthy that Heraclitus also emphasized change and discontinuity. Such differing approaches to "logo-centrism" would seem to reflect what Ruether terms an older cosmos theology. Christianity as a whole combines the two.

In *Speaking in Parables* McFague denotes the Judaic-Christian tradition as "strongly verbal" in comparison with "nature cults, mystic religions, liturgical and ritualistic traditions." She adds:

> Judaism and Christianity are "logos" religions: human beings are constituted by the Word as well as by words, or by the Word as made known to them through words. The Hebraic tradition is not visual but aural: Hear the word of the Lord, saith the prophet. And Protestant theology is agonizingly, painfully verbal and linguistic.[80]

This is to emphasize what Catholics and Protestants in their Hebraic tradition have in common with each other. If the Protestant tradition strongly affirms this verbal heritage, in what sense then could it enter into a broader sacramental world order?

77. McFague, *Super, Natural Christians*, 58.
78. McFague, *Models of God*, 212 n. 17.
79. See Ward, *Barth, Derrida and the Language of Theology*, 66.
80. McFague, *Speaking in Parables*, 27.

"Our thesis," says McFague, "is that the Catholic sensibility is greatly to be desired; that its insistence on sacred world order is right and needed but that such an order must be one that satisfies the steely-eyed Protestant head-shaking at how bad things really are and how different things are."[81] My question is: which elements of the Catholic sacred world order ought to be preserved and what contribution can rightly be gained from steely-eyed Protestant head-shaking? If the vertical route is factored into the Protestant mind-set, some aspects of the disjunctive, divided, skeptical, postmodern mind fall away. The Catholic insistence on sacred world order might then with advantage move a Protestant tendency towards the interior, vertical route into the exterior, message-bearing route. At the same time Protestant head-shaking might divest the sacred world order of its non-biblical speculative detail.

At this point one could ask if anything is to be gained from Buber's "I-Thou" approach to the natural world. Buber's vertical route would, I believe, have the tendency to guard against the possibility of what Mascall calls "falling into the fallacy of personifying the lower creation." Mascall disavows the charge, leveled by the followers of Martin Buber, that the scholastic "I-it" tradition is arid. It must be admitted, however, that the scholastic tradition was born in the age of the medieval model. As seen above, McFague emphasizes the Platonic and Aristotelian roots of the model, "the one focused on the otherworld and the other on this world." Such ancient boundaries between the "otherworld" and this world preclude interaction between creator and creation. But this distinction is not a biblical one. This is where the participatory Hebraic approach, expressed in Buber's "I-Thou" terms, could be helpful.

McFague detects the beginnings of what she calls the interior, vertical route in Augustine. But this is to leave something out. In his *Confessions* Augustine describes how he hears a voice saying, "*I am the God who IS.*"[82] Augustine recounts his spiritual journey away from the notion that creation was like a sponge in an infinite divine sea. In this earlier notion God was envisaged as permeating the finite creation in a material way.[83] Augustine rejects this notion on the grounds of theodicy. Catherine Keller sums up the question faced by Augustine: "how if God is everywhere is

---

81. McFague, *Super, Natural Christians*, 52.
82. See Augustine, *Confessions* VII, 10.
83. See Augustine, *Confessions* VII, 5.

Three Kinds of Sacramentalism

there space for anything but goodness?"[84] A horizontal view of God is liable to the problem of theodicy, as seen in chapter 5.

Augustine's vision stresses the distinction between the creator and material world but the redemptive journey draws the two together.[85] Augustine writes: "Your light shone on me with its brilliance, and I thrilled with love and dread alike. I realized that I was far away from you. It was as though I were in a land where all is different from your own." Augustine describes how he heard God's voice saying "I am the food of full-grown men. Grow and you shall feed on me. But you shall not change me into your own substance, as you do with the food of your body. Instead you shall be changed into me."[86] The difference between creator and creation is a prelude to a new kind of integration. We may recall here the legend of St. Francis and St Clare.

McFague objects to what she calls the vertical route on the grounds that it is "utilitarian."[87] I suspect that her conception of the vertical route is more Platonic than biblical. Yet she herself describes the traditional sacramental sensibility in terms of the Eucharist: "the bread and wine of the Eucharist are symbols of divine nurture; they do not merely 'point to' spiritual food, but really and truly *are* spiritual food. The things of this world participate in and signify what transcends our world."[88] It is the biblical emphasis on interaction and participation in the transcendent which overcomes the Platonic dichotomy.

This chapter began by suggesting that a sacramental world order might in some sense resemble the adventure of Dorothy and her friends in a land peopled by figurines made of china. The kind of sacramentalism that I envisage would differ from their adventure in a key respect. In the story, the relationship between flesh and blood and china is a rather uneasy one. Two incidents of breakage occur as the main characters of the story make their way through this strange land. One might say that the relationship between the figurines and their visitors is somewhat Platonic. Lewis describes the distinction between "Biological Life" and "Spiritual Life" as like the distinction between a statue and a real man. But Christianity, says Lewis, does not leave the distinction where it is. He

---

84. Keller, *Face of the Deep*, 81.
85. See Rom 8:19–23.
86. Augustine, *Confessions* VII, 10.
87. See McFague, *Super, Natural Christians*, 172.
88. McFague, *Metaphorical Theology*, 5–6.

writes: "This world is a great sculptor's shop. We are the statues and there is a rumour going round the shop that some of us are some day going to come to life."[89]

---

89. See Lewis, *Mere Christianity*, 135–56.

10

Metaphor or Better-For?

EVEN AFTER DOROTHY AND her friends find out that the supposed wizard is a Great and Terrible Humbug, they still believe that he will somehow help them to achieve what they desire. One by one the Scarecrow, the Tin Woodman and the Lion come to him to gain their wishes. The Lion who is supposed to be the brave King of the Beasts feels afraid of danger and concludes that he is a coward. He asks for courage. The old man tries to persuade him that it is not courage he needs but confidence in himself, in spite of his fears. "True courage is in facing danger when you are afraid," he tells the Lion, "and that kind of courage you have in plenty." But the Lion wants something tangible to convince him that he has courage. So the old man gives him a drink from a square green bottle in a green-gold dish, beautifully carved. "What is it?" asks the Lion. "If it were inside you, it would be courage," says the man. The Lion drinks until the dish is empty.[1]

In the story it is clear that the first judgment was correct. The Lion was no coward. He only thought he was. The drink from the green bottle gave him what he thought he needed. The drink had a placebo effect, convincing the Lion of a reality which was already there. The term "placebo" can also be used in a scientific experiment to mean a control or dummy sample. In this case the placebo and the substance being tested are both assessed for their effect in reality.

---

1. See Baum, *The Wizard's Illusion*, chapters 15–16.

McFague describes her metaphorical method as an experiment. "We are letting the metaphor of the world as God's body try its chance," she says. "We are experimenting with a bit of nonsense to see if it can make a claim to truth."[2] Her notion of metaphor could be said to resemble a placebo. It is, she says, a bit of nonsense. Nevertheless she wishes to test it, not as the dummy control but seemingly as the real sample making a truth claim. But the supposed reality has its own parameters: the dummy status defines what she means by "truth." She writes:

> As we begin this experiment we must once again recall that a metaphor or model is not a description. We are trying to think in an as-if fashion about the God-world relationship, because we have no other way of thinking about it.... One has to realize how not to apply a metaphor (to say God is the Father does not mean that God has a beard!) and also where it fails or treads on shaky ground. The metaphor of the world as God's body has the opposite problem to the metaphor of the world as the king's realm: if the latter puts too great a distance between God and the world, the former verges on too great a proximity. Since both metaphors are inadequate, we have to ask which one is better in our time and to qualify it with other metaphors and models.[3]

McFague goes so far as to point out a qualifying aspect for the metaphor "God the father": "to say God is the Father does not mean that God has a beard!" In terms of my illustration from *The Wizard of Oz*, this is to admit the loss of the Silver Shoes. But McFague's frame of reference (of the "as if") does not allow for any sense of arrival. On these terms the kind of reference supplied by metaphor (and the qualifying role of other metaphors) never occurs at the point at which a reality comes to language.

In McFague's thinking "metaphor" expresses, and refers back to, a prior concept. She states that the inadequacy of any one metaphor can be addressed by qualifying it with other metaphors. But what is the source of inadequacy? The ground on which the "metaphor" treads is shaky if it fails the test of what is "better in our time." Metaphors of the God-world relationship are judged to put too great or too little distance between God and the world, not by their descriptive potential but by their ethical application. The claim to truth is ethical, not ontological.

The loss of the ontological opens the door to the subjective. Ethics is built on a subjectivist judgment. There are two sides to this. In admitting

---

2. McFague, *Models of God*, 69.
3. McFague, *Models of God*, 70.

that her metaphor is a "bit of nonsense," McFague retains a kind of ontological awareness. Put in terms of the Lion's placebo, one may say that she places herself in the shoes of the supposed Wizard who knows the "bit of nonsense" only works because the Lion believes it does. But, in seeing if her bit of nonsense can make a claim to truth, McFague joins forces as it were with the Lion. The "bit of nonsense" is true because it produces the desired result. At the same time McFague relativizes what is meant by a claim to truth: what is true in this sense in one situation might not be true in another. On these terms, a drink from a green bottle could be tested in its effect against a drink from a red bottle. No longer in the position of the Wizard, McFague samples each bottle and judges accordingly.

The Lion drinks from a green bottle in order, as he thinks, to gain courage. But he only receives what he already has. In a sacramental universe, a lion is a symbol of courage.[4] In *The Wizard of Oz*, the symbol holds. The placebo only has a reassuring effect. But McFague's metaphors do not operate in a sacramental universe which is already there. They make their own sacramentalism. On her terms, the content of the green bottle produces the courage, a Dutch courage as it were. McFague wants this kind of courage to "try its chance . . . to see if it can make a claim to truth." One might ask what would happen in the story if the Lion's courage really rested on the drink from the green bottle.

McFague wishes to challenge the "monarchical model of the God-world relationship" which, she says, is dangerous in our time.[5] It resembles, we may say, a drink from a red bottle, dangerous because it "supports attitudes of control and use toward the non-human world."[6] McFague states that the "monarchical model" has had the tendency "to draw other models into its orbit, as is evident with the model of God as father."[7] In consequence, this challenge is lodged against the sacramental universe in which "God is somehow the true and original father."[8] I will return to the status of the "monarchical model" in the last section of this chapter.

At this point one may query whether McFague's method offers a remedy for attitudes of control and use toward the non-human world. Despite her rhetoric, I have already questioned whether McFague succeeds

---

4. Cf. McFague, *Super, Natural Christians*, 55.
5. McFague, *Models of God*, 69.
6. See McFague, *Models of God*, 68.
7. McFague, *Models of God*, 66.
8. McFague, *Speaking in Parables*, 106; cf. *Metaphorical Theology*, 29

in overcoming the subject-object divide. She equates "metaphor" with a projection of the self.[9] On this understanding, the subject remains king. The next step is to superimpose the projected world onto the real world. I would not call this "bit of nonsense" a metaphor. I call it a better-for.

WHY BETTER?

In *Models of God*, McFague goes so far as to offer a broad scope of what might be meant by "better for our time." She writes:

> There are, of course, different understandings of "better." Is it better in terms of our and the world's preservation and fulfillment? Is it better in terms of coherence, comprehensibility, and illumination? Is it better in terms of expressing the Christian understanding of the relationship between God and the world? All these criteria are relevant, for a metaphor that is all or mostly nonsense has tried its chance and failed.[10]

The "bit of nonsense," says McFague, will fail if it proves to be "all or mostly nonsense" when tested. This might sound as if she is conducting her experiment in terms of an external ontology. But McFague does not ask whether her metaphorical picture accords with what is "out there" because, in her way of thinking, that question cannot be asked. "We are trying to think in an as-if fashion about the God-world relationship," she says, "because we have no other way of thinking about it."

In asking whether one metaphorical picture is better than other pictures, McFague assumes that the question of what is better can be asked within a subjectivist frame of reference. She justifies her departure from tradition on the grounds of a limitation in the cultural milieu which allegedly gave rise to Christianity. She states: "It is possible to speculate that if Christianity had begun in a culture less dualistic and antiphysical than that of the first-century Mediterranean world, it might have been willing, given the more holistic anthropology and theology of its Hebraic roots, to extend the body metaphor to God."[11] McFague does not engage with the Hebraic roots on their own ontological terms. Rather, she draws on the Hebraic roots in a way which accords with her notion of a "better" metaphor.

---

9. See McFague, *Speaking in Parables*, 147.
10. McFague, *Models of God*, 70.
11. McFague, *Models of God*, 71.

McFague cites three general criteria for judging whether a metaphor is "better." I will leave the issues of coherence, comprehensibility and illumination to the third section of this chapter except where such matters impinge on the other two criteria. As seen above, McFague feels free to modify the Christian understanding of the relationship between God and the world to accord with what she judges to be "better for our time." The God of her model is then enlisted in her project for "our and the world's preservation and fulfillment." Consequently I will take her first and third criteria for testing her "bit of nonsense" together.

Let us consider the metaphor for "the world as God's body" in terms of the Christian understanding of the relationship between God and the world. As noted in chapter 5, the natural world in McFague's "ecological model" is to be perceived as soul or spirit: if "nature is part of us, so we are part of nature . . . not only are we body but nature is spirit (or subject, soul—whatever we call that part of ourselves that we consider 'more than' nature")[12] McFague admits that the metaphor is "in danger of reducing God to the world" which would be pantheistic.[13] To avoid this she wishes to modify this model with other personal metaphors (God as mother, lover, and friend), indicating a certain distance between God and the world comparable to the distance between humans and their bodies.[14] The model itself, she says, is "perhaps most precisely designated as panentheistic; that is, it is a view of the God-world relationship in which all things have their origins in God and nothing exists outside God, though this does not mean that God is reduced to these things."[15]

A God related to the world as spirit to body raises the problem of theodicy. McFague anticipates this problem. In contrast with an all-powerful monarchical God, McFague posits a God who is unable to interfere with nature: "God does care about and side with the outcast and needy, while working in accord with the inexorable caprices of natural selection—God cannot set aside the laws of nature to benefit a chosen few."[16] Given that "all things have their origin in God," McFague concludes that "evil is not a power over against God; in a sense, it is God's 'responsibility,' part of God's being, if you will." She goes on to say that "the other side of

12. See McFague, *Super, Natural Christians*, 104.
13. McFague, *Models of God*, 71–72.
14. McFague, *Models of God*, 71.
15. McFague, *Models of God*, 72.
16. McFague, *The Body of God*, 175–76.

this [responsibility for evil] is that God is also involved . . . in the suffering caused by evil."[17] The God of her model appears to take on something of the role of a Suffering Servant, not so much on behalf of nature but in recognition of divine complicity in evil. Panentheism on these terms entails the difficulty of God's complicity in evil, as was noted long ago by Augustine.[18] Chapter 9 drew attention to Grace Jantzen's observation that, in the absence of a God beyond the world, panentheism reduces to a form of pantheism.[19] It is difficult to see how these issues accord with a "better" metaphor for the Christian understanding of the relationship between God and the world.

I move now to an overlap between McFague's first and third criteria of "better." In arguing for a better metaphor in terms of "our and the world's preservation and fulfillment," McFague favors what I call a counter-ethic. McFague draws on the evolutionary story to suggest that God could "be understood as a continuing creator, but of equal importance, we human beings might be seen as partners in creation, as the self-conscious, reflexive part of the creation that could participate in furthering the process."[20] Given that God is said to be complicit in evil, one might ask who would be likely to act as senior partner in such an endeavor. McFague prefers "the common creation story" (or evolutionary history) to other cosmologies, including the creation stories in Genesis, because 'the common creation story' suggests that creation is still in the making. In other words, she sees value in the inexorable caprices of natural selection. But, as noted in chapter 5, McFague wishes the natural world to be viewed through "the loving eye." Somehow she hopes her model will have the effect of improving the natural world.

Taken on its own, the so-called common creation story does not supply the values that McFague is looking for. She links evolutionary history with a "holistic, organic view" of reality but this association is, she admits, an arbitrary one:

> On the issue of the mechanical versus the organic model, Robert John Russell asks whether Newtonian mechanics or Darwinian evolution should be considered as mechanical or organic, since "cases can be made for both interpretations in each case, e.g., in

---

17. McFague, *Models of God*, 75. Cf. McFague, *The Body of God*, 259 n. 18.
18. See Augustine, *Confessions*, VII, 5.
19. See Jantzen, *Becoming Divine*, 271 n. 5.
20. McFague, *The Body of God*, 105.

Newtonian gravity, presumably a mechanical theory yielding a 'clockwork universe,' all bodies are interconnected; in Darwinian evolution, presumably an organic theory yielding an ecological view of nature, the gene is the 'mechanism' of variation and is unaffected by the environment of the phenotype."[21]

In other words, the link between Darwinian evolution and holistic ecology is more rhetorical than scientific.

Chapter 7 noted her preference for an organic model over a mechanical model on the grounds that it offers "a stronger objectivity, a more inclusive view, a piecing together of various embodied research sites and agendas that will benefit more of the planet's creatures and supporting structures."[22] But the link between an organic model and evolutionary history undermines her argument in this respect:

> The problem of evil in its many forms, including natural evil and human sin, is heightened in an evolutionary perspective, for it is obvious that not all species, let alone all individuals in any species, *do* flourish, and this for a variety of reasons. A gospel of inclusive fulfillment for *all* of creation must face what the physical and biological sciences must also face: both the second Law of Thermodynamics as well as current evolutionary theory underscore what Robert John Russell calls "a world of dissipation, decay and destruction."[23]

Can McFague claim that her model of "the world as God's body" is, in this sense, better "in terms of our and the world's preservation and fulfillment"?

Despite her stated preference for evolutionary history or "the common creation story," McFague draws on Genesis 1 in advocating "a Christian nature spirituality."[24] She states: "The writer of the first chapter of Genesis leaves no doubt but that the goodness of creation is its message: it is repeated seven times in the space of thirty-one verses." She goes on to ask, "How have we missed this? Seven times it is repeated like a teacher drumming into a lazy student's head a bit of basic learning. We have not heard, 'It is very good.'" It is not clear how a "very good" creation is compatible with the "inexorable caprices of natural selection" and evil

---

21. See McFague, *The Body of God*, 217 n. 19. McFague says this comes from private correspondence.

22. McFague, *The Body of God*, 96.

23. See McFague, *The Body of God*, 259 n. 18. McFague cites "Entropy and Evil." McFague's italics.

24. See McFague, *Super, Natural Christians*, 164–65.

which is "part of God's being." In terms of the origin of evil, McFague leaves out the tragic history of disobedience in the Garden of Eden. If the God of the model is said to create everything good, one may ask what is meant by "good"? All things are said to have their origin in a panentheist God but the understanding of "all things" does not include the values of the model. As noted in chapter 5, McFague rejects the possibility, which she calls "Barthian," that God defines love and that all human love only conforms to the divine pattern.[25]

As already seen in this book, McFague wishes to superimpose what I call a redemptive umbrella onto evolutionary history. She does not confine the umbrella to Christianity. She states that "the common creation story is a public one, available to all who wish to learn about it."[26] She indicates its potential breadth of religious application: "This common story is available to be remythologized in different ways by any and every religious tradition, and hence is a place of meeting for the religions, whose conflicts in the past and present have often been the cause of immense suffering and bloodshed as belief is pitted against belief." But this place of meeting is posited at the expense of an external God. This does not sit well with McFague's appeal to the Hebraic roots of Christianity. The Yahweh who can make and unmake language in Derrida's dissertation on the Tower of Babel comes much closer to the Hebraic roots. In sum, McFague's model relies on rhetoric rather than science or established religion.

The morality of McFague's model depends on the ideology of the model-maker. Borrowing an illustration from *The Wizard of Oz*, I suggested in chapter 7 that, in such thinking, the notion of good and evil would be governed by whoever wore the Golden Cap. If there is no external standard of good and evil, who will judge the wearer of the Golden Cap? In the long run, the "loving eye" is answerable only to itself. McFague states that broadening the base of scientific endeavor could have the effect of strengthening scientific "objectivity" (by which she tends to mean the ethical focus of scientific research).[27] This would appear to suggest that the Golden Cap must be shared, as I observed in chapter 7. But I am not convinced that a broad-based sharing of moral focus is possible. If the "loving eye" were taken as the determinant of "objectivity," the principle would govern the selection of research activity. A likely trajectory

---

25. McFague, *Models of God*, 192 n. 37. McFague's italics.
26. McFague, *The Body of God*, 107.
27. See McFague, *The Body of God*, 94–96.

is a narrowing rather than a widening of the function of the sciences. I suspect that McFague's notion of a "sacred world order" would facilitate this narrowing effect. In such thinking, the space occupied by the "sacred" would seem to belong to a kind of cultural existentialism. But existentialism is by nature individualistic. The possibility of a "loving" elite comes to the fore.[28]

C. S. Lewis draws attention to the danger of basing morality on ideology. According to Lewis, the loss of faith in access to the external world has been accompanied by a loss of faith in access to an external morality:

> Until modern times no thinker of the first rank ever doubted that our judgments of value were rational judgments or that what they discovered was objective ... The modern view is very different. It does not believe that value judgments are really judgments at all. They are sentiments, or complexes, or attitudes, produced in a community by the pressure of its environment and its traditions.... To say that a thing is good is merely to express our feeling about it; and our feeling about it is the feeling we have been socially conditioned to have.[29]

Lewis goes on to describe the notion of "better" on such an assumption: "But if this is so, then we might have been conditioned to feel otherwise. 'Perhaps,' thinks the reformer or the educational expert, 'it would be better if we were. Let us improve our morality.'"

To my mind, McFague's "loving eye" fits the modern reformer's program comfortably enough. She claims a "stronger objectivity" for her notion of "better."[30] But, unlike earlier thinkers, she does not claim that her moral position is better because it is objective. Rather, she claims that it is objective because it is "better." Lewis finds grave danger in the notion that we can improve our morality:

> Out of this apparently innocent idea comes the disease that will certainly end our species (and, in my view damn our souls) if it is not crushed; the fatal superstition that men can create values, that a community can choose its 'ideology' as men choose their clothes. Everyone is indignant when he hears the Germans

---

28. McFague goes so far as to state that "in our [model] of God ... as lover of the world ... human beings, *particularly those human beings especially open and responsive to God*, are sacraments or signs of God the lover" (*Models of God*, 136). My italics. Cf. chapters 5 and 9.

29. Lewis, "Poison of Subjectivism," 99.

30. See McFague, *The Body of God*, 94–96.

define justice as that which is to the interest of the Third Reich. But it is not always remembered that this indignation is perfectly groundless if we ourselves regard morality as a subjective sentiment to be altered at will. Unless there is some objective standard of good, over-arching Germans, Japanese and ourselves alike whether any of us obey it or no, then of course the Germans are as competent to create their ideology as we are to create ours.[31]

In the absence of objective value, what is to distinguish the claim of "better for our time" from that which is the interest of the Third Reich?

Lewis states that the reformer may attempt to base his values on biology "and tell us that we must act thus and thus for the preservation of our species." (McFague also cites "our preservation" and adds the world's preservation to it.)[32] Lewis goes on to say: "Apparently [the reformer] does not anticipate the question, 'Why should our species be preserved?'" Lewis comments that the reformer "takes for granted that it should, because he is really relying on traditional judgments of value." Lewis points out that relying on traditional judgments of value is not logically consistent with the method. The reformer, says Lewis, "must awake to the logic of his position sooner or later; and when he does, what barrier remains between us and the final division of the race into a few conditioners who stand themselves outside morality and the many conditioned in whom such morality as the experts choose is produced at the experts' pleasure."[33]

McFague's "loving eye" still appears to follow an external standard. But, like Lewis's reformer, she does not acknowledge it. The rhetoric has changed somewhat since Lewis's day. But the method seems disquietingly similar. There are two ways of responding in her method. Either we are reminded of the distance entailed in thinking in an "as if" fashion or we are encouraged to "live within" the model. This twofold approach opens the door to the possibility of external conditioners for a conditioned majority.

We may find such a possibility in Turbayne's "linguistic" metaphor for the events of nature. Turbayne states that he could treat this metaphor "as a modern allegory" himself but offer it "for literal consumption at a later time, knowing full well that the generation to whom it is first told cannot possibly believe it, but that the next may."[34] He continues: "If

---

31. Lewis, "Poison of Subjectivism," 99–100.
32. McFague, *Models of God*, 70.
33. Lewis, "Poison of Subjectivism," 108.
34. Turbayne, *The Myth of Metaphor*, 216–17.

successful, I should attain to the full Wizardry of Oz, for the essence of full Wizardry consists in fooling others with our devices without being fooled by them ourselves." Could a similar thing be said of McFague's proposal?

ALLEGORY AND A MORAL REVOLUTION

The model of "God the father," says McFague, "has established a hegemony over the Western religious consciousness which it is the task of metaphorical theology to break."[35] She does not deny the "truth" of the model "God the father" but the kind of truth she has in mind is that which she associates with her alternative models. It is a relativized truth springing from the needs and sensibility of the time. McFague classes "God the father" as a projected picture. She wishes to expose what I would term its allegorical roots, to demythologize it in other words. The positive side of this demythologizing process for McFague is "remythologizing." The task of metaphorical theology, she says, "will be a reforming, transforming one."[36] The attempt to demythologize religion is not without precedent in Western history. This section outlines another reformation and transformation in the fate of the Hellenic gods.

Allegory became a literary genre in late antiquity due to a philosophical movement towards monotheism and a consequent decline of belief in the pagan divine pantheon.[37] The usage also arose out of a philosophical crisis: the moral depravity of the old gods had become a source of embarrassment in academia.[38] In response, pagan belief was explained allegorically; divine characters were understood as material projections of human qualities or of abstractions. Hence allegory and philosophy were connected. Lewis notes:

> During a period of religious controversy it is, indeed, the most obvious way of tuning primitive documents to meet the ethical or polemical demands of the moment. The Stoics, apart from their general doctrine of the gods as manifestations of the One, were always ready to explain particular myths by allegory.

---

35. McFague, *Metaphorical Theology*, 29.
36. See McFague, *Metaphorical Theology*, 28–29.
37. See Lewis, *Allegory of Love*, 57–61.
38. Augustine, *City of God*. See Book II.

> Saturn eating his children could be harmlessly interpreted as Time 'bearing all his sons away'.[39]

At first allegory is *demythologizing* in nature: myths about the gods are reduced to a philosophical idea.

Ricoeur describes two possible relations between myth and philosophical interpretation. It can be "a simple allegorical tie" which reveals the truth *behind* the myth:

> This was what the Stoics did with the fables of Homer and Hesiod. The philosophical meaning rises victorious from its imaginative shell; it was there all armed like Athena in the head of Zeus. The fable was but an outer wrapping; stripped off, it is rendered vain. Allegory implies that the true meaning, the philosophic meaning, preceded the fable, which was only a second disguise, a veil deliberately thrown over the truth to mislead the simple.[40]

But beyond this demythologizing movement is another response which McFague might recognize as *remythologizing*. Ricoeur states that speculative thought is in danger of "rationalizing symbols as such and thereby fixing them on the imaginative plane where they are born and take shape." The result is what Ricoeur calls "dogmatic mythology," which is the "temptation of gnosis."[41]

What Lewis calls "a profound change in the mind of antiquity" occasioned long-term demythologizing and "remythologizing" effects. "On the one hand," says Lewis, "the gods sink into personifications; on the other hand, a widespread moral revolution forces men to personify their passions."[42] An awareness of internal moral conflict was seen in terms of "contending forces which [could not] be described at all except by allegory."[43] He notes that in late antiquity, "the habit of applying allegorical interpretation to ancient texts naturally encouraged fresh allegorical constructions, and this method was freely practised by both pagans and Christians."[44] Consequently, says Lewis, allegory became a literary genre: allegory and a subjective element in literature go hand in hand from late

---

39. Lewis, *Allegory of Love*, 61–62.
40. Reagan and Stewart, *The Philosophy of Paul Ricoeur*, 46.
41. Reagan and Stewart, *The Philosophy of Paul Ricoeur*, 46.
42. Lewis, *Allegory of Love*, 63.
43. Lewis, *Allegory of Love*, 113.
44. Lewis, *Allegory of Love*, 58.

antiquity onwards. This kind of allegory is still evident in *Pilgrim's Progress* published in 1678.

From a literary point of view, the old gods did not die even when allegory was abandoned as a popular literary genre. Lewis describes the revival of the old gods in the Romantic period. While no longer worshipped or employed to personify a moral struggle, the gods were enjoyed for their aesthetic qualities. By this stage, according to Lewis, "the gods must be as it were, disinfected of belief; the last taint of the sacrifice, and of the urgent practical interest, the selfish prayer, must be washed away from them, before that other divinity can come to light in the imagination."[45] But here Lewis confines his interest to a particular literary fate of the old gods. As already noted, Jung describes another revival of a metaphysical world in the archetypes of the subconscious mind.[46]

What Jung terms a "rebirth of the Platonic spirit" may herald a further type of allegorical usage. This kind of metaphysic is based, not on belief in a pagan divine pantheon, but on the detection of motifs in the likeness of the old gods in a subjectivist inner world. There is a possibility, however, that such motifs, if projected as "symbols for divine mystery," may gain a certain credibility in themselves.[47] It is here that Ricoeur's remark about "dogmatic mythology" would appear relevant. According to Ricoeur, there is a Gnostic trajectory in which "represented materiality" is "transmuted into a pretended knowing where the letter of the image becomes solidified."[48]

Let us compare the direction of the moral revolution in late antiquity with the kind of approach recommended by McFague. Firstly the gods are dethroned. McFague states a similar wish to "break the hegemony" of the metaphor "God the father." The method is the same: the gods and "God the father" are demythologized. Secondly, there is in both cases an impetus of "remythologizing." The literary movement towards personification of human passions seems to have developed separately from

---

45. Lewis, *Allegory of Love*, 83.

46. Jung, *Aspects of the Feminine*, 122; cf. 119.

47. Cf. Johnson, *She Who Is*, 46–47. In stating that "the concrete, historical reality of women, affirmed as blessed by God, functions as symbol in speech about God," Johnson appeals to Ricoeur's axiom: "the symbol gives rise to thought." One might reply that, in Johnson's notion, the *thought* of "the concrete, historical reality of women affirmed as blessed by God" gives rise to feminist *symbolism* for God. The process is the reverse of that advocated by Ricoeur.

48. Reagan and Stewart, *The Philosophy of Paul Ricoeur*, 47.

the Gnostic trajectory described by Ricoeur. Whether this separation is likely to be sustained by McFague's method may be open to question. Her models of God as mother, lover or friend might take one direction while "the world as God's body," refashioned as "Nature which is," might take another. It is the validity of the method of demythologizing and "remythologizing" which is, to my mind, of most concern.

A LINGUISTIC MISTAKE?

I turn now to a further set of criteria against which McFague claims to test what constitutes a "better" metaphor. "Is it better," she asks, "in terms of coherence, comprehensibility, and illumination?"[49] In asking this question, one must be aware of the parameters that govern her kind of thinking. McFague states that her model-metaphors constitute "a bit of nonsense." Turbayne states that the operation of metaphor resembles what Gilbert Ryle calls a category-mistake: "the presentation of the facts of one category in the idioms appropriate to another."[50] Turbayne goes on to describe Ryle's definition of a category-mistake as "basic to [Ryle's] correction of the dominant modern theory of mind." Ryle's method of correcting the modern theory of "mind" is to demythologize "mind," as will be considered below.

In the Introduction, I drew attention to a historical tendency in Western thinking to demythologize the external universe. Lewis outlines this history:

> The process whereby man has come to know the universe is from one point of view extremely complicated; from another it is alarmingly simple. We can observe a single one-way progression. At the outset the universe appears packed with will, intelligence, life and positive qualities; every tree is a nymph and every planet a god. Man himself is akin to the gods. The advance of knowledge gradually empties this rich and genial universe: first of its gods, then of its colours, smells, sounds and tastes, finally of solidity itself as solidity was originally imagined. As these items are taken from the world, they are transferred to the subjective side of the account: classified as our sensations, thoughts, images or emotions.[51]

49. McFague, *Models of God*, 70.
50. Turbayne cites Ryle, *The Concept of Mind*, 8. (See *The Myth of Metaphor*, 12.)
51. Lewis, "The Empty Universe," 81.

Metaphor or Better-For? 209

But this is not the end of the matter. Lewis continues:

> The same method which has emptied the world now proceeds to empty ourselves. The masters of the method soon announce that we were just as mistaken (and mistaken in much the same way) when we attributed 'souls', or 'selves' or 'minds' to human organisms, as when we attributed Dryads to trees . . . Just as the Dryad is a 'ghost', an abbreviated symbol for all the facts we know about the tree foolishly mistaken for a mysterious entity over and above the facts, so man's 'mind' or 'consciousness' is an abbreviated symbol for certain verifiable facts about his behaviour: a symbol mistaken for a thing.[52]

Lewis is offering a general description of a certain way of thinking. He does not use the term "category-mistake" but it seems that this is the sort of understanding he has in mind.

"For we are given to understand that our mistake was a linguistic one," continues Lewis. "All our previous theologies, metaphysics, and psychologies were a by-product of our bad grammar":

> What we thought we were loving when we loved a woman or a friend was not even a phantom like the phantom sail which starving sailors think they see on the horizon. . . . It is as though a man, deceived by the linguistic similarity between 'myself' and 'my spectacles', should start looking round for his 'self' to put in his pocket before he left his bedroom in the morning: he might want it during the course of the day. If we lament the discovery that our friends have no 'selves' in the old sense, we shall be behaving like a man who shed bitter tears at being unable to find his 'self' anywhere on the dressing-table or even underneath it.[53]

This is the kind of understanding which seems to come to the fore in Turbayne's description of Ryle's *The Concept of Mind*. "In it," says Turbayne, "Ryle corrects a category-mistake. This mistake is mind-body dualism or 'the dogma of the Ghost in the Machine.'"[54]

Mind-body dualism is overcome at the expense of mind. The mind as an entity is said to be a category-mistake because, as Turbayne reports, it "represents the facts of mental life as if they belonged to one logical

---

52. Lewis, "The Empty Universe," 81–82.
53. Lewis, 'The Empty Universe', 82–83.
54. Turbayne, *The Myth of Metaphor*, 62.

type or category (or range of types or categories), when they actually belong to another."[55] Turbayne continues:

> [Ryle] notices that in the official or mistaken theory such entities as the will, volition, vanity and the mind are regarded as mental existents, some of which cause effects in the physical realm. Thus the impulse of vanity causes acts of boasting, while the mind itself exists in order to house impulses, volitions, and other incidents. These entities Ryle exposes as myths or occult qualities on a parity with phlogiston, vital force etc. . . . For example, the sentence, 'He boasted from Vanity,' which suggests that Vanity itself exists and caused his acts of boasting, is interpreted in terms of what might be called 'The Law of Vanity,' which explains particular occurrences called acts of boasting. This "Law," having been induced from, is testable by, observables.[56]

"Vanity" is capitalized here, presumably to indicate that it has been artificially personified. It is then demythologized. "Vanity" itself does not exist. Only the acts of boasting which are "testable by observables" can be said to exist. Correcting the "mistake" consists in reducing "Vanity" to the physical occurrences from which it was induced. "Vanity" is consequently identified as a projection of the physical occurrences.

This procedure would seem in one sense an extension of the old type of allegory, described in the section above. "Vanity" is no longer an allegorical character projected by the mind but "mind" itself is exposed as an allegorical house accommodating the allegorical figure (Vanity) which is projected by acts of boasting. Turbayne goes so far as to claim that Ryle's demythologizing method is incomplete. Ryle, he says, "proceeds to identify . . . new entities, specifically dispositions, propensities, or tendencies. Vanity is identical with a disposition to boast, etc., and the name 'my mind' 'signifies my ability and proneness to do certain sorts of things.'"[57] Turbayne critiques this depiction on the grounds that it claims an exemption from the method of demythologizing. Dispositions, says Turbayne, "might turn out to be just as ghostly as substances and other occult forces."[58]

55. Turbayne cites Ryle, *The Concept of Mind*, 16. (See *The Myth of Metaphor*, 62.)

56. Turbayne, *The Myth of Metaphor*, 63.

57. Turbayne cites Ryle, *The Concept of Mind*, 168. (See *The Myth of Metaphor*, 64.)

58. See Turbayne, *The Myth of Metaphor*, 64.

In this kind of thinking, says Lewis, "the [human] 'mind' or 'consciousness' is an abbreviated symbol for certain verifiable facts about [human] behaviour: a symbol mistaken for a thing." Lewis sums up the consequence of this:

> And thus we arrive at a result uncommonly like zero. While we were reducing the world to almost nothing we deceived ourselves with the fancy that all its lost qualities were being kept safe (if in a somewhat humbled condition) as 'things in our own mind'. Apparently we had no mind of the sort required. The Subject is as empty as the Object. Almost nobody has been making mistakes about almost nothing. By and large, this is the only thing that has ever happened.[59]

Lewis states that Hume is the "great ancestor" of this kind of thinking.[60] This is not to say (and Lewis is not arguing) that this conclusion is a necessary progression of the rules of logic. Ryle's depiction of the "category-mistake" of mind-body dualism might be open to question on this score. One might ask how Ryle's "particular occurrences" can be tested by observation if both the subject and the object are reduced to almost nothing.

Turbayne's critique of Ryle might seem to endorse a kind of infinite regress in which subjectivity is endlessly demythologized but Turbayne turns it in a different direction. As already seen, he recommends the conscious acceptance of the "mistake." One cannot avoid using model-metaphors but one can try to be aware of what one is doing. "One condition of the use of metaphor is awareness," he says. "More accurately speaking, this means *more* awareness, for we can never become wholly aware."[61] Put in terms of Lewis' description, Turbayne admits that the universe and "mind" are empty but claims the liberty to repopulate them on his own (enlightened) terms. He does not explain the possibility of consciousness on such demythologized terms.

---

59. Lewis, "The Empty Universe," 83.

60. See Lewis, "The Empty Universe," 84. Lewis says that this philosophy is difficult for our minds to sustain and adds that Hume "warned us not to try. He recommended backgammon instead; and freely admitted that when, after a suitable dose, we returned to our theory, we should find it 'cold, strained and ridiculous.'" Lewis cites Hume, *A Treatise of Human Nature*, Book 1, Part iv, section vii. Cf. chapter 1, "Knocking over the screen" for Turbayne's account of Hume's argument to dismantle the metaphor "God is a builder."

61. Turbayne, *The Myth of Metaphor*, 64.

Let us pause here. I am trying to address what happens if McFague's understanding of what constitutes a "better" metaphor is assessed in terms of coherence, comprehensibility and illumination. The parallels between her method and Turbayne's in the notion of "better" metaphors are revisited below. It is important to first be clear about the method itself and the function of demythologizing and "remythologizing." I have already noted a similarity between the exposure of the mind as a symbol of verifiable facts about human behavior and the exposure of the old gods as allegorical projections. In both cases this is a demythologizing exercise. In both cases the symbol is understood to have constituted a mistake if taken in a non-allegorical sense.

Let us now consider what McFague calls "remythologizing." If one accepts as a premise that the symbol is a mere allegory and then redeploys it as if it were the thing itself, one has parted company with the canons of coherence, comprehensibility and illumination as commonly recognized. The degree to which one parts company with these canons would seem dependent on how far one travels. It is one thing to demythologize the old gods and another to demythologize "mind." But "remythologizing" on the premise of a conscious mistake would be an *ab initio* parting of the ways.

There is, however, a complicating factor. Conscious "remythologizing" is not sustainable. In Turbayne's parlance, "we can never become wholly aware." At the level of unawareness, it could be added, we might fall into the error of claiming coherence, comprehensibility and illumination for our redeployed symbols. This could perhaps open the door to a new epistemology along the lines of what Ricoeur calls "rationalizing symbols as such" which is, he says, the "temptation of gnosis."[62]

McFague's method follows a similar direction to Turbayne's. The danger in religious and scientific metaphors, she warns, is that they will be "identified with reality."[63] In other words the "symbol" (or model) would be mistaken for the thing. Like Turbayne, McFague offers new models while at the same time endorsing an attitude of awareness about their lack of claimed reference. Both agree that it is not possible to avoid using metaphors. Given their understanding of metaphor, this is tantamount to saying that one can never say anything at an ontological level. At its most rigorous, the method would not allow any other valid discourse.

---

62. Reagan and Stewart, *The Philosophy of Paul Ricoeur*, 46.
63. McFague, *Metaphorical Theology*, 41.

But neither Turbayne nor McFague operates at that extreme. Far from demythologizing "mind," McFague endorses subjectivity. "What we *know*," she says, "are the metaphors or projections of the self, the worlds it creates . . . a moderate Kantianism (and we are all, one way or another, Kantians) insists that in a sense . . . all theology, philosophy, physics, and art is autobiography."[64]

Like Ryle, McFague wishes to overcome mind-body dualism. Unlike Ryle (and Turbayne) she does not proceed along the lines of demythologizing "mind." Rather, she consciously enters the territory of one of her projections. Here she follows Turbayne. But the content of McFague's ecological model undermines the model-maker. She writes:

> There is at least one significant difference that I need to emphasize between the "I" of classic Western religious autobiography and the self in the ecological model: the former epitomizes the humanist essentialist self that deconstruction has so roundly criticized, while the latter is, *by definition*, social. As I have emphasized throughout, the ecological self is a construction by other human selves as well as a myriad of natural contexts and influences. Thus, the private/public split or the individual/social dualism of the humanist essentialist split does not apply to the ecological self.[65]

The ecological self is part of the ecological model. The ecological self critiques an individual/social (or mind-body) dualism premised on the humanist essentialist (or Kantian) self which insists that in a sense all theology, philosophy, physics, and art is autobiography. But this is not the end of the matter because, in her capacity of moderate Kantian, McFague warns against identifying the ecological model with reality.

How far can one travel if the grounds on which one attempts to stand cancel each other out? McFague's ecological model sides with the tradition of deconstruction. Chapter 5 suggested a similarity between the thinking of deconstructionist poet-philosopher Rimbaud and what McFague terms "the most basic sense of self" said to be "in touch" with the natural world. At the same time deconstruction criticizes the humanist essentialist self with the result that subjectivity is undermined. The notion of an infinite regress in which subjectivity is endlessly demythologized is reminiscent of an emphasis on an infinite regress in which

---

64. McFague, *Speaking in Parables*, 147–48.
65. McFague, *Super, Natural Christians*, 199 n. 30.

metaphor is endlessly deconstructed. At these points the traditions of demythologizing (and "remythologizing") and deconstruction would seem to converge. Although she does not go so far as to canvas an infinite regress of subjectivity, I believe the method recommended by McFague has the potential to sit with relative ease at the point of convergence.

In the absence of "mind" or "the humanist essentialist self," the arguments for an infinite regress do not explain the possibility of being able to promote an argument. What McFague calls the "ecological self" exhibits a similar ambiguity. This sense of self operates within the model of "the world as God's body" in which, she suggests, human beings "might be seen as partners in creation, as the self-conscious, reflexive part of the creation that could participate in furthering the process."[66] Here the self-conscious Kantian functions *within* the model. What is the status of the Kantian self in such a context? What McFague calls "the common creation story" is of no assistance in this respect since it does not explain the shift of focus from material evolution to self-conscious reflection.

A sense of self in such a state of flux is not conducive to a sense of identity. Added to this is the loss of epistemology. There is a key difference between the demythologizing of late antiquity and demythologizing "God the father." Philosophically, metaphysics was not deconstructed in late antiquity since belief in the old gods was replaced by belief in the Judeo-Christian God. Here, as McFague reports, is the source of validation, and connection in and with the cosmos.[67] The loss of this footing may serve to explain the intensity of a postmodern search for identity. At the same time McFague notes a further destabilizing influence. She writes: "But deconstruction's critique makes clear the necessity of developing 'negative capability'—the ability to endure absence, uncertainty, partiality, relativity and to hold at bay the desire for closure, coherence, identity, totality." She adds: "It is a call 'to put away childish things' and grow up."[68] Perhaps, however, we do not need to "grow up" in this sense yet. Here I suspect that Turbayne (and McFague) offer some temporary, if spurious, relief.

This section began by citing one of McFague's areas of judging what she means by a "better" metaphor. Far from supplying coherence, comprehensibility, and illumination, the hallmark of her kind of thinking

---

66. McFague, *The Body of God*, 105.
67. See McFague, *Speaking in Parables*, 106.
68. McFague, *Models of God*, 25–26.

would appear to be ambiguity, if not absurdity. On the one hand, the metaphor, "the world as God's body" is a key source of ethics for McFague. On the other, like any other model, this metaphor is "a bit of nonsense." The "God" of the metaphor is not to be confused with the living God: that would be to mistake the symbol for the thing. Having in this sense demythologized the metaphor, McFague is at liberty to use the symbol (or model) independently of the thing. Both she and Turbayne recognize the linguistic error intrinsic to their endeavor. They are then free to go on making it, to plant "better" metaphors in the fruitful territory of illusion.

LOOKING OUTWARDS

What if the notion that metaphor is a "bit of nonsense" or a variant of a "category-mistake" is itself mistaken? What if the mistake about the "mistake" arises from the kind of mind-body dualism which countenances a dichotomy of outlooks from existentialism to materialism? What if the alleged "bit of nonsense" belongs to a frame of reference in which all our thinking would be nonsensical? What if such notions as a "bit of nonsense" and "materialism" fail to acknowledge the only frame of reference which would offer them validity? In terms of ontological access, McFague states that "there is no innocent eye."[69] In saying this, she also admits that the dominant "Kantian" self is by no means dethroned since it is the "Kantian" self which governs what the eye sees.

One must bear in mind that "Kantian" in this context is a misnomer. Broadly speaking, the Enlightenment era retained a metaphysical source of validation. Turbayne reports that Descartes' *Meditations* provided the foundations of his physics:

> For the same reason that an atheist can infer he is awake but can never be certain, so he cannot be certain of the existence of material objects and thus of the premises of physics. This certainty must come from God the non-deceiver, and His certainty must come from metaphysical proof. This the *Meditations* provided.[70]

---

69. McFague, *Super, Natural Christians*, 32.

70. Turbayne indicates that his source for the remark about lack of certainty for an atheist is Descartes, *Third Replies*. (See *The Myth of Metaphor*, 36.) In the attached footnote (n. 14) Turbayne adds: "The objector was Hobbes."

Certainty of the premise and some degree of "innocence" in observation go hand in hand, otherwise the inferences of physics are not open to correction by the observed behavior of material objects.[71]

Both Turbayne and McFague stop short of doubting the existence of material objects; they both appear to share positivist presuppositions in this respect. But to state that there is no innocent eye is to query access to the physical world. Further, this way of thinking leaves out the aspect of metaphorical reference in which, as Ricoeur claims, "a reality comes to language." The method does not engage with its own consequences. The arguments assume a loss of innocence and proceed accordingly.

In exposing the lack of innocence, Turbayne and McFague draw the moral: we must be constantly aware of the nonsense in our formulations. But they also look for "better pictures or better metaphors" to the extent that "when the 'initiated' say 'it is not true,' one is able to answer by acting *as if* it were true."[72] At this point metaphor becomes "better-for." McFague gives her style of "better-for" a metaphysical aura in linking it with "metaphorical theology." She admits to a feminist agenda. That is the "Kantian" eye at work. She also pursues an ecological agenda. In this she travels far in acting *as if* it were true, so far in fact that the loss of innocence might be in danger of being overlooked.

As part of her journey into the realm of the "as if," McFague wishes to learn from the medieval approach. "The culture of the Middle Ages was extroverted, not introverted," she says, "people looked outward to find signs of God in nature, rather than inward to find the divine within themselves."[73] It is this kind of looking outwards, however, which the so-called Kantian, or, rather, the existentialist, eye does not permit. McFague states that she is an "erstwhile Barthian" and here, I think, she reveals her existentialist roots. While differing from each other, Barth and Bultmann are alike in directing focus away from the world. McFague wishes to counteract this lack of engagement but her "better pictures" only operate *as if* they look outwards. It is ironic that McFague's kind of moral relativism, far from leading to engagement with, and preservation of, the natural world is likely, according to Lewis, to end our species (ironic that is, unless the end of our species might be considered to the world's advantage.)

71. Cf. chapter 3.

72. See Turbayne, *The Myth of Metaphor*, 217. Turbayne cites Stewart, *The Myths of Plato*. Cf. McFague, *Models of God*, 192 n. 37.

73. McFague, *Super, Natural Christians*, 53.

I believe that, in writing about "metaphor" as no more than a picture, McFague misses an opportunity. It is Ricoeur's notion that "a reality comes to language" which provides the means to look outwards.[74] The linguistic function of metaphor needs to be rediscovered. Lewis writes that "the truth ... won by metaphor [cannot] be greater than the truth of the metaphor itself."[75] Not all metaphors are equal in this respect but access to truth depends on reliable metaphors. The difficulty here is that McFague wishes to "break the hegemony" of the metaphor "God the father." At the same time she admits that the classical metaphor of transfer is premised on the notion that "God is somehow the true and original father, that all things are connected among themselves because they are connected in God."[76] In demoting this metaphor, McFague removes the branch on which she aspires to stand: if all things are not connected in God, how can they be connected among themselves? In removing the branch the ability to look outwards is undermined, hence the mind-body dualism noted above.

To rediscover the function of metaphor in Ricoeur's sense does not of course imply an uncritical acceptance of the medieval cosmos. Chapter 9 sketched a possibility of a new "sacramentalism" in which God would be known not as the unmoved mover of a medieval hierarchy but as the interactive God of the Judeo-Christian tradition. McFague might object to this on the score that a Judeo-Christian tradition would exclude other traditions. She posits what she calls "parabolic christology" which allows other religions to "make the claim that they also contain metaphorical expressions of divine reality."[77] But, on her terms, this is to confine divine reality to finding the divine within ourselves and our projections. On these terms other religions would be accommodated in a kind of internalized *pax Romana*. Lewis outlines a more outward-looking approach to other religions in his list of similarities in their ethical content. He describes the broad common ground of ethics as the "Tao."[78]

It is ironic that, in relativizing the Judeo-Christian tradition, McFague strengthens her reliance on the Hellenic side of the Western heritage with its existentialist, if not nihilistic, outworking. By contrast,

---

74. See Ricoeur, *The Rule of Metaphor*, 253–54.
75. See Lewis, "Bluspels and Flalansferes," 50.
76. See McFague, *Speaking in Parables*, 106
77. McFague, *Metaphorical Theology*, 51.
78. See Lewis, *The Abolition of Man*, 49–59.

I would suggest a fresh appraisal of our dual heritage in its Hellenic and Middle Eastern roots. The conversation between Mascall and the followers of Buber, touched on in Chapter 9, about the "I-it" and "I-Thou" approach to the world could offer a useful starting-point. It is in this context that I would hope for a rediscovery of the function of metaphor, as espoused by Ricoeur, in its twin aspects of creation and discovery. It is in this context that I would hope for an ethical approach to the natural world, something which I believe Lewis aspires to in *The Abolition of Man*:

> Is it . . . possible to imagine a new Natural Philosophy, continually conscious that the 'natural object' produced by analysis and abstraction is not reality but only a view, and always correcting the abstraction? I hardly know what I am asking for. . . . The regenerate science which I have in mind would not do even to minerals and vegetables what modern science threatens to do to man himself. When it explained it would not explain away. When it spoke of the parts it would remember the whole. While studying the *It* it would not lose what Martin Buber calls the *Thou*-situation.[79]

Lewis casts doubt on too easy an assumption of the innocent eye. But his cure is not to look inwards for a "better picture" but to look outwards towards Buber's "Thou-situation" which is anchored in the sacramental universe.

---

79. Lewis, *The Abolition of Man*, 47.

Conclusion

'One of my greatest fears was the Witches, for while I had no magical powers at all I soon found out that the Witches were really able to do wonderful things. There were four of them in this country, and they ruled the people who live in the North and South and East and West. Fortunately, the Witches of the North and South were good, and I knew they would do me no harm; but the Witches of the East and West were terribly wicked, and had they not thought I was more powerful than they themselves, they would surely have destroyed me.'[1]

THE WIZARD OF THE novel accepts an external morality. Good and evil cannot be redefined to suit his sensibility or that of the inhabitants of the City of Oz because good and evil have an existence beyond the bounds of the Emerald City. The good witches are not dangerous. The evil witches are a real threat. It is because they are evil that two of the witches wish to destroy the old man. It is because they are witches that they have the power to destroy him. In the story morality and reality go hand in hand.

When confronted with this threat the old man who has no magical powers resorts to trickery. The Scarecrow tells him that he ought to be ashamed of himself for being a "humbug" and Dorothy says that she thinks he is a very bad man. The old man denies that he is a bad man but

---

1. Baum, *The Wizard of Oz*, chapter 15.

admits that he is a very bad wizard. His devices can be explained. They have no real effect. The magic of the witches cannot be explained but produces real effects.

The contrast between scientifically verifiable trickery and the real power of creatures of fanciful mythology is reminiscent of Ricoeur's distinction between first and second-order linguistic reference. Philibert says of Ricoeur's understanding that poetic language suspends, and "builds on the ruins of," ordinary reference. Ordinary language "obeys our interest for control, manipulation, pragmatic activities." Poetic language has a second-order reference which is "actually our fundamental, first-order reference, and expresses our ontological belonging to life, to beings, to the world, to Being."[2]

The second-order reference of poetic or metaphorical language is intuitive as is its underlying first-order epistemology of ontological belonging. In her quest to fill the vacuum of the demythologizing movement, I find that McFague leaves out this intuitive element. It is because she leaves it out that her project does not go beyond the Wizard's counterfeit. For McFague, metaphors and models are constructs or pictures arising "largely [from] a functional, pragmatic view of truth."[3] This view of truth has a moral purpose: it stresses the implications of "certain ways of seeing things" with the aim to promote "the quality of human and non-human life." The ways of seeing invoke a God who "is on the side of life and its fulfillment" but the perspective does not go beyond ordinary reference with its interest in control, manipulation, pragmatism. There is no ontological belonging "to life, to beings, to the world, to Being" as outlined by Ricoeur in such thinking. McFague's quest for belonging is of a different ilk.

The Wizard of Oz presents two different kinds of magic. In describing the operation of metaphor, McFague appeals to the wizard's trickery. But there is a different kind. One does not have to be a witch to achieve wonderful things. This kind of wonder builds on the ordinary, as metaphor builds on the ruins of literal reference. In the writings of Ricoeur, Lewis, Tolkien, perhaps even in McFague's account of nature writing, I find a wonder as prosaic and as magical as that of a little girl and her dog. McFague wants to retain this kind of magic while denying its source but this magic cannot be kept on such terms. This kind of magic takes

---

2. Philibert, "Ricoeur as the Singer of Ruins," 133.
3. See McFague, *Models of God*, 192 n. 37.

traditional morality as a matter of course. In the story, even the supposed wizard subscribes to traditional morality. It is he who points out that courage is based on action, not feeling.

In this book we have been on a journey with parallels to Dorothy's journey in the Land of Oz. We have attempted to follow in McFague's footsteps since it is she who takes us to the Emerald City in the first place. I have described McFague's journey as a quest. As I judge, her enthusiasm to "remythologize Christianity" aims to turn us away from the desert lands of demythologizing and waft us magically into a land of milk and honey. In this kind of journey "metaphor" is the means to reconnect with reality and even with God, albeit not the God of tradition. In this land the old dichotomy of soul and body will be a thing of the past. One might suppose that ontological belonging in Ricoeur's sense would be a keynote of the journey. But this is precisely what McFague leaves out. Her journey begins in the wrong place. The green spectacles are a way of seeing, a trick which can be explained. The green spectacles represent McFague's notion of metaphor but it is not the real thing. This is the land of illusion.

McFague goes so far as to posit a loss for modern people of the intimate encounters of childhood. It is here, despite her claims to the contrary, that her divergence from Ricoeur would appear at its strongest. When Ricoeur writes of "a second naiveté" he envisages the bricks and mortar of language. In McFague's hands, Ricoeur's phrase comes to signify a distinction between the first naiveté of childhood in contrast with the interpretive paradigm of adulthood. For McFague, adults can only strive in various secondary ways for a lost intimacy with the cosmos; adults cannot walk, as children do, on the Yellow Brick Road. By her own admission, McFague's distinction between adults and children is a recent one. She states that the phrase, a second naiveté refers to "the possibility of returning to the most basic roots of our being by a conscious informed root when the intuitive acceptance found in our youth and the youth of the human community is no longer possible for us."[4] Not for McFague the biblical understanding that whoever does not receive the kingdom of God like a little child shall not enter it.[5]

Have we really lost the sacramental universe or do we just think we have? Does not the nostalgia of deconstructionist writers for a vanished world of "truths of substance" and "linguistic sacramentalism"

---

4. McFague, *The Body of God*, 247 n. 28. McFague states that the phrase "a second naiveté" is Ricoeur's. I argue that her definition misrepresents Ricoeur. See chapter 8.

5. See Luke 18:17.

bear witness to its persistent appeal? One might ask the same question of McFague's wish to borrow from a frame of reference which she rejects. Is there a rightness of the imagination, expressing our ontological belonging to life, a psycho-physical parallelism (or more) in the universe? A rightness of the imagination supplies the link between ontology and ethics. Its instrument is metaphor. McFague wants to replicate this sense of connection in a "sacred world order." But hers is a constructed world. The link with reality is severed.

Both McFague and Turbayne acknowledge the linguistic importance of metaphor but on what terms? Lewis writes that the truth won by metaphor cannot be greater than the truth of the metaphor itself. For Turbayne and McFague, metaphor is a "mistake" or "bit of nonsense." Admittedly, McFague wishes the "bit of nonsense" to make sense in terms of contemporary science and the Christian faith. To my mind, her attempt to make sense out of a bit of nonsense resembles Barthian Protestant's assertion that nonsense can be given sense by a sheer act of divine omnipotence. I have asked whether McFague situates the indirect mediation of interpretation in a place similar, in terms of method, to that of Barth's saga. If McFague advocates taking a bit of nonsense and placing it in its immediate relation *pro nobis*, does it not follow that epistemology for "modern people" operates through a sheer act of existentialist omnipotence?

The truth (or otherwise) won by metaphor is at the heart of the discussion. McFague draws attention to "the contemporary crisis of language" which, she says, "both elevated the importance of metaphorical language and, on the part of theologians as well as of others, made us painfully aware of its limitations, so much aware that the desire to escape is at times irresistible."[6] She cites Iris Murdoch: "We can no longer take language for granted as a medium of communication. Its transparency is gone. We are like people who for a long time looked out of a window without noticing the glass—and then one day began to notice this too."[7] McFague is very conscious of the glass. Metaphors, in her thinking, are productive of reality.[8] She claims that metaphorical language "knows no subjective-objective split,"[9] but the kind of linguistic reconciliation which she has in mind occurs in a constructed space. "To see the form

---

6. McFague, *Speaking in Parables*, 35.
7. See McFague, *Speaking in Parables*, 27.
8. McFague, *Models of God*, 26.
9. McFague, *Speaking in Parables*, 32.

of theological reflection in metaphorical terms takes the Kantian limits seriously," says McFague. "There is no way *around* the metaphor."[10] The window glass of language defines the view as the green glasses define the view of the Emerald City.

This book has offered a critique of McFague's notion of metaphor and drawn attention to its negative consequences. On the positive side, McFague has opened up many useful avenues of enquiry. Not least of these is the status of what she calls the Kantian limits and the effect of such limits on the sciences. To my mind, her project to overcome the subject-object dichotomy straddles the existentialist-positivist dichotomy on subjectivist terms. Where in such thinking is the logical status of "hard-nosed" evolutionary theory? Is it not largely accommodated *within* "the contemporary picture of reality" supposedly coming from "the sciences of its day"?[11]

McFague writes of "the radical limits of language and the possibility of dealing with those limits in metaphorical language."[12] In this context she locates Bultmann in a "subjective cul-de-sac" and in some sense purports to offer a way out of it.[13] Yet her constructed world order still belongs in an existentialist cul-de-sac, coming close perhaps to its subjectivist extreme. Conceivably, however, the end of the subjectivist cul-de-sac, while far removed in terms of access, may be close, in terms of distance, to the world outside. The reverberations of the world may be clearer here, hence the nostalgia for it. One cannot find a way out of a cul-de-sac without significant retracing of steps. But one must first get one's bearings. While it may be less than helpful as a staging-post out of "the contemporary crisis of language," McFague's project offers an excellent listening-post for the causes of the crisis. What McFague overhears is perhaps best retold in terms of *The Wizard of Oz*. But I will take further liberties with the story.

If McFague's project resides in a cul-de-sac which is close but without access to the Main Road, its position may be said to resemble that of the Deadly Poppy Field which is tantalizingly close to the Yellow Brick Road. The Deadly Poppy Field is the Land of the "as if." The Deconstructionist River laps its shores. There are backwaters here of Jungian archetypes and

---

10. McFague, *Speaking in Parables*, 33.
11. See McFague, *The Body of God*, 66.
12. See McFague, *Speaking in Parables*, 33–34.
13. McFague, *Speaking in Parables*, 34.

"the common creation story" with its superimposed counter-ethic. From the vantage point among the poppies one may observe the meandering course of the river, upstream and downstream.

Up river beyond the Yellow Brick Road is the far view of medieval sacramentalism. It looks calm and peaceful, at least from a distance. One can see the remains of a bridge that once spanned the river. As the eye travels downstream, one sees the rocks and cascades of upheaval until one reaches the place where the river divides in two. This is the place of post-Cartesian epistemologies. Parts of the old bridge must have been carried here by the historic force of the water. Now they form two islands around which the waters swirl and eddy. The islands are called Positivism and Existentialism. A new form of "horizontal sacramentalism" seeks to construct an integrating bridge which will cross the river by way of these islands. But, as McFague's project reminds us, this is only a bridge of the "as if." Its foundations are not solid.

By this stage the Deconstructionist River is swollen with a plethora of waters, including those gritty with the sand of demythologizing. The river has deposited temporary shoals of sand beside the Land of the "as if." These shoals offer a salutary reminder to those who live there. One may inhabit the "as if." At the same time one must be aware of its deceptive potential. But only the initiated are aware of the deception and the state of awareness is of no assistance in reaching the Yellow Brick Road. In fact, McFague's project has set its face against the Yellow Brick Road along with the narrow footbridge of metaphorical transfer which still offers a means to cross the river for those who have eyes to see it. McFague's project does not offer the initiated a place of residence beyond the Land of the "as if." The shoals of sand have a tendency to break up underfoot. There is always the possibility of being transported downstream as the river travels towards a nihilistic sea.

While McFague's project does not engage directly with the nihilistic sea an appraisal of her work must take that prospect with due seriousness. McFague's "metaphorical theology" joins forces with the feminist agenda to break the "hegemony over the Western religious consciousness" supplied by the model "God the father."[14] This agenda constitutes a radical exercise in demythologizing, more radical than the type of demythologizing espoused by Bultmann, because what McFague describes as "a hegemony over the Western religious consciousness" is the source

---

14. McFague, *Metaphorical Theology*, 29.

of connection with the cosmos. McFague admits this. "The metaphor of association or transference," she says, "seems to rest on a confidence that . . . God is somehow the true and original father, that all things are connected among themselves because they are connected in God."[15] In wishing to demythologize the metaphor "God the father," McFague's "metaphorical theology" poses a challenge both to metaphor (along with its effect on language in general) and to ontology. The shifting sands of relativism compromise the validity of the feminist agenda. There is nowhere to stand. One must take seriously the remark by Irigaray's editor, that postmodernism poses a challenge to identity and subjectivity.[16] One must soberly contemplate Graham's observation that Irigaray's attempts to construct female "bodies" risk being "immaterial and rhetorical, rather than empirical and rooted in social relations."[17] The connection with reality is severed. I will return to the real questions posed by the feminist movement below.

McFague states that "to imagine the world as God's body is to do precisely that: to imagine it that way."[18] In the course of her project, the imaginary picture of the "world as God's body" becomes a "subject-subjects model" or "functional cosmology" for how Christians should love nature.[19] She wishes to impose her imaginary picture onto the relationship between God and the world. I have suggested that she may owe something to Barth in her wish to superimpose her "better" models onto an otherwise remote external reality. But one may also suspect that the procedure is intrinsic to the method since "better" models which make no claim to ontological validity can only operate in this arbitrary manner. This kind of thinking promises a form of ethics which is divorced from an external ontology and epistemology and can only be deployed *within* the model. What then of the hermeneutic of suspicion *towards* the model?

I stated above that McFague's project offers insight into the causes of what she calls "the contemporary crisis of language." But in failing to engage directly with the prospect of nihilism, McFague herself would seem less than aware of the implications of her project. She does not pursue these possibilities, I believe, because the allure of the "as if" is

15. McFague, *Speaking in Parables*, 106.
16. Whitford, *The Irigaray Reader*, 12–13.
17. Graham, *Making the Difference*, 137–38.
18. McFague, *Models of God*, 61.
19. See McFague, *Super, Natural Christians*, 2–3.

at the heart of her project. She looks to its "remythologizing" aspect to restore warmth and color to what Tyrrell calls "the cold constructions of intellectualism."[20] But her pictures do more than feed a starved imagination. They persuade the imagination to take moral responsibility for the fate of humanity and the earth.[21] This is metaphor turned "better for," a prime instrument for a new rhetoric. Turbayne raises the possibility of what he calls "the full Wizardry of Oz" in which those who control the rhetoric will fool others with their devices without being fooled themselves.[22] He does not recommend this course of action. But is it avoidable?

Despite her continued reminders about the deceptive potential and, at best, temporary nature of her models I believe that McFague underestimates the practical difficulty of sustaining what I have called the Wizard's perspective. I suggested above that "modern people" might give credibility to their own models by means of existentialist fiat. I also suggested that only the initiated are sufficiently detached to be aware that they are doing this. The mind-set of the cool-headed initiate is far removed from that of the impassioned activist, too far removed for most people. Hence Lewis's prospect of a division between conditioners and conditioned cannot be ignored. Those who continue to "live within" the model are likely to forget that the epistemology belongs to the model, that nonsense has been given sense by those who control the rhetoric. In all probability the "better" ethics of the model will become for many a psychological necessity. The stage is set for confirmed inhabitants of Oz.

But perhaps it is not too late for a different outcome. Is it possible to stem the tide and divert the river? Can we travel back to the sacramental uplands, alongside McFague and deconstructionist writers, but with different eyes? The Western world inherits a linguistic tradition dating from antiquity. Steiner calls it the covenant between the word and the world. The tradition is strongly ontological. "At the outset," writes Lewis, "the universe appears packed with will, intelligence, life and positive qualities; every tree is a nymph and every planet a god."[23] The Middle Ages retains the ontological thrust of this tradition but tempers its content. Trees are no longer nymphs but message-bearers of the creator. It is this message-bearing function which underwrites what Steiner calls "presence" in

---

20. See Tyrrell, *Christianity at the Cross-Roads*, 207.
21. See McFague, *Models of God*, 21.
22. See Turbayne, *The Myth of Metaphor*, 217.
23. Lewis, "The Empty Universe," *Present Concerns*, 81.

language. The current linguistic crisis results from the loss of this sense of "presence." McFague admits that the ontological thrust is underpinned by the understanding that God is somehow the original father. Can we class McFague's opposition to this understanding as a missed opportunity?

McFague presents the model of "the world as God's body" as an alternative imaginary picture to the "monarchical model" in mainstream Christianity. She states that the "monarchical model" of the God-world relationship is dangerous for our time: the model threatens the continuation of life itself because it supports attitudes either of domination of the world or of naïvely trusting passivity rather than responsibility.[24] McFague claims that this model has had the tendency "to draw other models into its orbit, as is evident with the model of God as father."[25] But elsewhere she presents another view of God as father:

> The first thing to notice... about Jesus' characteristic address to God as "father" is not the foundation it provided for a patriarchal model to God, but its relational, personal character. It was for Jesus a term of great intimacy and affection which described his own sense of utter trust in God. Likewise, the thrust of his teachings as well as his healings was toward persons, their way of relating to others, their wholeness and health, both physical and spiritual. Most importantly, that mode was exemplified or modeled in his own person, in his dealings with the poor, with women, with outcasts, and with foreigners.[26]

McFague wishes to demythologize the metaphor "God the father" on feminist grounds, because of its alleged implications in terms of "ecclesiastical, social, political, economic and personal oppression."[27] Does she miss the opportunity of detaching the metaphor "God the father" from its political and oppressive associations?

It is the associations of the model of God as father (and not the model itself) which appear detrimental. McFague writes:

> This model could have gone in the direction of a parent (and that is clearly its New Testament course), with its associations of nurture, care, guidance, concern and self-sacrifice, but under the powerful influence of the monarchical model, the parent

---

24. See McFague, *Models of God*, 68–69.
25. McFague, *Models of God*, 66.
26. McFague, *Metaphorical Theology*, 52.
27. McFague, *Metaphorical Theology*, 29.

became the patriarch, and patriarchs act more like kings than fathers: they rule their children and they demand obedience'.[28]

McFague reports that Jürgen Moltmann objects to the "monarchical monotheism" associated with Christianity "which supports hierarchalism and individualism, and insists instead that a social, trinitarian doctrine of God is needed."[29]

The model of the parent turned patriarch is the source, says McFague, of post-medieval alienation from the world:

> The model's anthropocentrism (the other side of its lack of concern for the natural world) can be seen, for instance, in classical Protestantism's emphasis on the Word of God. The monarchical model and an aural tradition fit together naturally, for kings give orders and subjects obey, but the model has no place for creatures who cannot hear and obey.[30]

As a remedy, McFague advocates a return to what she calls a visual tradition in which it is not "just a book, the scriptures, that is special as the medium of divine presence, but the world is also God's dwelling place."[31] Ruether goes so far as to discern a similarity in this respect between McFague's view and that of an "older cosmos theology" in which the divine Logos "as Ground of Being [bodies] forth in not only human being, but all visible things."[32] An engagement with word and being in relation to the divine Logos appears in the linguistic theories of pre-Socratic philosophers, Heraclitus and Parmenides. But if McFague wishes to re-engage such thinking, where does this leave "modern people," said to be deprived of a naïve harmony with the sacred cosmos?

McFague attributes a loss of harmony with the cosmos to the scientific model of modernity. "Because we inhabit the machine model," she remarks, "we have lost the sense of belonging . . . in our world . . . and we have lost the sense that we are part of a living, changing, dynamic cosmos that has its being in and through God."[33] By contrast, McFague wishes to promote a "holistic, organic view" with which theology should be in

---

28. McFague, *Models of God*, 66.

29. See McFague, *Models of God*, 199–200 n. 7. McFague cites Moltmann, *The Trinity and the Kingdom of God*.

30. McFague, *Models of God*, 66.

31. McFague, *Models of God*, 67.

32. See McFague, *Models of God*, 200 n. 9.

33. McFague, *The Body of God*, 34.

conversation. She discerns some parallels between the organic model and the Platonic World-Soul or Logos viewed as intermediary between mind (God) and matter.[34] She goes so far as to find a similarity between her suggested "subjectification of the world" and the *anima mundi* in medieval times and the early Renaissance.[35] But her linguistic theory denies the ontology of earlier thinking. Her alleged affinity with it lacks substance. Does McFague miss the opportunity of promoting a more robust (and Judeo-Christian) Logos theology in Protestantism, along the lines suggested by Moltmann?

We have lost the sense of belonging in our world, says McFague. She attributes this to a linguistic aural tradition allied with a monarchical theological model and a scientific machine model. We might find echoes here of the various types of oppression associated with a feminist perception of the metaphor "God the father." McFague purports to find an antidote for modern isolation in the visual tradition of an older cosmos theology but such thinking did not separate the aural and the visual. McFague's endorsement of a visual tradition runs counter to her endorsement of the deconstructionist emphasis on "the absence of God over our presumptuous insistence in Western religious thought on the presence of the divine."[36] Her "metaphorical theology" tends to discard, rather than modify, the aural tradition. Ruether reports that the older cosmos theology flows into Christian sacramentalism. But this is the point of connection with the cosmos which McFague wishes to break.

How can the sense of belonging be regained? I query the usefulness of current feminist trends in this respect. I stated in the Introduction that Ruether endorses the kind of feminist thinking in which "God" is a construct of the imagination. Jantzen goes so far as to withdraw from the ontological realism of process theology as "somewhat less promising territory for the new ground of a feminist philosophy of religion intent on developing a feminist symbolic of the divine."[37] Far from promoting a sense of belonging in the world, the loss of ontological realism heralds a further movement in an inward direction. On Jantzen's terms, an "I-Thou" relationship with the world would be a chimera rather than a reality. On Jantzen's terms, the "divine" is consonant with "what we consider

---

34. See McFague, *The Body of God*, 31–32.
35. McFague, *Super, Natural Christians*, 112.
36. See McFague, *Models of God*, 195–96 n. 13.
37. Jantzen, *Becoming Divine*, 257.

most worthy and to be valued." The arrogant eye is not really dethroned in such thinking. This is the territory of the "as if" in which morality accords with a projected "divine horizon."[38] As such, the so-called "loving eye" would offer only a pseudo-abdication.

If McFague invokes an older cosmos theology on less than helpful terms this is not to devalue the possibility of an alternative approach. But something radical is at stake. It has to do with the nature of truth and meaning. Despite the appeal to an older way of thinking, the new way is very different. We have seen that the moral momentum of McFague's project is equaled by the thrust of the ontological disclaimer. The issue may lie even deeper. Lewis writes that "reason" is the "organ of truth" while "imagination" is the "organ of meaning."[39] If imagination projects its own world in defiance of ontological realism what is the result? I suspect that Lewis would not have recognized such projection as an exercise of the imagination. In writing about *The Lord of the Rings*, Lewis asks whether mythopoeia is not the least subjective of activities. It helps us, says Lewis, to "escape the illusions of our ordinary life."[40] But McFague's notion of "remythologizing" is of a different genre. This is the domain of what Ricoeur calls "demythologized myth" and Barth "anthropocentric mythology."

Truth and meaning in the old sense flow from sacramental belonging. But McFague's project has a relativistic approach to truth. Despite its emphasis on imagination, her project has a relativistic approach to meaning and redirects the imagination inwards. McFague says that her kind of theology is "not a theory to be *applied to* literary genres of the Christian tradition but a kind of reflection that arises *from* them."[41] She wishes to persuade the reader that the details of the parables and poems which she cites "can be shown to substantiate, even to demand, such an approach." I submit that this is an illusion. McFague has her ear to the door of such writings but she cannot open the door because she has intentionally thrown away its key. What her kind of myth-making does to human thought is yet to be charted.

While her theory of metaphor operates according to the "contemporary crisis of language," McFague does not seem at ease in a situation of

---

38. Jantzen, *Becoming Divine*, 269.

39. See Lewis, "Bluspels and Flalansferes," 49.

40. Lewis, "Tolkien's *The Lord of the Rings*," 115–16. Cf. the Preface to *Of This and Other Worlds*, 14, for Lewis's rejection of cheap introspection in favor of "the real imagination" of the poetry of Wordsworth.

41. See McFague, *Speaking in Parables*, 10. McFague's italics.

Conclusion 231

linguistic isolation. She comes closest to ontological engagement perhaps in her remarks about a non-linguistic base to metaphor:

> While in many ways we are the "metaphorical creature" and language is profoundly metaphorical, if we are not to absolutize metaphor we must view it as *one* way—albeit a highly suggestive and fruitful way—by which to understand particular aspects of the human being . . . I do not believe, however, that it is an adequate perspective from which to view our sensuous, affectional, and active lives at their base level. Of course, this level of human existence, when expressed and interpreted, comes under the metaphorical, but it also lies beneath it, is its funding, and is more basic than it. In a sense, we feel more than we can express, we know more than we can interpret. Metaphor deals with expression and interpretation, not with the depths of human existence that lie even beyond words . . . There are some things that lie too deep for words, among them, for instance, the touch of another human being, what occurs in human silence, the terror that can grip us in the night, or an act of human compassion. These are not metaphors but the stuff from which metaphor is made.[42]

But this kind of apprehension stops short at the base level of human experience. It does not engage the Ground of Being of all visible things.

The issue comes to a head in McFague's understanding of Ricoeur. She finds a similarity between her understanding of the non-metaphorical base for metaphor and Ricoeur's distinction between symbol and metaphor. She states that, for Ricoeur, symbols "are rooted in reality at a cosmic prelinguistic level, while metaphors are the linguistic innovation of symbols, interpreting and reinterpreting them."[43] But the kind of interpretation and reinterpretation that Ricoeur attributes to metaphor does not produce a hiatus between metaphor and its non-metaphorical base. For Ricoeur, as seen above, poetic or metaphorical language has a second-order reference which is "actually our fundamental, first-order reference, and expresses our ontological belonging to life, to beings, to the world, to Being."[44] Failing this, I have suggested that McFague's search for connection could have more affinity with Rimbaud's mind experiments.

I stated above that McFague offers a listening-post in discerning the current crisis in linguistic reference. We appear to have a choice, in terms

---

42. McFague, *Metaphorical Theology*, 36–37. McFague's italics.
43. See McFague, *Metaphorical Theology*, 202–3 n.12.
44. Philibert, "Ricoeur as the Singer of Ruins," 133.

of linguistic philosophy, between Hume's empty universe, McFague's sacred world order, and Ricoeur's sacramental sense of belonging. The first two choices are perhaps two sides of the one alternative. McFague herself does not journey very far along the route of Hume's nihilism. In the long run, however, I suspect that the twofold nature of her project straddles the empty universe and the sacred world order since the latter belongs within the model. On his own terms, Turbayne's linguistic Wizard can have no external motive for his ethical choices or even, if demythologizing is taken to its logical extreme, a solid basis of belief in his own existence.

As I judge, Lewis documented or foresaw most of these developments. But I think McFague's project adds something which Lewis did not discern. Lewis wrote about metaphor but general interest in metaphor as a key to language seems to postdate him. Lewis predicted a development in ethics which would facilitate a division of conditioners and conditioned. What he did not predict, as far as I am aware, was the role that an understanding of metaphor would seem likely to play in this. A further element is McFague's alliance with feminist thinking. Her appeals to Ricoeur could have offered a genuine way forward for a reality to return to language, had not the hermeneutic of suspicion towards the metaphor "God the father" prevented her from following that direction. Nevertheless, she opens a way for others to do so, including me.

Let us return to my reason for writing this book. I said in the Introduction that this discussion of metaphor was an unanticipated precursor to my original starting-point. I began by asking: what does it mean for a woman to be created in God's image? This brought me to the prior question of how the language of analogy functions or how metaphor works. If one demythologizes the metaphor "God the father" where does this leave the *imago Dei*? On McFague's terms, the *imago Dei* reappears only within the model. The deconstruction of epistemology overlaps a deconstruction of the subject with the risks, discerned by Irigaray, in terms of subjectivity and identity for women. I think there is an alternative to this essentially negative direction. I hope to develop the alternative in a companion volume to this book, entitled *The Metaphor of Gender*.

Bibliography

Abrams, M. H. *A Glossary of Literary Terms*. New York: Holt, Rinehart and Winston, 1966.
Augustine. *The City of God*. Translated by Henry Bettenson. London: Penguin, 1984.
———. *Confessions*. Translated by R. S. Pine-Coffin. Harmondsworth, Middlesex: Penguin, 1987.
———. *The Trinity*. Translated by Edmund Hill. New York: New City, 1991.
Barth, Karl. "Evangelical Theology in the Nineteenth Century." Translated by Thomas Wieser. In *The Humanity of God*, 11–32. London: Fontana, 1967.
———. "The Humanity of God." Translated by John Newton Thomas. In *The Humanity of God*, 33–64. London: Fontana, 1967.
———. *Church Dogmatics* I/I: *The Doctrine of the Word of God*. Translated by G. T. Thompson et al. Edinburgh: T. & T. Clark, 1960.
———. *Church Dogmatics*, III/I: *The Doctrine of Creation*. Translated by J. W. Edwards. Edinburgh: T. & T. Clark, 1958.
———. *Dogmatics in Outline*. Translated by G. T. Thomson. London: SCM, 1966.
———. *The Word of God and the Word of Man*. Translated by Douglas Horton. New York: Harper, 1957.
Baum, L. Frank. *The Wizard of Oz*. Reprint, London: Penguin, 2012.
Black, Max. *Models and Metaphors: Studies in Language and Philosophy*. Ithaca, NY: Cornell University Press, 1981.
Bonaventure, St. *The Life of St. Francis of Assisi*. Translated by E. Gurney Salter. New York: E. P. Dutton, 1904. http://www.ecatholic2000.com/bonaventure/assisi/francis.shtml (accessed Jan 14, 2022).
Bunyan, John. *The Pilgrim's Progress*, edited by Roger Sharrock. Harmondsworth, Middlesex: Penguin, 1968.
Chesterton, G. K. *St. Francis of Assisi*. Garden City, NY: Image, Doubleday, 1957.
Christensen, Michael. "We see through a glass darkly." In *C. S. Lewis on Scripture: His Thoughts on the Nature of Biblical Inspiration, the Role of Revelation, and the Question of Inerrancy*, 57–58. Nashville: Abingdon, 1989.

Derrida, Jacques, "Des Tours de Babel." In *Acts of Religion*, edited by Gil Anidjar, 102–34. New York, NY: Routledge, 2002.

Fiddes, Paul S. *Participating in God: A Pastoral Doctrine of the Trinity*. London: Darton, Longman and Todd, 2000.

Graham, Elaine. *Making The Difference: Gender, Personhood and Theology* Minneapolis: Fortress. 1996.

Hay, Denys. *The Medieval Centuries*. London: Methuen. 1967.

Hunsinger, George. *Disruptive Grace: Studies in the Theology of Karl Barth*. Grand Rapids: Eerdmanns, 2000.

Jantzen, Grace M. *Becoming Divine, Towards a Feminist Philosophy of Religion*. Manchester: Manchester University Press, 1998.

Jaspers, Bernd and Geoffrey W. Bromiley, eds. *Karl Barth–Rudolf Bultmann Letters 1922–1966*. Grand Rapids, Michigan: Eerdmanns, 1981.

Johnson, Elizabeth A. *She Who Is: The Mystery of God in Feminist Theological Discourse*. New York, NY: Crossroad, 2007.

Jung, Carl Gustav. *Aspects of the Feminine*. Translated by R. F. C. Hull. London: Routledge, 2003.

Keller, Catherine. *Face of the Deep: a Theology of Becoming*. London: Routledge, 2007.

Kidner, Derek. *Genesis: An Introduction and Commentary*. Leicester: Inter-Varsity, 1967.

Lewis, C. S. *The Abolition of Man*. London: Fount, 1978.

———. *The Allegory of Love: A Study in Medieval Tradition*. Oxford: Oxford University Press, 1958.

———. "Bluspels and Flalansferes." In *The Importance of Language*, edited by Max Black, 36–50. Englewood Cliffs, N.J.: Prentice-Hall, 1962.

———. *The Discarded Image: An Introduction to Medieval and Renaissance Literature*. Cambridge: Cambridge University Press, 1995.

———. "The Empty Universe." In *Present Concerns*, edited by Walter Hooper, 81–86. London: Fount, 1986.

———. "Fern-seed and Elephants." In *Christian Reflections*, edited by Walter Hooper, 191–208. London: Fount, 1983.

———. "The Funeral of a Great Myth." In *Christian Reflections*, edited by Walter Hooper, 110–23. London: Fount, 1983.

———. "Historicism." In *Christian Reflections*, edited by Walter Hooper, 131–46. London: Fount, 1983.

———. "The Language of Religion." In *Christian Reflections*, edited by Walter Hooper, 164–79. London: Fount, 1983.

———. *Mere Christianity*. London: Fontana, 1956.

———. "Preface." In *Of This and Other Worlds*, edited by Walter Hooper, 9–24. London: Fount, 1985.

———. "The Poison of Subjectivism." In *Christian Reflections*, edited by Walter Hooper, 98–109. London: Fount, 1983.

———. *Reflections on the Psalms*. London: Fontana, 1973.

———. "A Reply to Professor Haldane." In *Of This and Other Worlds*, edited by Walter Hooper, 97–109. London: Fount, 1985.

———. "Some Thoughts." In *First and Second Things*, edited by Walter Hooper, 91–95. London: Fount, 1986.

———. "Tolkien's *The Lord of the Rings*." In *Of This and Other Worlds*, edited by Walter Hooper, 112–21. London: Fount, 1982.

McFague, Sallie. *The Body of God: An Ecological Theology*. Minneapolis, MN: Fortress, 1993.

———. *Metaphorical Theology: Models of God in Religious Language*. Philadelphia: Fortress, 1982.

———. *Models of God: Theology for an Ecological Nuclear Age*. Philadelphia, PA: Fortress, 1987.

———. *Speaking in Parables: A Study in Metaphor and Theology*. Minneapolis: Fortress, 2007.

———. *Super, Natural Christians: How We Should Love Nature*. Minneapolis, MN: Fortress, 1997.

Martis, John. "The Self Found Elsewhere: Phenomenological Faith meets Deconstructive Doubt." *Pacifica* 22, no. 2 (2009) 198–214.

Mascall, E. L. *Existence and Analogy*. London: Darton, Longman & Todd, 1966.

———. *Words and Images: A Study in Theological Discourse*. London: Longmans, Green and Co., 1957.

Neumann, Erich. *The Great Mother: An Analysis of the Archetype*. Translated by Ralph Mannheim. Princeton, N. J.: Princeton University Press, 1974.

Parmée, Douglas, ed. *Twelve French Poets 1820–1900: An Anthology of 19th Century French Poetry*. London: Longmans, Green & Co, 1966.

Philibert, Michel. "Ricoeur as the Singer of Ruins." In *The Philosophy of Paul Ricoeur*, edited by Lewis Edwin Hahn, 127–37. Chicago: Open Court, 1995.

Prior, A. N. "Can Religion be Discussed?" In *New Essays in Philosophical Theology*, edited by Antony Flew & Alisdair MacIntyre, 1–11. London: SCM, 1963.

Reagan, Charles E. and David Stewart, eds. *The Philosophy of Paul Ricoeur: An Anthology of His Work*. Boston: Beacon, 1978.

Resch, Dustin. *Barth's Interpretation of the Virgin Birth: A Sign of Mystery*. Farnham, Surrey: Ashgate, 2012.

Ricoeur, Paul. "Biblical Hermeneutics." *Semeia* 4 (1975) 29–148.

———. *The Rule of Metaphor: Multi-disciplinary studies of the creation of meaning in language*. Translated by Robert Czerny et al. London: Routledge & Kegan Paul, 1986.

———. "Reply to Stephen T. Tyman." In *The Philosophy of Paul Ricoeur*, edited by Lewis Edwin Hahn. *The Philosophy of Paul Ricoeur*, 472–76. Chicago: Open Court, 1995.

Ruether, Rosemary Radford. "*Imago Dei*, Christian Tradition and Feminist Hermeneutics." In *The Image of God: Gender Models in Judaeo-Christian Tradition*, edited by Kari Elisabeth Børresen, 267–91. Minneapolis: Fortress, 1995.

Smith, James K. A. *Jacques Derrida: Live Theory*. London: Continuum, 2005.

Steiner, George. *Real Presences*. London: Faber and Faber, 1991.

Thiselton, Anthony C. *New Horizons in Hermeneutics*. Grand Rapids: Zondervan, 1992.

Turbayne, Colin Murray. *The Myth of Metaphor*. Columbia, S. C: University of South Carolina Press, 1971.

Tyrrell, George. *Christianity at the Cross-Roads*. London: Longmans, Green & Co., 1909.

Ward, Graham. *Barth, Derrida and the Language of Theology*. Cambridge: Cambridge University Press, 1995.

Whitford, Margaret, ed. *The Irigaray Reader, Luce Irigaray*. Oxford: Blackwell, 1994.

Index

Abrams, M. H.: 4, 4n9
absurdity
  in pretense in allegory extended as "metaphor," 8,14
  unmasking pretense, means of, 13–15
allegory
  description of (tenor and projected vehicle in), xv, 11–12
  example of, xv; "literal truth" behind; 15; exposed (demythologized), 205–6
  history of, in academia and literature, 205–7
  See also "metaphor" as extension of allegory; Turbayne, Colin, modern allegory, "linguistic" example of
Apostles' Creed
  as not a "mere historicism", 136–37, creation not accessible to human thought in (Barth), 137
  as template for understanding world history (Lewis), 137–38; creation not found in pagan religion, 137
  See also historicism

Aquinas, Thomas
  Aristotelian essence in "logocentrism," 48, 64
  doctrine of analogy, presuppositions of, 65
  God as self-existing "He who is," 99–100
  natural law as way to God, 174
  ways of speaking of God (*via negativa* and *via analogia*), 64–66
archetypes. *See under* Jung, Carl
Augustine of Hippo
  ancient theories on world history, 133n41
  God not material (except in Incarnation), human participation in God who IS, 100, 192–93
  moral depravity of old gods, 205n38, 205–6
  "sponge" theory of creation in infinite divine sea rejected, theodicy in, 192–93, 200
Autobiography
  existentialist view of, as metaphor of the self (master form), 161
  Paul's letters as, 161–62

Autobiography (*cont.*)
  philosophy, theology, physics and art seen as, 160
  portraits of Jesus (in synoptic gospels, omitting doctrine of person and work) interpreted as reader self-discovery, 161–62

Bacon, Francis, on received systems as worlds of own creation ("stage-plays"), 56
Barth, Karl, xvii
  admits departure from orthodox approach, 107, 137, method of, retrospective, 107–8, projection in, 112–13
  against *analogia entis*, 109–10, divine perspective claimed, 108–10, 118, 125
  God as "wholly other" revised to God enclosing humanity, 106–8; divine institution (Jesus Christ) prior to creaturely reality (biblical history), 109–10, mystery of Incarnation (thing) prior to miracle of Christmas (sign), 119
  Jesus Christ detached from world history, 107–8 (*see also* Bultmann, Rudolph, on Barth's idealism)
  parallel seen between pagan mythology and evolutionary history (concept of creation distinct from either), 113–14; saga in relation to concept of creation, 114–15
  poetic picture (saga) in immediate relation to God, 115, 131, creation against chaos in, 116, 116n38 (*see also under* Keller, Catherine)
  position differentiated from Bultmann's and anthropocentric mythology, need to speak of God before speaking of "man," 120–21
  See also Apostles' Creed; historicism

better,
  "as if true" pictures as "better", 17–18; better for our time, 44
  criteria for McFague's "better" model-metaphor outlined, 198–99, 208 loss of ethical basis in, 203–4
  models imposed on otherwise remote reality, 225, "loving eye" ideology, not better because objective but vice versa, 144, 203
Black, Max
  on metaphor: examples ("man is a wolf"; "war is a chess game"), 7–10, external reference of, 5–6, 11, 25; taken literally (naïve usage of), 15, 28
Bultmann, Rudolph,
  on Barth's idealism, 107, 136
  on demythologizing, 113, 136
  on evolution (worldview of objectifying science), 113, 140

Cartesian legacy
  dichotomy in, 67–68: modern objectivity (I-it relationship in, literalism in) and subjective epistemology (as cause of ecological crisis), 175–79
category mistake, definition of, 3, 4. *See also under* Ryle, Gilbert; Turbayne, Colin
Chesterton, G. K., 102–3, 183. *See also* Francis of Assisi
Christensen, Michael, 64
critical realism, 49n22

dead metaphor. *See under* McFague, Sallie (Turbayne compared with Lewis on); Ricoeur, Paul; Turbayne, Colin
deconstruction, xiii, 38, 40–42, 70–71
  absence of God in, 47–48, 53; effect on Western communicative tradition, 46
  "break in covenant between word and world," 46, 61, 63, nothing outside the text, 46

Index

memory of linguistic
sacramentalism retained, 66–67,
Romantic nostalgia for linguistic
purity in, 72–75
demythologizing, xiii
concept retained (unlike
deconstruction), 54
"God the father" demythologized, 78
demythologizing/"remythologizing"
process, 44, 113–15, 164, 205–6
Lewis on, 44–45, 205–6
Ricoeur on, 29, 45, 206, 230
Derrida, Jacques, xiii
connection of meaning and God-
concept, 48
quasi-ontology (trace or presence-
in-absence), 71, 74
networks of "signification" as Other,
71
nostalgia for linguistic transparency,
72–73,
problems of translation, Babel story
as allegory of, 73n42
rubbed coin image, 71, undermined
source of language in, 76
Yahweh's imposition of break in
Logos-order, Wagnerian cost of,
73–75, 75n46. *See also* Lewis, on
Wagner
Descartes, Réne
axiom of "logocentrism" in, 48
God as source of certainty in
science, 215
See also epistemology, subjective:
Cartesian legacy for; Turbayne,
Colin, Descartes

ecological model of self and world
Christian nature spirituality in, 84–
85, 94, panentheist God in 97–98
contrasted with true Franciscan
spirit, 102–3
detachment in, ethical vision of,
83–85, 94 (*see also* subject-
subjects model)
distinct from hard science, 83, 132
way of thinking, sub-rational,
embodiment, identity in, 90,
93, 153

epistemology
Barthian: thing (divine institution)
prior to sign (creaturely reality),
109–10 subjective: Cartesian
legacy for, existentialist
expression of, 67–68, 145,
177–78
traditional, 48, 64, as retained in
Cartesian legacy, 46, 67
See also "I-it"; "I-Thou" orientation
ethics
good and evil: as external values,
219–20; in ecological model
(McFague), 124–25, subjectivist
basis for, 196–97; in model of
election (Barth), 125
model of "loving eye," patterned on
human loves, 98, answerable to
itself (God as defining love ruled
out), 127, 202
possibility of conditioner/
conditioned distinction in,
203–4, 226
evolution
entropy in, 200–201, fang and claw
in, 101
non-relevant myth of (Barth and
Bultmann), 113–15
popular myth of, 132–34
role in *pro nobis* interpretive
paradigm (McFague), 108–9,
167–68
See also under "metaphorical
theology," "theology of nature"
as "working cosmology"
exteriority. *See* "things out there"
"eye of beholder" approach
history of, xvi–xvii, 226;
demythologizing of external
world in, xvi–xvii, 208;
demythologizing of "mind"
(Hume as ancestor of), 209, 211,
211n60
"Kantian" self (no innocent eye)
in, 215–16, against positivist
assumption of access to material
objects, 216
model of "loving eye," 96, opposed
to "arrogant eye," 96, 98

"eye of beholder" approach (*cont.*)
  not too easy assumption of innocent
    eye (Lewis), 218

feminism
  emancipation of women and
    postmodern deconstruction
    of subject, conflict between,
    127–28
  view from the body in, 144, loss of
    "bodiliness" in, 128
  See Whitford, Margaret; Graham,
    Elaine
feminist theology, x, xi n.6, 224–25. *See
  also under* patriarchal construct,
  "God the father" as
fiction
  external standard for good and evil
    in, 163, 221
  heuristic aspect, discovery beyond
    poet's control (Ricoeur), 36,
    148–51; meaningful language
    of, in children's story, Jumbo
    (Lewis), 163, 167–68
  not always allegory, xv
  view of in "metaphorical theology,"
    43, 54–60
Fiddes, Paul S., 100
Francis of Assisi, 85
  attitude to nature, 100, horizontal
    approach, attributed to, 101–2
  true Franciscan spirit, 100, 183,
    legends about, 102–3.

Graham, Elaine
  Derrida's skepticism on "truth," as in
    male/female binary, 128
  female body as projection, 128, 225
God
  categories of God-talk not always
    clear, 97–98; Jesus's relationship
    with God the father seen as
    distinct from patriarchal model
    (McFague), 227–28
  God as present, in linguistic transfer,
    63; source for Western theology,
    metaphysics, epistemology,
    aesthetics (Steiner), 64

"God the father," mystery of,
  perceived as absent (McFague),
  53
hermeneutic of suspicion towards
  tradition, 33, 33n37, 58;
  demythologizing of "God the
  father," 11, 78–81, relativist
  assumption in, 205
patriarchal construct, "God the
  father" as, x, xi n.6, danger of,
  12–13; unmasked, xii, xv, 37,
  40–41
"world as God's body" as model
  for God, 97, Christian
  nature spirituality in, 84–85;
  panentheistic God in (all things
  in God except values of model),
  98, evil and suffering of, 97;
  modified by other metaphors
  (mother, lover, friend), 98, 196
Yahweh at Babel, deconstructionist
  view of, 73–75, 73n42, 74n44,
  188
gods (Hellenic), fate of,
  demythologized as projections of
    concepts, 205–6
  "remythologized" (allegorized): as
    Gnostic projections, 207; as
    personified passions, 206–7; as
    purely literary figures, 207
  Jungian archetypes, rebirth of
    Platonic spirit, 70, 207

Hay, Denys, on Great Chain of Being,
  172–73
historicism
  Barth compared with Lewis on,
    136–38
Hume, David
  demythologizing of "mind," ancestor
    of, 211, 211n60
  metaphor "God is a builder," 13–15,
    14n32, unmasked by "literal
    truth" (patriarchal model
    assumed), 15–16
Hunsinger, George, 111n25

Index

"I-it"; "I-Thou" orientation
"I-it" relationship and Cartesian ideas (Mascall), 174–76
"I-Thou" relationship with a tree, mystical element in (Buber), 174–75
looking outwards to "Thou situation" of sacramental universe (Lewis), 218
scholastic tradition likened to "I-it" relationship by Buber's followers, 174–76

identity
deconstruction, on loss of, 86–88, rejection of search for, 214
in redemption (Rom 8:19–23), 100–101
in subject-subjects model, two sources of, 92–93

illusion, x, xiii
awareness/unawareness/promotion of, in metaphor as extension of allegory, 12–18, 60
"optimistic arrow" of popular evolution as, 133–34
mythopoeia as escape from, 230
positivist view of metaphor as, xiiin10

imagination
as organ of meaning, Lewis on, 37, 54, 230, fittingness of some metaphors (Ricoeur), 147, 221–22, rightness of (Lewis), 148; as product of "right" brain, 155, 155n27
attributed to sub-rational mind, 87–88, 90, carrying responsibility for fate of earth and humanity, 51, 88, 226
in mythopoeia, 167, poetry, 230n40
in nature writing, 91, 153–54
in traditional sacramentalism, 179–80
in "world as God's body" and other constructs, xi, 225, 229–30
imago Dei, xi; fate of, if "God the Father" demythologized, 232.

Incarnation
as concept (Barth), 114
explodes idealistic categories, 139
historical event (Lewis compared with Barth on), 136–38
lack of credibility for, on Platonic and postmodern terms, 139

infinite regress
of metaphor, deconstructionist argument for, 37; Ricoeur on, 37; Lewis's avoidance of, 37
of subjectivity, 213–14

"is" and "is not," 19
applied to God, 40–41, 53
"is not," no identity in assertions of, 44, 97; projection/bit of nonsense/placebo, 195–96
on "low view," "high view" terms, 31–32
"is" projected as "as if", 53, 55;
"as if" true, 17–18; as picture, better for our time, 33, 196
experiment making claim to "truth," 97;
linguistic error, as basis for (illusory) model-metaphors, 214–15
living within "as if", 84–85, 89, model making its own sacramentalism, 197
scientific "is" at risk in, 146
"truth" claim of, ethical, not ontological, 196

Jantzen, Grace
ethics in terms of "symbolic," connection between women and material in, 187
feminist panentheism reducing to pantheism, 185–86, 200
process theology, rejection of ontological realism in, 187, 229–30,

Jung, Carl,
archetypes, xvii–xviii
subconscious as source of epistemology, 68, rebirth of Platonic spirit in, 70, 95
Johnson, Elizabeth A., 96, 207n47

Kant, Immanuel, as logocentric
(transcendent logic), 48
Keller, Catherine
Barth viewed as "logocentric,"
115–16 but unorthodox on
chaos, 116
feminized chaos (*tehom*) as timeless,
materialized myth (against
Barth's masculinized creator),
116

Lewis, C. S.
evolution, as popular Myth, 132,
arising from Romantic era
(as liberation, "fact" about
improvements), 132, 134, as
illusion (enchantment), 134;
predates scientific theory (about
changes, mostly regressive),
132; rationalist assumptions of
science at odds with, 145–46
making sense: xi; access to truth
via metaphor, 37, 55, 77–78,
imagination as organ of meaning,
rightness in, 37, 54, 148; literal
language dependent on metaphor
(language of senses excepted),
22–24, 37, affective consequences
of amnesia about, 22–25
Masters/Pupil's approach to
scientific models, "Flatlander"
example of, 23–24;
Medieval Model, sacramentalism
(message-bearing in), 188;
syncretistic nature of, 67, 172
metaphor, examples of, xn4; external
reference not wholly vain in, 22,
25, 62, compared with Ricoeur,
27–28; scientific models,
provisional, open to testing,
56–57, 62
moral relativism as destroying
humanity, 203, 216, ethics
traditionally rational in basis,
ideological basis risking
conditioned/conditioned
distinction, 203–4
mythopoeia as least subjective
of activities, 165–67, 230,
meaningful language in
children's books, 163; nature of
scientific accuracy in science
fiction (Jumbo), 167; real
imagination 230n40
on Bultmann, 163
on Tyrrell, variation on *via negativa*
in, 44–45
on Wagner, Romantic hero in, 74n45
redemption, pictured as statues
coming alive, 193–94
See also "eye of beholder" approach,
history of; allegory, history of,
in academia and literature; "I-it",
"I-Thou" orientation
literal truth
concept/s (tenor/s) behind
allegorical projection (vehicle),
12; revealed in unmasking of
allegory extended as "metaphor,"
13–14
metaphorical meaning confused
with (in naïve usage of
metaphor), 11
positivist assumption on, xiv, 25, 18
three meanings of, 170–71
logocentrism (*Logos*-order)
Logos as Ground of Being, 185,
"presence" of and many avenues
to, but one ultimate source, 48,
64
message-bearing from, 226–27;
metaphor as way of knowing in,
76, 48
something in what we say, 76
Ricoeur's presentation of Being
compared with McFague's, 153
Barth's method viewed as (Keller,
contrary to Ward on), 117 (*see
also under* Ward, Graham)

making sense/nonsense; sense/
sensibility
"contemporary crisis of language,"
222–23
"God the father" as source of
connection with external world,
78, psycho-physical parallelism,
148

God giving "sense" to "nonsense,"
119–20, 120n49, existentialist
variant on, 222
if mind demythologized, whether
all thinking nonsensical,
consciousness possible, 208–15
"imagination" projecting its own
world, 230, 230 n. 40
metaphor, all truth beyond language
of senses dependent on, 55
"metaphor," as bit of nonsense, 97,
120, as category mistake, 3–4,
208, category mistake possibly
mistaken, 215
postmodern sensibility and
Christian ethic in relation to, 38,
51, 90; role for ecological model
in, 101–2; separation of truth
and value in, 140–44
retrospective method, promotion of
"bodiliness" claimed, 124–26;
models not open to external test
in, 58, 128–29
self-conscious "Kantian" in relation
to evolutionary paradigm,
212–14
trajectory of convergence
for deconstruction and
demythologizing, 213–14
See also under "metaphorical
theology," "incarnational"
Christianity and contemporary
science, making sense between
Mallarmé, Stéphane
subjectivist frame of xiii, xiv–xv,
46–47; "purity" within language
itself, 50, 59, 69, 72–73
philosophy and translation valid
through nostalgia for linguistic
transparency, 72
Mascall, E. L.
doctrine of analogy, presuppositions
of, 65–66
medieval access to transcendent
via external world contrasted
with Kantian categories of
understanding, 67
scholasticism and followers of
Buber, 175–77, 179

Martis, John, 86n11
McFague, Sallie
as "erstwhile" Barthian, resistant to
"nature" spirituality, 125; values
dependent on God described as
"Barthian," 98, 202
influenced by feminist epistemology
("view from the body"), 144,
process theology, 127
on Barth's view of creation as
enclosed within election, 125;
biblical revelation excluded from
"Kantian limits" in, 140–41;
on Bultmann, subjective cul-de-sac
of, 140–41, 223, New Testament
meaningful as *pro nobis*
(*Geschichte*), not as objective,
factual (*Historie*), 121–22,
164–65
on Descartes as father of modern
objectivity and subjective
epistemology, 67–68, 178, loss
of relationship with nature in,
178–79, "metaphor" mooted as
remedy for, 181
on existentialism, critique of, 146,
164–65
on "low" and "high" views of
scientific models, 30, likened
to Lewis's distinction between
Master's and Pupil's metaphor,
30–31
on "metaphor," definition of, xiv,
20, 39, 59, from amalgam of
theories on, 20, 38: Black's
example ("war is a chess game"),
9–10, Richard's definition, xiv,
16, Ricoeur's "is" and "is not",
25–27, Turbayne's three stages
of, 2; two types of, 78–79
on "metaphor," potential for illusion
in religion and science (affective
power in), 2, 4–5, 10, 20–21,
212; juxtaposition in, 10, 79,
projection in, 41, 45, 178,; taken
literally (danger of, awareness
in), 10, 12, 25; unmasked,
12–13, 33

McFague, Sallie (*cont.*)
  on nature writing (as subject-subjects model) contrasted with whole earth picture (as subject-object model), 84–85; imagination in, 91, intimate encounter, scientific accuracy in 153–54; "second naïveté" attributed to (but as interpretive paradigm in modern loss of direct encounter with nature), 152–54
  on Ricoeur, as critical realist (as in "high" view of models), 31, 55; hermeneutics of restoration in, 33, 33n37; on "is and is not" of metaphor, 19, 25–26; ontological wager in, 32–35; on parables 156, relativity in, 158–59; on symbolic bonds with cosmos, 35, 78, on Scripture accessed in poetic language, 160n52; usage of Ricoeur's phrase "second naïveté," 150–53, 221; viewed as unsatisfactory on broad interpretation of models, 151, 151n15
  on traditional sacramentalism, history of, 179–80, 191; rejection of, 12–13, 187–89, 207, 217; modern consciousness detached from, 135, 155, 170–71; Platonic and Aristotelian/Thomist roots of, 174; Thomist doctrine of analogy critiqued, 65–66; 69
  Turbayne compared with Lewis on dead metaphor, 22–23
  See also God; "metaphorical theology"; nature spirituality, Christian; Nature which is
"metaphor" as extension of allegory
  allegory as pretense ("mask"), 11–12, duality (similar to zeugma) in, 3–4, literal tenor/s behind, 3, 12
  illusory potential of, x, xiii, 17, awareness or lack of awareness of, 196–97; positivist assumption in, xii–xiii, 18
  potential as dominant model, 10–11
  taken literally (unaware of "mask"), 8, 11
  treated "as if" true (better picture), 17;
  unmasked, method of, 13–14, 18, 28
  See also Turbayne, Colin, modern allegory, "linguistic" example of
metaphor (live), ix–x
  etymology of, xiv, xviii, defined as figure of speech, 4, vehicle and tenor in, xiii–xiv, 11–12; examples of, x, xiii–xiv, 7; metaphorical tension in, xiv, 20
  description of: by Black, 1, 6; by Richards, xiv, 20 ; operation of, xi, 6, 15; scope of, xi; source of cognitive language, xii, 22–25
  positivist assumption on, xi, 18
  taken literally, xvi, 15, 18
metaphor (dead). *See under* McFague, Sallie (Turbayne compared with Lewis on); Ricoeur, Paul; Turbayne, Colin
"metaphorical theology," x,
  "contemporary crisis of language," 222–23; constructions as productive of, not testable by, reality, 48–49, 58; "no innocent eye" towards external reality, 96–97, 154, but non-linguistic access to, 51–52, 231; non-speech as reality test of, 53–54
  expression of "religious idea," 45, contemporary expression of Christian faith, 38, as in ecological subject-subjects model, 62; need for reforming of Christian faith, as response to modern "positivistic scientism," 170–71
  form of pretense, 2, 4, 16–17; God absent in, 38, 40–41, 49–50, mystery of, including other religions, 53–54; "mostly fiction" but some fictions ("metaphorical" pictures) better than others, 43
  "incarnational" Christianity and contemporary science,

compatibility with, 129, 132, "making sense" between, xi, 124, 155; "metaphor" as link factor, contrary to positivist perception, 140–41; objectivity redefined on ethical terms, 144; personal/organic model, 117n40, in conversation with theology, 143, successful research linked with machine model, 143–44 (albeit doubt cast on distinction), 200–201; traditional Incarnation rejected as absurdity, 139

Jesus seen as "parable of God," expressing cosmic Christ, 125, 155, 156n34, not exclusive of other religions (relativity of models), 139, 156–57, 217; "parabolic" theology", 58–59: genres for, 149, 160, example of, 159; story of Jesus as reader self-discovery, 161

"loving eye" contrasted with "arrogant eye" in, 90, 96, 154–55 (see also under "eye of beholder" approach)

loss of sense of belonging in machine model, 228, agency as means of belonging in personal/organic model, 129; "Kantian" model-maker and self of ecological model, 213–14

"metaphor" as way of knowing in literary sense, 59, 63, as autobiography ("metaphor of the self"), in Paul's letters, 160–63; corrective to conceptual approach, 149

pragmatic view of truth, 94, 220, ethic based on 127; in touch model, 90, via deepest sense of self, 69, 88, 90–91, 127, 152–53

"remythologizing" Christian faith, reconstructing Jewish and Christian symbols as "planetary agenda,"133, "world as God's body," 89, 97, 184, 201

summary of series on, progression of method in, 89

"theology of nature" as "working cosmology", 130–31, contrasted with "Genesis myth," 132, 134; ethic based on, 127, theodicy, 201; evolution as narrative ("common creation story"), 131, "historical" because unfinished, 131–32; "optimistic arrow" and natural theology rejected, 109, 130, 133; retrospective method of, salvation direction of creation, creation place of salvation, 108–9, 112

via negativa and deconstruction as absence of God, 37–38, 40–42, 46, 49–50, 63, 81, Julian of Norwich, 53, Nietzsche's "coin," 70–71; loss of linguistic sacramentalism (Foucault's description of), 66–67; loss of traditional "sacramental universe," 169–70, 173, 193

wager that God is on side of life and its fulfilment, 62, 84, 113

Model, Medieval
elaborate correspondences in, 173
linguistic sacramentalism via book of nature, 172–73
looking outwards in, 189, 216, Plato as source of vertical truths, Aristotle as source of horizontal truths, 174
non-biblical accretions, possible divesting of, 189
sacramentalism (message-bearing in), 188, 192
syncretistic nature of, 67, 172
trans-sensory meaning in, 67, 172

myth, 163
mythopoeia as least subjective of activities (Lewis) 167
non-referential "is not" in (McFague), 164, 166.

nature spirituality, Christian,
   case studies for: Buber's "I-Thou"
      approach to nature as, 174–75;
      Francis of Assisi, 100–102;
      medieval book of nature,
      173–75; also Gerard Manley
      Hopkins, 180, Genesis myth,
      201; Logos theology, 185
   "Christian nature spirituality" in
      relation to "survival of fittest",
      98–99, 101; human experiences
      of liberation projected onto,
      108–9, 112, 123, 134
   desire for "horizontal" approach,
      100–102, 180, 182–83, "as if"
      terms of, 184; cosmological
      terms of, 186, "Catholic"
      symbolic connections in,
      "Protestant" scepticism towards,
      187–88, 190, 192
   ecological model of self and world,
      51, 69, 83, 90; ethic towards,
      96–98, 124, sin in ecological
      model, 125
   human beings as *imago Dei* in,
      105, 181–82, as signs of God's
      "incarnation," 94, 139–40;
      sacramentalism ("sacred world
      order") of, 187
   subject-subjects model, 62,
      84–85, nature as subjectified,
      spiritualized in, 90–91, 93,
      similar to *anima mundi*, 186
Nature which is
   language for God in, xvii–xviii, 96
   language of model, dependent on
      human model-maker, 99
   limited by viewer's perspective, 96
   panentheist God ("world as God's
      body", God as "mother of
      creation") in, 94, 97–98, 117,
      135, 155, 185, 199–200
   variant on Thomist "He who is," 96
natural world
   "fang and claw" in, 101, 134; role
      of "loving eye" towards, 101,
      153, source for "loving eye"
      (McFague), 101–2
nature writing. *See under* McFague,
   Sallie

Neumann, Erich, on feminine self, xvii–
   iii, 70, 95
   See also under Jung, Carl, on
      archetypes
Newton, Isaac
   conscious pretense regarding
      metaphor attributed to, 16–17,
      31; mechanical model of, 29;
      scientific method of, 56, whether
      model mechanical or organic,
      200–201
Nietzsche, Friedrich, on metaphor
   as illusory source of truth
      (rubbed coin image), 70–71, 86,
      compared with Lewis, 77–78,
      Derrida on, 71n36

parable. *See under* "metaphorical
   theology," Jesus seen as parable
   of God; Ricoeur, Paul, Jesus,
   parables of, Jesus as parable
Parmée, Douglas, 69, 86–88, 90
patriarchal model, 12–13. *See also under*
   God, patriarchal construct "God
   the father" as
Philibert, Michel
   on Ricoeur's understanding of
      metaphor, second order
      reference of ontological
      belonging in, 80–81, 95, 220,
      231
positivism
   view of metaphor in, xii–xiii, 18, 25,
      as leading to illusion, xiiin10.
      See also under literal truth;
      metaphor as extension of
      allegory, positivist assumption
      in; Ricoeur, Paul, on Turbayne,
      positivist parameters in; "eye of
      beholder" approach
Prior, A. N.
   "Barthian Protestant" on God giving
      "sense" to "nonsense," 119–20,
      120n49, 222
process theology, agential nature of, 129
   See also Jantzen, Grace, process
      theology, rejection of ontological
      realism in

religious traditions, other major
  as included in God's absence, 41–42
  as internalized *pax Romana*
    (McFague) in contrast with Tao
    (Lewis), 217
"remythologizing" (Christianity as "as
    if")
  xii, xvi, alternative to
    demythologizing, 44, 54–55, 90,
    95, 113, 226, anthropocentric
    nature of, 230
  See also under "metaphorical
    theology"
Resch, Dustin, on Barth, myth, saga and
  "genuine history" (in immediate
  relation to God), 115, 118–19,
  137
Richards, I. A., metaphor, definition of,
  xiv, 20
Ricoeur, Paul:
  dead metaphor as extension of
    literal meaning, 36
  hermeneutics of restoration
    (metaphor as wager), 33, 35;
    first (pragmatic) reference
    and second order (ontological
    belonging) linguistic reference
    in, 81, 220; symbol, symbolic
    thought, 35, 36
  history of allegory, demythologizing
    and dogmatic mythology in,
    206, 211
  "is" and "is not" (operation of
    metaphor), 25–27, Black's
    organizing process in,
    79–80, demythologization in,
    metaphor-faith beyond, 35, 45,
    61–62 (*see also under* second
    naïveté), external reference of
    (fictional element "as if" and "is"
    beyond poet's control), 35–36,
    54, 61, 147, 217, rightness of,
    147–48; ontological naïveté
    about, 28n22
  Jesus, parables of and Jesus as
    parable, 156, religious language
    at extreme of experience (but
    not beyond it, unlike Barth's
    "Wholly Other"), 158–59,
    160n52
  on making sense, xi; positivism as
    not sole verifying realm, 36
  on positivist view of metaphor, xi,
    30, 36; rejection of, xiiin10
  on Turbayne, his "pretense"
    likened to bad faith, 146n92;
    on demythologized "myth"
    (ontological abstinence), 28–31,
    39, 45, positivist parameters
    in, 30, 52, 141; whether
    demythologized "is not"
    sustainable, 62, as in "mastered"
    scientific models, 30–31, 36
Rimbaud, Arthur, xiii
  "I" as "other" in, 69, 85–87,
    subjectivist frame, sub-rational
    and ethical vision (social
    responsibility) in, xiv–xv, 46, 87.
Ruether, Rosemary Radford, xi, xin6
  on older cosmos theology, 185
  on patriarchal model, 16n35
  See also under God, patriarchal
    construct, "God the father" as
Ryle, Gilbert, category mistake,
  definition of, 3–4, correction to
  idea of "mind" as mind-body
  dualism, 208–10

sacramentalism, traditional, xvii
  God as ultimate Subject in, 95;
    linguistic sacramentalism until
    sixteenth century (Foucault) but
    origins of it older, 66, 169–70;
    "second order" language still
    means of access to (Ricoeur),
    sense of belonging in, 95
  Judaeo-Christian God, not
    unmoved mover, 77, 135,
    217; redemptive journey,
    integration with personal God
    in (Augustine), 192–93; possible
    integration between "Catholic"
    and "Protestant" sensibility,192,
    proposed further dialogue
    between scholastic tradition and
    Buber's followers, 192
  message-bearing (Judaeo-Christian)
    compared with pantheism, 188
  sacramentalism abandoned, reborn
    as model

sacramentalism, traditional (*cont.*)
  contemporary Western culture, positivistic leaning in, loss of sacramentalism in, 170, rejected also on feminist grounds, 188–89
  horizontal sacramentalism mooted (McFague), 181–88, "Catholic" sensibility, as symbolic, promoting "sacred world order," 183, 187, "Protestant" sensibility promoting skepticism, 187–88
  rebirth of Platonic spirit in subconscious mind (Jung), 70
scientific models, xi
  language of, xiii; "low view" and "high view" of, 30–31, 42; Lewis's Master and Pupil's approach to, 30–31
second naïveté, 29, 35
  in Ricoeur's critique of Turbayne, 29, on "metaphorical truth," 35, 151–52; means to connect modern people with sacred cosmos (McFague), 151–52, 164
Smith, James K. A., 46, 70, 73, 74n43, 74n44
Steiner, George
  on deconstruction anti-God as Father of meaning, deconstructionist rejection of logocentric tradition on logocentric terms, 75
  on Mallarmé, 59
  on Rimbaud, 88
  remythologization via arts as "discipline of unknowing," 81–82
  "semantics of correspondence," 46–49, semantic trust *and* inadequacy in, 76–77;
  "something in what we say," xvii, 48, 64, 66, 126, truth values, "presence" or "absence" in, 61, 63, 226
  See also under logocentrism (*Logos*-order), 46, 48

subject
  as deconstructed, 86, 128–29; as elusive, 89
  natural world as, 90–91
  projection from, causing loss of embodiment in, 128
  self-reference, self-authentication in, 129
subject-subjects model, 84–85
  basic sense of self in touch with, constituted by nature, world "subjectified" in, 91–94; circular nature of (diagram), 93
  compared with nature-writing, 91
  detachment, as pretense in, 85, compared with subject-object model, 62, 84–85, 89, 98
  equivocal on orientation to reality, 92
subject-object model: 84–85; as oriented to reality, 92; viewed as arrogant, 90, 98, 153
symbol: description of, xiv; example of, xv; vehicle and tenor in, xv; Ricoeur on, 35
symbolists, French, subjectivist frame of, xiii, xiv–xv; vision (ethical) in, xiii, 46. *See also* Mallarmé, Stéphane; Rimbaud, Arthur

tenor (principal subject), 6. *See under* metaphor (live), (vehicle and tenor in); allegory (tenor and projected vehicle in)
"things out there,"
  poetic access to (Ricoeur), 150–51, 151n15
  sub-rational access to (McFague, Rimbaud), 86–88, 153
Thiselton, Anthony
  on positivist view of metaphor and Ricoeur's rejection of, xiii n.10; on Ricoeur's ontological wager (via symbol), 35
Turbayne, Colin, xii
  accessibility of "facts" in doubt, 142; misallocation of "facts" (category mistake) in

Index

"metaphor," awareness (of trespass) in, 4; non-awareness of (hidden metaphor), 13–15, 21
Bacon's "stage-plays," as hypothesis which may be "undressed", 56–57, putting back "stage-plays," as conscious masks, 56
Descartes, God as source of certainty in science, 215; approach to mechanical models interpreted, 29
dead metaphor as exempt from pretense, 21–22
Hume's demythologizing method, Hume's example ("God is a builder"), 13–14, 13n32, applied to Black's example ("man is a wolf"), 13–14
"metaphor" as based on figure of thought (as in zeugma), 3–4; affective power of, 22–25; duality in, 3, 12; pretense (absurdity) in, 3–5, 14, three stages of, 2, allegorical component in, 12, 34
model-metaphor, Black's examples of ("man is a wolf"; "war is a chess game"), allegorical interpretation of, 7–9, viewed as mask, 8, unmasked, 14, 18, 28
modern allegory, "linguistic" example of, three responses to (taking literally, deceiving others in "full Wizardry of Oz", 226, treating "as if" true), 17–18, 19–20, 31–32, 43, 143, 204–5, 216
on Newton, whether aware of pretense in model-metaphor, 16, 56
on Ryle, category mistake, definition of, 3–4, correction to idea of "mind," 208–10; possible infinite regress of subjectivity in, 210–11, loss of coherence in, 212
See also under metaphor as extension of allegory; Bacon, Francis; Hume, David; Newton, Isaac; Ryle, Gilbert

Tyrrell, George
on "religious idea," inadequate expression of, 44–45, 113
"symbol" as projection, compared with "cold constructions of intellectualism", 45, 58

vehicle (subsidiary subject), 6. *See also under* metaphor (live), (vehicle and tenor in); allegory (tenor and projected vehicle in)
via negativa, 38, 40–45, 63–64
modernist versions compared with tradition, 44–46; tradition open to external reference (Julian of Norwich), 53–54, 84
via analogia, 55, 63–64
analogies for God, as useful (Christensen), 65; epistemology in subconscious mind apparently similar to, 68, 70

Ward, Graham
Barth's method viewed not as *analogia fidei* but *allegoria fidei*, similar to différance, 112, revelation in relation to ordinary reality in, 111–12, 138
"logo-centrism," in Parmenides and Heraclitus, 191, 228
Whitford, Margaret, 127–28, 134, 225
Wizard of Oz, The, illustrations based on: balloon flight, destination uncertain, 62; focus on aspiration, as modernist *via negativa*, 40–42
Dorothy's house in cyclone, ecclesiastical model (Barth), 104, 110, 112
Deadly Poppy Field, as living within model ("as if"), 61–62; 222–23; illusory potential of, awareness or lack of awareness of, 224
Dresden China Country, as traditional sacramentalism, 169
flight from Witch of the West's castle, as retrospective method, 146, ecological soteriology in relation to popular evolutionary history, 123–24

Wizard of Oz, The (cont.)
    Golden Cap, ethics as ideology, dependence on wearer of, 125–26, 202; suggested possibility of sharing, 144
    green glasses, metaphor as "eye of beholder" approach x–xi , as starting point of subjectivist quest, 221, as means of pretense/illusion, 2, 21, 117–18, 146
    homecoming (minus Shoes), metaphor as journey (from vehicle to tenor) towards belonging (beyond poet's control), 19, 147, 152
    Lion's placebo courage, as constructed "sacramentalism," 195–97; not necessary for lion in traditional sacramentalism, 197
    River, Deconstructionist, cross-currents in, 61, 63; loss of bridge (connecting word and world), 61–63, 223; islands of Existentialism and Positivism in as soul/body divide, 223; trajectory towards nihilism of, 222–24
    Silver Shoes, metaphor as means of linguistic transfer, 27–28; 62–63; loss of literal reference in (homecoming in "stocking feet"), 19, 152
    Wizard's address from tethered balloon, as masquerade, detachment from, 83, 89
    Yellow Brick Road, as traditional epistemology, sure footing of, sacramental approach in, 76–82; seen as only accessible to children and pre-moderns, 221–23

zeugma, definition, 4; example of, 3
See also under "metaphor" as extension of allegory

www.ingramcontent.com/pod-product-compliance
Lightning Source LLC
Chambersburg PA
CBHW050346230426
43663CB00010B/2012